The Mining Industry and the Developing Countries

A World Bank Research Publication

Rex Bosson
and
Bension Varon

The Mining Industry and the Developing Countries

Published for
The World Bank

Oxford University Press

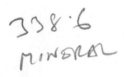

Oxford University Press

NEW YORK OXFORD LONDON GLASGOW
TORONTO MELBOURNE WELLINGTON CAPE TOWN
IBADAN NAIROBI DAR ES SALAAM LUSAKA ADDIS ABABA
KUALA LUMPUR SINGAPORE JAKARTA HONG KONG TOKYO
DELHI BOMBAY CALCUTTA MADRAS KARACHI

© 1977 by the International Bank
for Reconstruction and Development / The World Bank
1818 H Street, N.W., Washington, D.C. 20433 U.S.A.

Library of Congress Cataloging in Publication Data

Bosson, Rex, 1943–
  The mining industry and the developing
countries.
  Bibliography: p. 273
  Includes index.
  1. Mineral industries. 2. Underdeveloped
areas—Mineral industries. I. Varon, Bension,
joint author. II. Title.
HD9506.A2B67   338.2'09172'4   77–2983
ISBN 0–19–920096–3
ISBN 0–19–920099–8 pbk.

Contents

Contents

Appendixes

Figures

Tables

Acknowledgments

THIS BOOK HAS ITS ORIGIN in a comprehensive paper on the mining sector prepared by the staff of the World Bank in 1972 and 1973, and much of our research for the book was carried out in connection with that paper. The first persons we wish to thank, therefore, are Hans Fuchs and Mahbub ul Haq—at once bosses, friends, and sources of inspiration—who gave us the permission and encouragement to embark on a book. Mr. Fuchs was intimately involved in all aspects of the original paper and was, in fact, the guiding light behind it. We would also like to acknowledge Turgut Ozal's contribution to the original paper, from which we have benefited greatly.

We are also extremely grateful to Raymond Mikesell of the University of Oregon and to John Carman and Wolfgang Gluschke of the United Nations Centre for Natural Resources, Energy, and Transport for commenting on an early draft of the book and for their useful suggestions. Mr. Carman's influence represents a special case. His enormous, lifetime contribution to the mining field—as an accumulation of facts and perceptions and a standard of candor—served as a model and a catalyst for our own thinking. We also wish to thank Barbara Varon for her constant refrain of "say what you mean."

The very difficult and exacting task of typing the first draft fell to Mary Shannon and Farida Dossani, and they handled it admirably. Katharine Tait edited the final manuscript, Rachel C. Anderson prepared the index, and Brian J. Svikhart directed production of the book.

Last, we wish to make it clear that this book is in large measure the product of the opportunities for learning, field experience, contacts, and open discussion afforded us by the World Bank. Yet we would not want to attribute any errors in the text to the Bank or to the individuals whom we have thanked for helping and encouraging us.

REX BOSSON
BENSION VARON

The Mining Industry and the Developing Countries

Introduction and Summary

THIS BOOK is designed to provide an overview of the world mining industry—its structure, objectives and operation, and the major factors bearing on them, such as the physical characteristics of mineral resources, economies of scale, capital requirements, and economic and political risk; its production, consumption and trade characteristics; the behavior of mineral prices; and the industry's impact on economic growth with particular reference to the developing countries. The book examines the principal problems and challenges facing the industry, both in the short term and over the long run, and the needs and interests of the various players. It reviews the role that policy, both public and private, can and must assume to meet the needs of society while safeguarding the interests of nations, especially those of developing countries. If the professed goal of greater international economic cooperation is progress for all, above all the neediest countries, then a vital sector such as the mining industry must make a positive contribution toward that goal. We address ourselves to this issue throughout the book, and especially in chapters 5 and 6, devoted to mineral sector development in the developing countries.

The analysis is limited to nonfuel minerals and thus excludes such vital sources of energy as petroleum, natural gas, coal, and uranium. Although there are many similarities in the basic characteristics and policy implications of fuel and nonfuel minerals, today's market, with its prospects of massive transformation in the fuel sector, introduces important differences that warrant separate treatment. The analysis also excludes construction minerals such as stone, sand, and gravel. Even though they serve to meet important needs and account for a large proportion of world mineral output (measured in value), international trade in them is insignificant.

While we cover the centrally planned countries in the statistical analysis, we do not deal with the particulars of mineral development in these countries nor how their experience may relate to new nations. Nevertheless, in dealing with the institutional and policy steps to be taken for establishing and administering a mining sector, we suggest alternative ways of implementing these steps depending on a country's political and structural preferences. We do this only within the bounds of the mining sector; that is, we do not consider the case where the entire economy is centrally planned and integrated with other centrally planned economies through a network of commercial and political agreements. Under such conditions, the determinants—even the definition—of savings, investment, risk, and profit are significantly different. Furthermore, the information base for such economies is not nearly as complete as that obtaining for the market economies. To proceed on a sketchy basis might lead to wrong conclusions and therefore to an unjustly distorted profile.

Although we do not hesitate to express opinions, the book's emphasis is largely on facts, for on this topic there is a plethora of judgments but a dearth of facts. The adage "knowledge is power" fits the mining industry like a glove. Understanding of the fundamentals plays a key role in shaping expectations and harnessing bargaining power. National policymakers especially must recognize and come to terms with the industry's complexity, no matter how frustrating the process, in order to legislate realistically. Without such effort, policies as well as international arrangements are likely to miss their objectives, and their failure would come as a surprise only to the policymakers. Although the modern age has increased man's capacity for empirical analysis (especially in response to crisis), it has not necessarily increased his ability to make objective judgments. In the evaluation of the ramifications of the energy crisis, the grace periods allowed by nonrenewable resource inventories, and the sharing of benefits between producers and consumers, identical figures are being used to support different diagnoses and policies. For some analysts the cup is half empty while for others it is half full. It is important, under these conditions, to reach agreement on facts as prelude to agreeing on interpretation, before agreeing on solutions.

This book cannot hope to clear up all the confusion about the mining industry and its role in developing countries. Our objective is the more modest one of providing a view of the industry as an organic whole so that the problems posed by the new market realities can be put in an operational perspective. Though we hope to be informative in the eyes of all readers, we specifically set out to address those who, while not experts in the field of mining, are informed and sympathetic participants in the ongoing debate on international economic relations and development. The approach is, therefore, selective with a view to providing these readers with a manageable information base on which, we feel, our perceptions and judgments can comfortably rest. We have tried to avoid inundating the reader with raw data.

Statistical information about the mining industry is incomplete, difficult to assess, and, particularly for intercountry evaluation, lacks comparability; in addition, the reliability of the data can at times be questioned. Much of the difficulty can be traced to measurement problems and incomplete disclosure. While we believe that our major conclusions are not materially affected, readers should be cognizant of these shortcomings.

The Pressure of Change

The postwar era has been characterized by the emergence of new nations with specific sets of needs and urgent demands summarized most clearly in the recent call for a new international economic order. While some of the excessive rhetoric can be dismissed, the root causes for the discontent among developing nations and the need for reviewing the present configuration of economic strength cannot.

A review of the income distribution trend during the last three decades reveals no appreciable closing of the gap either within or among countries. Clearly, the promise of the postwar period has not been fulfilled; in the light of this, the workings of the marketplace have to be examined and brought into line with the goals of fairer income distribution and an improved standard of living on a worldwide basis.

The foundations for that hoped for improvement include ample and stable resource supplies—in food, energy, and industrial raw materials. The first step, then, is to examine who produces what, how, for whom, and how the answers bode for the ideal of a growth-sustaining economic environment for all.

This ideal ought to be the yardstick against which we measure performance. Who are the "we" in this case? First, governments in their role as participators, stimulators, integrators, and regulators of economic activity and, second, the large producers in the private sector. It is these large, powerful units that can most easily bring about needed results in response to changing aspirations. The major part of world economic activity does not take place in the extremes of either a totally planned or a totally free economic environment. It is, therefore, in the mixed market situation, where governments subscribe to broad economic and social goals, that we must look for answers. In such a situation, each large unit of production must make a positive contribution to the dynamics of overall social and economic development and, as a consequence, the large companies' role has to go beyond the traditional objective of maximizing company profits.

In the case of the mining industry specifically, the role of the large companies is crucial in terms of sheer dominance in the field and their power, therefore, to withhold or extend benefits to the economic system in which they operate. These giant companies can be powerful agents for development in developing countries. Their incentive to become such agents is determined to a large extent by how they perceive the success of their ventures in a host country. Traditionally, they have based their investment decisions on their assessment of the comparative stability, especially political stability, of the host country.

In today's world nothing is stable compared to past decades. The present era is one of fundamental change, when poor countries are striving for well-realized developed nationhood with all the attendant turmoil; and developed nations are asked to reevaluate their internal and external economic life. Ironically, at a time when change is the only viable solution to the ills of a world economically divided into haves and have-nots, the companies are unwilling to give up the old yardstick of stability in making investment decisions. For stability to be regained, the changes in perception and aspiration on the part of the developing countries must first be accommodated. This accommodation, however, can take place only with the agents and mechanisms at hand in the marketplace. These must be brought into a more perfect partnership with the host countries rather than replaced; for the immediate problem, at least, would be with what? There is, after all, very little time.

Weighing the Contribution of the Industry

The contribution of the mineral sector to civilization, especially in the Industrial Age, and to material progress is immeasurable; all major advances in meeting human needs in the past—for food, housing, health care, education, jobs, and transport—have been predicated upon the use of additional minerals, more efficient use of minerals, or use of better minerals—indeed, very often a combination of all three. Throughout history, the discovery of a new mineral, or of a new alloy, or of a new method of extracting or processing a mineral, or of a new orebody has had a major impact on industrial growth and consumption. If this crucial function is not revealed in global or regional measures of the contribution of mining to gross national product (GNP), industrial production, or employment, it is because available statistics stop showing the contribution of minerals once the resources move from the mining sector to the manufacturing sector. The problem is one of categories as defined in the present system, which vanishes with historical perspective.

Substantial benefits can accrue to a country from a properly structured and administered mineral industry. In addition to providing foreign exchange earnings, mining activity may produce additional revenue through taxes and royalties; stimulate development of depressed regions; improve the professional and technical skills of nationals; and, for some countries, provide a nucleus for economic development. In the past two decades, mining has become a major source of public and private revenue for many newly emerging nations. Most mineral projects are by and large independent of the size of the local market; with proper policies and assistance, the industry can be competitive in any country suitably endowed with natural resources.

There is no doubt that the mining industry can also have adverse effects, directly or indirectly, on the economy of a developing country. By their very nature, mineral export projects have remained enclaves, better integrated with the outside world than with the host economies, and have allowed little backward integration. The enclave industry label is well deserved. This fact, however, should not be used in the tradition of the forceful cliché, namely, that mining is bound to have gross adverse effects in the developing countries and, therefore, should be given low priority on the development plan. This would prevent the establishment of a properly operated, regulated, and economically integrated mining industry—the only model we advocate on the basis of the unacceptability of current experience.

Unfortunately, the enclave character is but one of several negative features of the mining industry as it now exists. The industry shows insufficient concern for environmental damage and exhibits a skewed income distribution. To be sure, these are not characteristic of the mining industry alone (its skewed income distribution is all but dwarfed by that existing in agriculture as a result of the unequal distribution of landholdings) but they are the more glaring in an integrated industry dependent on host countries, where a responsible and responsive company ethic should be the order of the day. Yet in imagining the ideal contribution of the industry and the multinationals, one can easily fall into the trap of asking them to fill a role beyond their purview. It is one thing to ask an industry not to aggravate the maldistribution of income—indeed to assist in its correction—quite another to look to it for a model. That would imply quasigovernmental powers on the part of the multinational company and the spread of its influence over other sectors. It is inconsistent to complain about the power of the companies while deriding their lack of initiative in areas which are government prerogative. Maximizing the industry's positive contribution to overall economic development requires intelligent cooperation between governments and companies.

Attributes and Performance of the Industry

The mining industry is extraordinarily complex because of the physical characteristics of mineral resources: their heterogeneity and nonrenewability, their uncertain occurrence and often deep underground location, the remoteness of some sites, and the requirements for processing before mineral ores can be turned into useful products. Mineral resources have to be discovered and, even after discovery, the true value of a deposit cannot be known until the deposit is depleted. The extent, rigor, and cost of preproduction activities in mineral resource development are far in excess of those required for the development of other industries. Three distinct and lengthy stages—broad geological surveys, regional and detailed exploration, and detailed orebody delineation—have to precede mine development. The elapsed time between the start of exploration and commercial production can be considerable: on the average more than ten years and often as much as twenty years.

Although exploration expenditure generally amounts to only a small part of total project cost, exploration constitutes the high-risk element of any project, and in most cases the expenditure is made without proving up a viable deposit. The major investment in mining itself is made at much lower levels of risk; yet the total risk in mineral resource development is in most cases considerably higher than in the manufacturing industry because of the uncertainty surrounding the results of exploration. Since no returns can be assured or in some cases even assumed, the funds required for exploration must be provided strictly as risk capital. In the past, therefore, the private sector has borne the burden of exploration expenditure.

The mining industry is very capital intensive and is becoming even more so; the economies of scale that can be realized are significant; and infrastructure requirements can be enormous in comparison to most other industries. All this points to extremely large capital investment requirements which, coupled with attendant risks much higher than for other industries, has led to an industry structure dominated by corporate giants capable of spreading risks over geographic and commodity areas. Very large mining companies, international in outlook and sophisticated in financial and technical analysis and operations, control the mining cycle from exploration to marketing of the refined mineral, even to fabrication and production of consumer goods. The continued presence of the multinationals in all phases of the sector increases their knowledge and skills through accumulation of experience, and this gives them a further competitive edge over the small firm.

Detailed analysis does not support the popular notion that the mining industry is one of high or excessive profits, since the data offered to support this claim tend to be drawn only from brief periods of immensely high profits in the larger and more successful projects, and are not representative of the industry as a whole. If all exploration expenditures are included, the industry can probably be said to be one of average-to-above-average profitability, but also one in which numerous entities too small to spread their risk have failed. But the profit picture varies from year to year and by company. In periods of economic buoyancy the mining companies generally do better than companies in other industries, but in periods of economic instability and decline the mining industry generally lags behind other industries. There is no doubt that highly profitable projects do exist, and that in areas of political instability mining corporations tend to consider only projects of high profitability. While there is reason to suggest that profitability and income returned to parent companies have been higher in operations in the developing countries than in projects in developed regions, there is insufficient information on this point by country and by commodity.

Geographic concentration

World consumption, production, processing, and trade of mineral commodities are characterized by uneven distribution among economic regions and heavy concentration in individual countries. Developed market economies consume over two-thirds of the world output and import 90 percent of the exportable surplus in order to meet 60 percent of their requirements. Developing countries consume less than 10 percent of the global output; yet they produce one-third of that output and supply fully half of the domestic requirements of the developed market nations. Underconsumption of raw materials of such proportions is a true indicator of the severe underdevelopment of the developing countries. Viewed negatively, the interdependence of developed and developing countries in mineral resources and their heavy reliance on imports and exports, respectively, can be considered a source of potential conflict. On the other hand, trade in mineral commodities can be an important tool not only for bridging the gap between the have and have-not nations, but also for assuring efficient global exploitation and use of resources.

A cause of gross dissatisfaction on the part of the developing countries is the heavy concentration of mineral processing facilities in the developed regions. The current value of developing countries' mineral output is no more than 30 percent of the potential production value had all ore mined been processed through the metal bar stage there. Although there is great scope for increasing value added in this sector in the developing countries, progress will be slow because the major impediment is transfer of technology and capital rather than limited access to markets. While the latter can be remedied by governmental action, the other two constitute constraints on production that will be difficult to remove. Besides, the current processing facilities in the developed countries cannot be dismantled, especially at a time of high unemployment. It is true that permanent closings in the developed countries took place in cotton textiles, but mostly in places where the machinery was nearly a hundred years old. The modern mineral processing facilities of Japan are a different matter. Furthermore, aside from the need to have the requisite inputs such as energy, there are technical factors at play. For example, one reason why the processing of some metals is centered in the developed countries is that it requires mixing of mineral ores of different grades and composition and from different origins to produce the necessary intermediate product; another reason is the existence of a skilled labor force and a tradition of industrial performance. Considerations of economies of scale, energy, and mixing imply that there is considerable scope for cooperation in joint ventures among developing countries. Some already exist and others are under consideration.

The skewed distribution of production and processing should be viewed against the backdrop of the geographic distribution of reserves and exploration expenditures. Developing countries possess nearly 40 percent of world reserves. Future discoveries are likely to expand this ratio, since there are large areas which have not yet been systematically explored, especially in the tropical regions, whereas exploration saturation is being approached in the developed regions. Nearly 85 percent of world exploration expenditures have been channeled to the developed countries. Correcting the maldistribution of production, therefore, requires investment of capital, time, and effort in expanding exploration in the developing regions.

Peformance record

The record of the world mining industry in responding to the needs of the developing countries is dismal. The industry's total effort has been directed to obtaining sufficient supplies for the consuming nations, namely the developed countries—a task in which the industry has been very effective and innovative. Only recently has the industry even shown awareness of the needs of the developing countries, and very few consuming nations and firms have reacted earnestly to meet the challenge; the record remains largely uncorrected.

The international companies' pattern of project selection, investment, location of processing facilities, and revenue-sharing arrangements—while defensible on narrow microeconomic and political grounds—has not always been consistent with the development needs, legitimate interests, aspirations, and sensitivities of the developing countries. The leverage of developing countries over the mining industry has been kept low by the industry's history of guarding its knowledge of reserves and resources, technology and markets, overstressing its complexity to prevent easy intervention. In a number of instances the multinationals have been less than candid with regard to the results of exploration, the parameters of investment and expansion decisions, processing and marketing properties of the product, technological and economic trends, and market value. Host countries have thus been deprived of knowledge about their own resources and of the basic tools with which to evaluate decisions deeply affecting their self-interest. In a number of areas the multinationals have themselves been the major source of the information needed for independent evaluation of their performance, fostering suspicion and placing them at odds with host countries and with legislators in their own countries.

The industry has performed reasonably well on the standard of efficiency. It has provided consumers with an expanding variety and steady source of mineral raw materials, many of which are exploited as efficiently as man is able to; but there are some glaring gaps. For example, the best deposits are not alway brought on stream first in accordance with the relative economics of alternate deposits. Political climate has had a major impact in the past on the industry's decision where to mine and has tended to discriminate against the developing countries. This is particularly apparent in the distribution of exploration expenditures with their disproportionate allocation to developed regions.

There is also reason to question the industry's efficiency with respect to use. The proportion in which mineral resources are exploited and used today does not reflect their relative abundance, largely because of imperfections in the orientation of research and in the pricing mechanism. Far from being directed systematically toward abundant materials, research in end use is sporadic, particular in its application, and very uneven among minerals and over time. Often, major breakthroughs have been achieved during and in response to emergencies (wars) or as a by-product of advances in other fields (space). Traditionally, mineral prices have been determined on the basis of capital, operating, and distribution costs modified by bargaining power. No allowance has been made for the inherent value of the mineral in the ground. The imperfection of the pricing mechanism has undoubtedly led to inefficient use, aside from maldistribution of benefits.

Mineral Sector Development in the Developing Countries

Both developed and developing countries have a common interest in cooperating to expand the flow of mineral resources to world markets. Developed countries will have to rely increasingly on the supply of minerals from developing economies, although they have considerable flexibility in slowing down this trend. On the other side, modern mining and processing methods have become so capital intensive and the capital requirements of most modern mines and their attendant infrastructure so large that few of the developing countries can expect to bring a sizable project into operation on their own. While over the long run the developing countries will be able to negotiate their more abundant supply situation into better leverage over joint exploration and production ventures, their revolution of expectations and growing absorptive capacity will intensify the pressure on the development of their mineral resources. The interdependence of the developed and developing countries is real and will grow.

At the project level, however, it is unlikely that the objectives of a multinational firm will coincide with those of the host government; in fact, these objectives may diverge considerably. The multinational company will act to maximize profits and spread the risks of the company as a whole, not necessarily those of the affiliate in a particular producing country. In determining the distribution of production between subsidiaries in different countries, a mining company will take into account the relative costs (including taxes) of the different subsidiaries, the preferential access to some markets of various suppliers, the need to maintain minimum production levels as specified by contracts, and the degree of political risk in each country. Companies, moreover, tend to specialize in commodities experiencing high growth rates and to shift incremental resources out of a commodity whose growth rate has fallen off to one with a higher growth rate. The companies are themselves deeply involved in influencing the growth and displacement of commodities through their large research and development establishments, which are constantly putting forward new products and promoting product uses based on their mineral resources.

A government, on the other hand, is more concerned with maximizing total revenues of the subsidiaries operating within its territory, and especially its share of revenues, with little interest in overall corporate profits. Governments also seek to influence the level and geographic pattern of resource development; encourage backward and forward linkages in the economy; and expand the processing, refining, and fabrication of raw materials, both for domestic use and for export.

The divergence of objectives can lead to serious conflict. In a recent investigation of two copper mining projects, Raymond F. Mikesell concluded: "The two case studies confirm the generalization that conflicts between the host government and the foreign investor tend to be more or less continuous, and the greater the profitability of the mine the more intense will be the demand for renegotiation of the contract on the part of the host government."[1]

The bargaining position of each party changes according to the amount of knowledge of the resources to be exploited available at the time of negotiation, favoring the multinationals in the early stages of exploration but the host government later, as knowledge of the mineral increases. This points to a real need to promote exploration by the host government and requires funds from sources other than the traditional source of the multinationals. Most developing countries can ill afford to supply these funds from their own coffers—which leaves the multilateral and bilateral aid agencies as

1. *Foreign Investment in Copper Mining: Case Studies and Mines in Peru and Papua New Guinea* (Baltimore: Johns Hopkins University Press for Resources for the Future, 1975), p. xxii.

possible sources. The use of these sources, however, can have many pitfalls; developing countries should be cognizant of them and incorporate the appropriate safeguards. Nevertheless, in our opinion, a major increase in multilateral and bilateral aid is needed to promote mineral exploration and development in the developing countries.

It is also of paramount importance not to overlook the already significant and expanding opportunities for cooperation between the developing countries, not only in training and research and development, where joint facilities may be established, but in all areas, including processing. Here, too, aid agencies and the UN Regional Commissions in particular can play a useful role as catalysts.

Establishing a mineral sector

Mineral sector development in any country, whether developed or developing, constitutes only one element of total national development and must therefore be structured to fit within the framework of the total economic plan. The broad objectives of mineral development normally include: ensuring optimal use of indigenous mineral resources; earning or saving foreign exchange; creating employment, directly or indirectly, often in remote areas; promoting backward and forward linkages in order to maximize value added within the country; assuring an adequate supply of raw material inputs for industry; and stimulating regional development. To attain these goals, a national mineral policy must be enunciated and stated clearly, so that all parties with a role to play can move in the same direction. Formulation, dissemination, and carrying out of mineral policy is the responsibility of the government.

As a first step in formulating a national mineral policy, the country must decide whether to develop its mineral sector on the basis of a private, public, or mixed system. The selection of one of these options or a combination will depend on political, structural, and social preferences but must also take into account the exploration, operating, and marketing characteristics of the sector. In the case of state-run mineral development, success will depend wholly on the effectiveness with which the state can plan, commit financial resources, provide managerial and technical expertise, and secure markets. Development under the private sector approach depends for its success on more detailed consideration of the respective responsibilities, privileges, and obligations of private companies and the government. These should have as their objective assuring not only the efficient operation of the sector but also maximizing its contribution to national well-being on a broad scale, for example, by encouraging conservation, training of nationals, and reinvestment of profits in productive activities.

Any plan of action for effective mineral sector development requires a factual basis. An inventory of the mineral resources is fundamental and, therefore, knowledge of the geology and mineral occurrences is a prerequisite. In the field, in the laboratory, in the administration, and in operations, moreover, mineral sector development requires highly specialized personnel. Mineral resources can be of such potential significance to a country that they require specific legal status. Legislation would include a mining code and a special taxation regime compatible with existing investment codes and social legislation. The taxation regime is perhaps the most important element of any national mining policy, for it constitutes an important means for realizing many policy objectives.

The government, therefore, needs to set up six or seven administrative nodes beginning with a policy, planning, and administrative agency; this usually means a Ministry of Mines, although, depending on the size of the sector, it may be combined with Energy or, at times, with Transportation or Economic Development. An institute for geological surveying is also an early requirement; it can be set up as an autonomous agency but under the direction of the Ministry of Mines. Educational facilities, such as separate departments in local universities, are also needed. It is possible that a research and development institute will be required to undertake research and provide technical assistance to the sector. In countries where there is a strong national desire to develop mining under the administration of the state, a government-owned enterprise needs to be established. Often it is also necessary to provide channels for making financing available to the sector, especially to medium and small-scale operations. This may entail setting up a separate mining bank or "opening up a new window" at the development bank. Finally, the government may wish to centralize the marketing function to strengthen its role as controller or coordinator, and this may require new institutional arrangements.

In each of these areas, the actions taken by governments are often seriously deficient. For example, in many cases, the Ministry of Mines is a large, bureaucratic, and ineffective institution. It suffers from overstaffing, low salaries and inability to attract qualified personnel, inadequate budget, incorrect procedures, lack of planning and ability to formulate policy or monitor relevant legislation, and ineffective decisionmaking. Although some of the staff may have sufficient academic qualifications, it is rare to find many with practical experience as well. In numerous cases, lack of experience makes it difficult for the staff to relate to the reality of the industry, and assignment of sector priorities often constitutes a bewildering task. The linkages between projects are often ignored, as is the dependence of mining and processing operations on infrastructure. All too often political considerations override what should be strictly technical considerations in the assignment of priorities.

The choices open to governments in taking action at every step are broad. The total ramifications of alternative courses of action should, however, be properly evaluated. For example, while many governments' increasing desire to exercise control over marketing may be justifiable, it should be appreciated that the setting up of a separate marketing agency for this purpose—whether it is to market part or all of the production—requires special care and caution. The marketing of minerals is a highly specialized field where inexperience can be costly. Besides, the cost of setting up a fully integrated marketing agency with foreign offices can be immense. Furthermore, as the principal marketing agents which have traditionally performed this role have usually been important sources of finance as well, replacing them by a state monopoly can retard the growth of the sector. Short of government takeover of this function, control can be exercised by laying down the ground rules (for example, in terms of the level of domestic processing required), including the basis for establishing prices (a particular international quotation), and exercising the right of prior approval of all sales contracts. Marketing arrangements for each mineral should be reviewed independently; arrangements suitable for one mineral are not necessarily suitable, or even feasible, for another.

Although there can be no single blueprint for the establishment of a viable mining sector in the developing countries, it is possible to draw up broad guidelines on the basis of past experience. Even when such guidelines draw heavily on the experience of the developed countries, where the modern mining industry is of longer standing, they need not be viewed with the disfavor attached to indiscriminate copying, especially in areas where experience has shown them to lead to efficiency. Efficiency ought not be the prerogative of developed nations; it must inform the actions of any government involved seriously in mineral development.

Dealing with multinational companies

Unmistakably, control by multinationals will decrease as host nations, developed and developing alike, assume more of it. Host governments' right to make basic policy decisions is indisputable; however, they will have to continue to rely on the large companies for both execution and such basic inputs as capital, technology, and management—for it is there that the experience is concentrated for the time being. Transfer of this experience is a relatively slow process.

Even with a well-defined mineral policy and legislative system, a country relying on private foreign capital for development of its mineral sector should pay particular attention to its policies and procedures as they apply to the foreign enterprises. The precise relation between the multinational corporation and the host country must therefore be clearly defined and a mechanism established for coordinating and monitoring this relation. These functions are often widely scattered among various ministries, few of which are even remotely equipped to deal with the whole range of problems that may arise, or in a position to play a central role in developing a consistent set of policies.

A major problem area is that of negotiation between the multinationals and host governments. Most developing countries lack the expertise to conduct these negotiations so as to ensure that their interests are protected. Results may vary from giving away excessive concessions—in order to buy the participation of the corporation—to a hard line which frightens away potential investors. Either extreme is unsatisfactory. The negotiators on both sides must strive for a partnership that is mutually beneficial and can endure.

Governments must respect their agreements except when national interest has been grossly, illegally, or unfairly violated. Belligerence toward companies is bad practice; curtailing excesses is a sound policy objective. Companies, on their part, must learn to recognize and respect the needs and aspirations of the countries in which they operate. Be they national or foreign, they must show increased social awareness in their economic contribution.

The Future

The world mining industry faces a dynamic future. Continued population growth and universal demand to improve physical standards of living guarantee that. While the intensity of use of nonfuel minerals (the volume of consumption per unit of GNP) has been declining in the industrially advanced countries and is bound to bring about a deceleration in the growth rate of world demand, this need not be fully manifested in the next ten years, constitute an open-ended trend, or simply that the task of meeting future requirements will become progressively easy—far from it. In the next five to ten years, world demand for nonfuel minerals is likely to grow at rates not materially different from those of the 1960s. The force of declining intensity of use in the large producers will very likely be felt more strongly in the late 1980s and the 1990s. Available projections for the year 2000 point to considerably slower growth rates in the last quarter of the century than in the third quarter. Because of the progressive expansion of the consumption base, however, additional yearly requirements are hardly likely to decline in absolute terms and, given the fixed stock of resources, meeting these requirement will pose a constant challenge.

With regard to the very long term, it suffices to note that the deceleration in the growth rate of demand need not last indefinitely or give way to stable growth rates of unlimited duration. Not only the hoped-for industrialization of the developing countries but also programs to eradicate pockets of relative poverty, to redistribute income, or to reallocate and improve the volume and quality of mass consumption in the rich countries can revitalize, even revolutionize, demand for minerals. Therefore, the decelerating trend in demand may be interrupted by spurts or even sustained periods of rapid growth.

Current expansion plans point to substantial increase in the supply of several major minerals by 1980, in some cases significantly above anticipated levels of demand. Several projects will inevitably be postponed because of lack of finance, hesitancy brought about by political instability, and limitations on the absorptive capacity of the industry. Overall, supply is not likely to fall below demand in the medium term, although short-term imbalance cannot be ruled out.

For the longer term, there is little information that permits pinpointing with confidence—by year and commodity—shortages and surpluses of major consequence. Present known reserves for most minerals are adequate to the year 2000, with only moderate increases in the real price needed to precipitate new mine development.

How about the indefinite future? Present knowledge does not provide an adequate basis for judging how long terrestrial mineral reserves will be able to keep pace with the rapidly rising exploitation of minerals. It should be emphasized that a reserve or resource is at best an intelligent guess based on quite limited information applying only to a brief moment in time; reserve figures are usually only slightly related to total quantities which may be available in the future; definition of what constitutes a reserve is extremely dynamic and, in global terms, changes in reserve estimates have almost always been upward; the oceans are a true frontier whose potential yields may be so vast as to make it impossible at this stage of development to assess definitively their ultimate impact upon the total supply picture. Nevertheless, it is almost certain that minerals will be increasingly difficult to discover and the cost of extraction and beneficiation will increase. Whether, how soon, and for whom, the availability of mineral resources becomes an insurmountable problem will depend on advances in resource creation and use; the application of every tool, such as technology, recycling, and conservation; the coordinated management of resource discovery and exploitation in an atmosphere of cooperation rather than confrontation; and the realization that there must be limits to the frivolous consumption of minerals.

Problems and challenges

The principal problems and challenges facing the industry in the short run are: the business cycle and the excessive volatility of prices which make planning difficult; the industry's tendency to overreact to business cycles; the rapidly weakening fiscal stability of some of the large mineral-producing countries; and rapidly rising capital and financing costs, coupled with the decreased availability of finance for mining.

In the long run, the industry faces and has to respond to: changes in the rules of the game, increased nationalism, and inevitable changes in ownership; the limited absorptive capacity of the developing countries for their own mineral development, coupled with problems of transfer of technology caused by the recalcitrance of the developed countries as well as the shortsightedness of many developing countries in not recognizing their own limitations; and the need to respect the national self-interest of the developing producing countries in joint ventures. Energy and pollution should not prove major problems for the industry except in specific areas or projects.

The problem of investment and finance has three components: size of investment, fluctuation, and distribution. With regard to the first, capital requirements have increased enormously in recent years, not only because of inflation but also because of greater infrastructure costs (as most of the new mines are in remote areas), and sophistication in equipment which, though leading to high productivity, formidably increases the investment cost. Total capital requirements for the next ten years, excluding exploration costs, are estimated at about \$100,000 to \$120,000 million (in 1975 prices),[2] or 50 percent more a year than in the last few years.

Historically, the principal source of such capital has been the internally generated funds of the large mining companies, but in the future a large part will have to come from commercial sources, at high interest, with internal cash flow continuing to play an important role. Raising this capital is predicated on improving the profitability of the industry, which requires a recovery of prices from their present levels, coupled with mechanisms designed to smooth out the excessive volatility of mineral prices. Assuring an equitable distribution between the developing and developed countries necessitates improved political and economic climates in the former. Investment is already down, especially in the developing countries, because of the recession and greater risks in the eyes of the investors, although we do not know by how much. The situation is reported to be serious enough to threaten large shortages seven or eight years from now if it is not soon corrected. This raises the question of the possible need for an agency to monitor the flow of investment into mining in order to warn off, and play a role in, smoothing dangerous cyclical movements. Such an agency exists for agriculture in the form of the Consultative Group on Food Production and Investment established jointly in 1975 by the World Bank, the United Nations Development Programme, and the Food and Agriculture Organization.

Prices

Perceptions of the determinants and role of mineral prices are in the process of reevaluation and undergoing fundamental transformation, however without commensurate refinement of the analytical tools required to evaluate the merits of, and if necessary assist in, the transformation. Historically, under assumptions of competition, prices have been viewed principally as a function of demand and supply in the short run and cost determined in the long run. Recently, persisting inequality in the global distribution of income and the view that international economic developments such as global inflation are working against them have induced many developing countries, mineral producers among them, to reexamine the determination and function of prices, moving away from the market-clearance concept toward a resource transfer concept. Though this new view, implicit in the demands of many

2. All currency figures are in U.S. dollars unless otherwise stated.

nations that produce raw materials, has strong economic and moral underpinnings, economic theory is unable to provide a means of optimizing prices by this method.

What characterizes the present scene, therefore, is certainty of fundamental change—in the very rules of the game, with prices as a major target—but unpredictability as to the nature, degree, and extent of the change and the adjustment required, since the outcome depends on bargaining among political bodies, namely, governments. Even though the final destination and conditions of the journey are not clear, the course has been set and it points toward the not yet fully explored waters of a massive readjustment of relative prices, if need be through unilateral action.

In the past, bargaining power has been disproportionate with consuming industrialized nations, which have enjoyed control over capital, technology, processing, marketing and shipping. In some ways, this bargaining power has been increasing (for example, through vertical and horizontal integration, technological advances, and regional economic arrangements) rather than decreasing. What appears to be at issue today, at least in the eyes of developing countries, is not so much the merits of competition compared to other forms of market organization in the abstract, as the need to counterbalance the real and substantial power of consuming countries to influence the terms and rate of exploitation of the world's scarce natural resources. One thing is certain: a market situation where competing and unorganized sellers confront a strong buyer favors sellers least among all possible forms of market configuration. In light of this, and given the successive disappointments on the part of the developing countries with aid flows, transfer of know-how, trade liberalization, and especially with attempts at drawing up international commodity agreements, it is neither an historical anomaly nor an economic violation for the developing countries to seek more equitable returns from the exploitation of their scarce natural resources through producers' alliances.

The prospects for achieving significant and lasting increases in mineral prices through unilateral action, however, are limited. But perhaps the issue has been stated the wrong way. In nonfuel minerals, at least, the objective ought not to be raising prices for its own sake but rather *allowing* them to rise—something which the structure of the industry has not permitted in the past—in order to ensure a much needed expanded flow of investment, keeping ahead of costs and inflation, permitting improvement of working conditions, and adoption of environmental safeguards. Attacking the structure also promises greater and more lasting success to the developing countries. Although price-related issues are important, one should not lose sight of the fact that what needs to be assured is a bigger share of the expanding market for developing countries. The benefits of this have far greater multiplier effects and can outweigh those obtained through higher prices alone. Developing countries need both better prices and a bigger share, but demands on prices should not be such as to deter developed countries from relying more on the developing countries.

Goals

With regard to the future, the following observations are justified. First, the trend toward aggressive attempts to influence prices seems irreversible. Mineral prices are likely to ascend in the foreseeable future, depending on the stance of the producing countries, yes, but as much, if not more, on global economic trends, cost factors, technological change, and policy decisions affecting global investment in exploration, mining, and processing. Second, while alliances among mineral producers probably cannot go too far in trying to achieve price increases in the style of the oil-producing countries, this does not preclude the possibility that some developing countries can and will benefit from such action—or that some subsectors in the consuming countries can and will be hurt by it. Third, stable prices are important for the smooth functioning and steady expansion of the mining industry, and commodity agreements can perform a useful role in this respect. Finally, it is in the long-term interests of both the developed and developing countries not to interrupt the flow of investment into the mining industry. Although some of the acts need changing, the show must go on.

Minerals have been as much a development agent of civilization as agricultural products and communication, and a steady supply of them is essential to its continuation. Though the primary challenge to the mining industry will continue to be, as in the past, the provision of adequate supplies, in the coming decades the industry itself, rather than its product, will have to become a conscious agent for worldwide economic development. This is admittedly an enormous task.

All the complex difficulties the industry faces in its normal course of operations are now compounded by the unrelenting pressure for additional supplies. Population growth and improvement in individual income translate into one basic imperative: more! While steadily increasing production, the industry must also find ways to safeguard the environment in which its activities are located and to conduct them harmoniously in a more demanding political and social setting. Governments increasingly seek a role in the making of decisions or, at the very least, demand compliance with sectoral goals and guidelines. The world has become feverishly aware of the importance of natural resources for the survival of civilization and anxious to know how well their providers are safeguarding the future. A fundamental requirement of the mining industry, therefore, is to respond to the challenge by planning, investing—in knowledge and capacity—and operating in such a way as to inspire confidence in man's ability to manage natural resources on a global basis and over time.

The mining industry is truly international in character, by definition and necessity. Mineral development requires the combination of physical, financial, and technical resources from varied sources, and its products travel across national boundaries. The industry thrives best in a climate of cooperation among disciplines, countries, investment sources, the public and private sectors, management and labor, and the various elements of the research and information networks. The potential for cooperation will be enhanced by the industry's efforts to distribute its investment and earnings equitably over countries. This accomplishment will require a continuous resolve on the part of the industry to commit its vast know-how and in-house resources to international development, particularly that of the developing countries.

It is widely argued that the mining industry should shift its base of operations to the developing countries because the developed countries are depleting their existing mineral resources. This has to be pursued systematically, as a matter of policy, both because, over the long run, intelligent resource planning and management must truly cover the globe, and because the strain on civilization, over the short and medium term, of a world divided into economic classes—of a standoff between the have and have-not nations—is insupportable.

1 | The Nature and Structure of the Industry

THE PRODUCTS OF THE MINERAL INDUSTRY are numerous and extremely diversified. Individual ores and metals widely used today number more than eighty, of which thirty-five have a world annual output greater than $100 million each and ten in excess of $1,000 million. The products obtained and processed by the industry vary in a number of respects, such as abundance and geological formation; incidence of undesired elements or impurities; degree and nature of processing; by-products of processing; physical and end use properties, including substitutability, destructibility (recycling characteristics), and the degree to which these can be modified or imparted to other products through chemical treatment or alloying; and transportability over long distances. Furthermore, different ore deposits of the same mineral, for example, nickel ore, can display significant dissimilarities in extraction and processing technology, principal by-products, final products for which they are mined, and end uses of these products. All the variable physical properties listed above are translated into economic characteristics which affect the value of a deposit, investment costs and operating expenditures, size of operation, rate of exploitation, the form in which the product is marketed, profitability, and prices.

Of course, complexity and diversity make generalization difficut. Yet there are basic factors underlying the operation of the mining industry, no matter the specifics of location and product. We deal with the most important of these in the current chapter to provide the essential outline from which all variations issue.

General Characteristics

The mining industry has a number of characteristics which distinguish it from other industries—even from other activities based on natural resources such as hydropower production, primary agriculture, and forestry. Mining involves the exploitation of nonrenewable and finite resources often found in isolated areas, the development of which requires heavy investment in infrastructure facilities. The geological unknowns of mineral deposits and the characteristics of mineral markets and prices cause the industry to operate at levels of risk—physical, commercial, and political—which are significantly higher than those for other industries. The structure and control of the industry have historically been highly concentrated and display extensive vertical integration from exploration to marketing of minerals.[1]

The nonrenewable property of mineral resources requires that they be exploited and used efficiently as well as equitably. The interests of the nations in which the resources are located must be given prime consideration where ownership and control of those resources are involved. It is not surprising that this causes controversy between major parties with fundamentally different interests: the host country, which can be either a developed or a developing nation; those who extract the mineral resource, often a multinational corporation; and the ultimate users, mainly in the industrialized countries.

The incompleteness of geological knowledge and the difficulty of geological interpretation always cast doubt on mineral reserve and grade statistics; generally, the true value cannot be known until the deposit is depleted. When such a high-risk industry competes for funds with lower-risk industries it often has to pay higher financing costs. These and other characteristics of the mining industry have promoted the growth of large multinational firms which have been responsible for exploration, extraction, processing, and marketing and have made it a deliberate policy to spread the risks not only over geographic regions but also over mineral and other activities. Furthermore, these firms have been primarily responsible for technological developments within the industry, as well as for product development and the stimulation of consumer demand.

A fundamental aspect of the mineral industry is the unequal

1. Most of these are characteristics of the preproduction stages of mineral development and have no close parallels in other sectors. Thomas N. Walthier writes, "When the decision is finally made to put the discovered mineral deposit into production, we enter the phase where mining most resembles other kinds of heavy industry." See "Problems of Foreign Investment in Natural Resources" (paper presented at the International Minerals Acquisition Institute, Denver, October 1974, mimeographed), p. 7.

distribution of known mineral resources among countries and continents, by types of deposits, and by economic usefulness. Demand for minerals is also unevenly distributed geographically, being heavily concentrated in the industrialized regions. Minerals are therefore not only an important factor in world trade and trade policy, and a source of economic growth, but also the subject of national and international dispute—as is increasingly evident today. Changes in conditions of demand and supply, including new discoveries and technological innovation, or the recent energy crisis and subsequent escalation in transport and equipment costs, together with increasing nationalism, affect the competitive position of companies and countries, causing instability as well as structural changes in the market.

Stages of Mineral Resources Exploitation

Preparation of any project, in mining, manufacturing, agriculture, or other fields, requires comprehensive study leading to an investment decision. The extent, rigor, and cost of the preproduction activities in mineral resource development, however, are far in excess of those required for the development of other industries. To emphasize this point, the successive stages leading to mineral exploitation are briefly summarized below.[2]

Broad geological surveys

Broad geological surveys consist of regional topographical, geological, and more recently, geophysical and geochemical surveys, as well as mapping with the important new tool of space photography. This stage in mineral exploration, commonly referred to as infrastructure geology, is designed primarily to identify areas of mineral potential and should ideally be conducted by government agencies. Evidently, the step can be and often is omitted in the search for minerals. Many of the mineral deposits being exploited today were found quite by accident, by some shepherd tending his flock, some crew building a road, or a prospector on a hunch. As areas are

2. Experts at the United Nations have been emphasizing the need for a systematic approach to mineral development for years, although this is still not fully appreciated by nonspecialists. For a recent account of the stages leading to mineral production in a specific context, see Sir Ronald Prain, *Copper: The Anatomy of an Industry* (London: Mining Journal Books, 1975), chap. 15.

ever more extensively and intensively explored, however, the need for a systematic approach in the search for minerals becomes vitally important. Such an approach allows more efficient use of scarce exploration funds and provides countries with knowledge required for incorporating mineral development in their overall development strategies. While most developed countries had a well-developed mineral sector before the systematic approach to exploration, the latter has pushed them even further ahead in mineral development. Only a few of the developing countries have made much progress in the modern systematic mapping of their mineral potential.

Regional and detailed exploration

Areas identified as possessing potential mineral resources need to be further surveyed and mapped through detailed prospecting and geophysical and geochemical surveys to single out those with the highest mineral potential. These activities are generally accompanied by preliminary pitting, trenching, and drilling of the deposit, followed by laboratory testing to ascertain whether the ore can be processed by available technology. The result, if successful, is the outline of a potentially economic mineral deposit with estimates of the size of the deposit, its mineral content, and its other characteristics. A prefeasibility study is completed, reviewing the technical and financial viability of mining and processing the deposit, in order to decide whether further exploration and study are justified.

Detailed orebody delineation and evaluation

Potential orebodies identified in the previous steps are reviewed in detail to ascertain in precise terms the technical and financial viability of exploitation. This review requires systematic drilling, often supplemented by additional pitting, trenching, and tunneling, accompanied by metallurgical tests in the laboratory and pilot plants and, in some cases, test marketing of the product. The completion of this stage is marked by the preparation of a detailed feasibility study, containing definite extraction plans and cost estimates, upon which an investment decision is made.

Mine development and plant construction

Following a positive investment decision, financing is sought and the project implemented. The orebody is developed to expose the ore for extraction: for open-pit mining this means removal of overburden; for underground mining it involves the sinking of shafts and construction of accessways to the ore. Processing plants are constructed and infrastructure facilities (such as transport, water, power, communications, townsite, and social facilities) installed. Management teams are formed, staff and workers trained, administrative and work procedures established, equipment tested, markets secured, and operations started up.[3]

Exploitation

The exploitation phase, which is also referred to as the operational phase, begins with extraction of ore from the orebody. The ore is transported to a concentrating plant where it is upgraded, most simply by crushing, sizing, washing, drying, and hand sorting, or by separating the valuable minerals from the waste by a variety of methods.[4] The concentrates are either used directly, as is the case with construction materials and most of the nonmetallic minerals (asbestos and gemstones, for instance), or submitted to further processing. For most of the metallics this involves smelting, whereby the concentrates containing the mineral in its natural state are subjected to a high temperature and reducing environment and the metal separated from the oxygen, sulfur, and carbonate to produce a molten bath of metal which is cast into ingots. Some concentrates go through a further stage, refining, which involves the removal of remaining impurities.[5] The two stages are more and more being replaced by a single stage as pyrometallurgical processes give way to hydrometallurgical processes, whereby the mineral content of the concentrates is recovered by leaching and electrolysis. The end product is one with marketable properties;

3. For most large projects, markets are secured before obtaining finance and before an investment decision is made.

4. These methods include: magnetic separation (separating magnetic and nonmagnetic minerals); gravity separation (separating minerals according to density); sizing (separating large from small particles); flotation (causing some minerals to attach to air bubbles and hence float to the surface of a tank for recovery); chemical reaction; or heating to drive off impurities, organics, or liquids.

5. Aluminum is a notable exception to this smelting-to-refining pattern; bauxite is first refined to produce alumina (an aluminum oxide) and subsequently smelted to produce the metal aluminum. Refining can be done electrolytically by ion exchange, with the impurities dropping to the bottom of the tank, or by volatilizing the impurities by blowing oxygen or other gas over the molten metal.

for metals this product has very small amounts of impurities (99.95 percent pure copper or 99.995 percent pure lead); for nonmetallics merely a minimum mineral content is required, and often maximum limits are established for the quantities of impurities contained. Further processing of this end product (extrusion of copper and aluminum, acid manufacture, and so on) is considered part of the manufacturing industry, not of the mineral industry.

The time, risk, and expediture required for each of the five phases outlined above differ significantly as indicated in figure 1.[6] This chart can be considered representative of the industry. The time between the start of exploration and commercial production can be considerable, often up to twenty years and only in exceptional circumstances less than five years; on the average, more than ten years are required. Exploration alone can take ten years, depending on whether the project begins from regional exploration, accidental discovery, or an already identified deposit. The construction period may vary from two to five years according to the size of the project and the availability of financing. (With staged construction, this can run to ten years or more, though this is uncommon today.) The inevitably long period required to develop a mineral resource has significant implications for both consumers and producers, but most of all for planners, when viewed against the backdrop of resource scarcity, bargaining power, and the broader question of resource management.

Exploration and feasibility work generally account for 5 to 10 percent of total project cost, although this percentage has reached 30 to 40 percent in some recent projects. Mine development, plant erection, and installation of infrastructure facilities account for the remainder. Although exploration expenditures generally amount to only a small part of total project cost, exploration remains the high-risk element of any project, and in many cases these expenditures are made without proving up a viable deposit. The major investment in mining itself is made at much lower levels of risk; yet the total risk in mineral resource development is often considerably higher than in the manufacturing industry because of the uncertainty of the results of exploration. The dominant feature of the other stages—mining and processing—is technological change; together with risk it plays a key role in shaping the ownership and investment pattern of the industry.

6. See also the timetable drawn by John S. Carman on the basis of UN experience in "Forecast of United Nations Mineral Activities" (paper presented to the World Mining Congress, November 3–8, 1974, Lima, Peru).

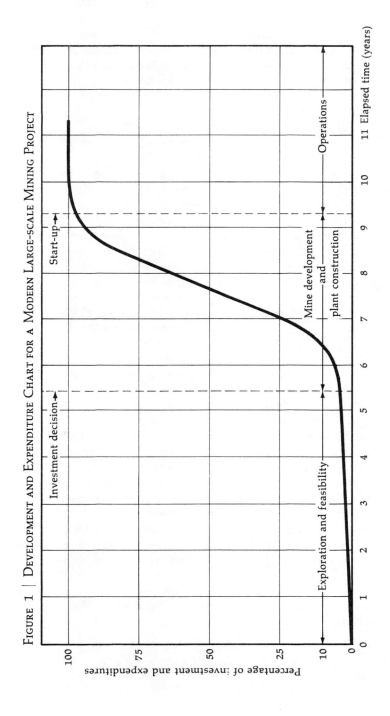

FIGURE 1 | DEVELOPMENT AND EXPENDITURE CHART FOR A MODERN LARGE-SCALE MINING PROJECT

Costs and Patterns of Mineral Exploration

Outlining the pattern of exploration expenditures is difficult, since the results of mineral explorations can constitute a major asset and are therefore kept confidential by companies. Nevertheless, sufficient sources exist to indicate the broad range of costs, risks, and patterns of expenditure. Data specific to the Canadian and U.S. industries are presented in appendix A.

The availability of risk capital for mineral exploration is of paramount importance—the lack of it can be a barrier to growth in the mineral industry. During the early 1970s, about $12 million was spent for each major mine discovery in Australia and $30 million in Canada. Average exploration expenditures in the United States appear to be even higher; for each dollar value of ore discovered in Canada and the United States they have more than doubled since 1960. The higher costs of exploration in the United States and Canada (compared to those in Australia and elsewhere) indicate the degree of exploration saturation taking place there as economic reserves become more difficult and costly to find. One industry spokesman stated several years ago that a five-year exploration program with *annual* expenditures of $1 to $3 million is the minimum for finding an economic deposit. Another claimed this kind of effort would provide little better than a 50 percent chance of success.[7]

Very little comparable data are available on exploration expenditure in the developing countries. In the past, announcements of discoveries in these countries were often withheld and underplayed to minimize political and marketing risks. Rough estimates indicate that in the early 1970s approximately $300 to $350 million were spent annually on nonfuel mineral exploration activity worldwide (excluding centrally planned economies), compared to $7,000 million of annual expenditures for plant during the same period. Exploration expenditures were heavily concentrated in the developed countries rather than in the developing countries, the ratio being 85:15 despite the generally higher exploration costs and greater exploration saturation in the developed countries. About 80 percent

---

7. A third expert, Thomas N. Walthier, Director, Corporate Exploration, St. Joe Minerals Corporation (New York), concluded more recently: "Assuming a capable staff (and this is assuming a tremendous amount), I would not recommend a mineral exploration programme of a general nature in North America budgeted at less than an average of 3 to 4 million dollars annually spread over 4 to 5 years—or smaller amounts for more years (but not vice versa)." "Problems of Foreign Investment," p. 4.

of all exploration expenditure was in four countries: Australia, Canada, South Africa, and the United States. This skewed distribution of expenditure is attributable to the stable political and economic climate of the industrialized nations in the eyes of the private investors rather than to any geological advantages. Countries such as Chile, Peru, Zambia, and Zaïre would receive a much larger portion of the total exploration budget if allocations were made on strictly technical grounds. Restrictive changes in mining and taxation legislation in Australia, Canada, and Ireland may bring about a major shift of exploration expenditures toward the developing countries, assuming that the concern over security of investment and supply does not outweigh the economic and technical consideration.

Since no returns can be assured (or in some cases even assumed), the funds required for exploration must be provided strictly as risk capital. In the past, therefore, the private sector has borne the burden of exploration. Most exploration activities are undertaken by large companies, often multinational corporations. In Canada, for example, during the late 1960s, 20 to 25 percent of all exploration expenditure came from only four companies. The reason for this is obvious: large exploration programs (measured in dollar terms) have a higher probability of success and therefore attract the resources of the larger companies. In many cases the amount of exploration activity seems to be a function of company size, as indicated by figure 2.[8] Not only can large companies benefit from the lower risk associated with larger expenditure, they can also spread their risk over many mining activities, essentially reducing their exploration decision to one based on profitability of ongoing operation. For the smaller company, probability of discovery is the crucial variable, a few unsuccessful exploration programs usually meaning financial disaster. Furthermore, the trend in exploration methods has given the larger mining company an added advantage. The changing techniques of exploration have introduced economies of scale into the exploration process. The use of these techniques is expensive and usually accessible only to large companies, increasing the absolute cost of engaging in exploration while simultaneously lowering the unit cost of discovery.

The advantages enjoyed by the large international mining companies can be countered to some extent by government-supported

8. For comparison, in 1954–68, Canadian oil companies spent proportionately ten times more of their sales revenues on exploration than the mining companies.

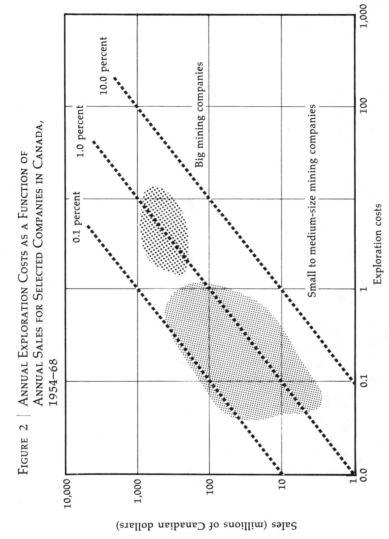

FIGURE 2 | ANNUAL EXPLORATION COSTS AS A FUNCTION OF
ANNUAL SALES FOR SELECTED COMPANIES IN CANADA,
1954–68

Source: F. G. Kruger, "Mining—A Business for Professionals Only," *Mining Engineering* (September 1969), p. 87.

programs. Brazil, for example, has established a public exploration company which has been successful in exploring on a large scale and similar steps are being considered throughout the world. Bilateral and multilateral technical and financial assistance has contributed to expanding the explortion effort of the developing countries and can be counted on to play a greater role in the future.

Technological Change and Economies of Scale

Technological change has been a powerful force in the development of the mineral industry through the ages, especially following the Industrial Revolution which vastly expanded and diversified the demand for minerals. Although the most dramatic breakthroughs occurred in the distant past, we shall focus here on developments in the last ten to fifteen years, in order to illustrate that technological change is a continuing process and to provide an overview of the industry's present situation.[9]

The past decade has seen a trend toward massive mining operations which take advantage of the economies associated with large production capacity and the use of large mining equipment. For instance, in hard rock mining the typical twenty to forty-ton truck of 1960 has become the eighty to two hundred-ton truck of 1970; shovel size increased from two to four to eight to fifteen cubic yards during the same period. Mines and processing facilities are becoming heavily capital intensive and labor is becoming a diminishing factor. In the United States, for example, mine production of copper has doubled over the past thirty years while, because of decreasing copper grades, ore handled has increased fourfold, yet related manhours have decreased by 60 to 70 percent. Nevertheless, because of continuously rising wage rates, labor costs remain a significant component. Labor still accounts for 30 to 50 percent of operating costs throughout the world.

Large open-pit mining and processing technology have reduced operating costs considerably, making many low-grade deposits economically exploitable. For example, in the United States, the average value of metallic ore mined in 1969–70 was about $5 a ton for open-pit mining, compared to about $12 a ton for underground mining; roughly the same differences existed for nonmetallic ores. In the early 1960s, a cutoff grade of about 0.8 percent copper was

9. For a more technical discussion, see United Nations, *Proceedings of the Interregional Seminar on the Application of Advanced Mining Technology*, Ottawa, May 21–June 3, 1973 (DP/UN/INT-72-064) (New York, 1975).

considered the economic minimum for porphyry copper deposits; by 1970 this was reduced to 0.3 to 0.4 percent copper, despite the fact that prices increased by only about 20 percent in real terms over this period. Large open-pit mining methods have also allowed the exploitation of orebodies with higher overburden-to-mineral ratios than were previously viable, and have made it possible to greatly reduce reliance on more expensive underground mining. Furthermore, technical risks currently are lower for open-pit operations. As a result, a much greater portion of mineral output is now being produced in open-pit operations than in the past. It is estimated that in 1970 some 65 to 70 percent of all ore mined in the world came from open pits; in the United States the proportion was as high as 90 to 95 percent.[10]

In addition, the introduction of large equipment to underground mining has permitted the exploitation of many deep-seated deposits previously considered uneconomic. This has served to increase mineral reserves substantially, a development which in the long run may affect the distribution of mining between developing and industrialized areas. The industrial economies, deep in the process of depleting their higher-grade deposits, will still have to rely increasingly on the mineral reserves of the developing countries, but these technological developments may act as a brake on the speed with which that occurs.

To summarize, there are substantial economies of scale in mining and ore-concentrating operations with regard to both capital and operating costs, as illustrated in figure 3. This gives the large producer, typically the multinational firm, a significant competitive advantage over the small operator and explains the history of corporate mergers within the industry.

The 1960s also brought continued advances in mining and processing technology, with associated cost reductions. For mining, these advances can be summarized as follows: general sophistication of machinery and improved alloys allowing for increased production rates and longer equipment life; improved rock fragmentation technology such as better explosives and blasting techniques; increased use of automation and remote-controlled equipment, with lower manpower requirements and increased productivity, particularly in haulage, hoisting, and loading; and widespread application of rock mechanics to optimize extraction and increase the safety of operations. Basically, however, mining

10. The recent energy crisis has led to increases in production costs, countering the gains achieved by economies of scale. Output prices continue to lag but may catch up in the near future.

FIGURE 3 | COMPARISON OF COSTS AND SIZE OF OPERATION

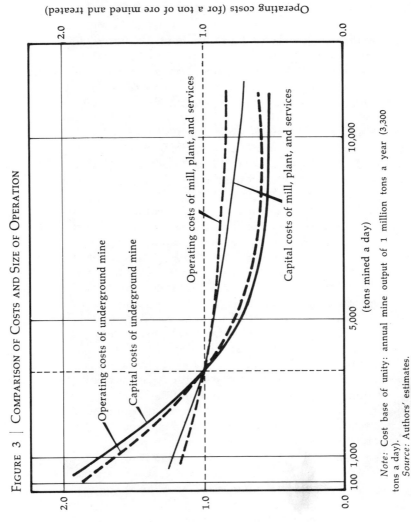

Note: Cost base of unity: annual mine output of 1 million tons a year (3,300 tons a day).

Source: Authors' estimates.

remains a repetitive process of drilling, blasting, loading, rock support, and hauling; although considerable progress has been made in soft rock mining with continuous methods which reduce manpower requirements to a minimum. Considerably more progress must be made, particularly in equipment design, before continuous mining can be applied to hard rock mining on a large scale.

In mineral processing, developments are characterized by sophistication of traditional equipment; larger scale; increased use of automatic process control; and introduction of new technologies to process lower grade and more complex ores, improve recovery ratios, produce purer products, and reduce pollution. For example, over the past decade, methods for processing some previously unexploitable oxide ores have been developed, and the sophistication of leaching–electrowinning technology has served to increase the economic viability of several deposits.

For both mining and processing, a point has probably been reached where further increases in scale can do little to reduce costs significantly.[11] Nevertheless, some of the new technology actively studied at present should be able to achieve some cost reductions, yield economic methods for extracting minerals from ores not currently exploitable, and diminish the undesirable ecological effects of mineral exploitation. For instance, developments in on-site leaching technology will assist in solving the ecological problems of strip mining and underground caving methods. Research to develop new technology has been conducted mainly by the private sector in the past, but public sector research activity is increasing.[12]

Mineral exploration continues to evolve from a more or less haphazard scratching of the earth's surface to a systematic examination of an area's mineral potential. The past decade has seen no major breakthrough in exploration technology, but rather a refining

11. It should be noted that, in principle, economies of scale can be achieved only in the case of ample ore reserves. Since most deposits contain only a limited tonnage of ore amenable to processing, increasing the production capacity (and reducing the unit cost) results in a shorter life for the project (and higher capital charges). In contrast, a longer operating life requires reduced production and higher unit operating expenditure. An optimum solution through incremental financial analysis has to be found.

12. For instance, mining and mineral research and development expenditures by the U.S. Bureau of Mines increased from $28 million in 1966 to $46 million in 1970. The French government in 1973 provided $10 million for research in metal extraction and $25 million for research into new uses of nonmetallic minerals.

of existing methods and tools. Improvements in transport (such as helicopters) have expedited exploration considerably, as has the use of mobile laboratories, portable sampling equipment, improved survey devices, and automatic mapping techniques. Also, greater application of geophysical and geochemical prospecting, space photography, and radar and other sensing devices has significantly increased the effectiveness of exploration. Although the new techniques have raised the cost of setting up an exploration program, they have resulted in important economies of scale, improved discovery ratios, and lower costs for each exploration target or area explored. Although most of the exploration effort so far has been directed to mineral outcroppings at or close to the surface, there has recently been a concerted search for methods of locating deeper deposits. Intensive programs are under way to reduce drilling costs by a factor of ten. Considerable interest has recently been shown in developing methods for use in tropical areas covered with heavy vegetation and deep overburden; the unsuitability of existing methods for these areas is reflected in the lack of mineral development in tropical regions.

Infrastructure and Shipping

Since it has the dual function of making exploitation feasible and integrating it into the overall economy, infrastructure plays the central role in mining more frequently than in other industries. It may form the major part of investment requirements. Large investments are required for water supply (dams, boreholes, pumping stations, pipelines, treatment plants, recycling and recovery plants); power supply (generating facilities, hydrostations, thermal stations, fuel pipelines, oil tank farms, transmission facilities); transport facilities (rail track, rolling stock, loading and unloading facilities, storage and stockpile installations, roads, vehicles, aircraft landing strips, port facilities, piers, waterways, and even ore ships and tugboats); social and municipal facilities (housing, schools, hospitals, electricity, filter plants, commercial and recreational facilities—in short all the services required by any sizable community); and communication (telephone, two-way radio).

Historically, especially in the developing countries, the mining companies have borne the cost of building the complete infrastructure, opening themselves to charges of double control. Currently, more and more of the infrastructure is being provided by the host country, reflecting a desire on the country's part to assume more control over it, to integrate it firmly into other sectors, and to increase the government's share of the benefits flowing from the mining venture.

Perhaps more than the mining activities themselves, the infrastructure brings the political elements of mining to the fore. Routing of road, rail, water, or power transmission facilities entails obtaining rights of way or purchasing private property (often fertile farmlands). It may also mean heeding the needs of other sectors, regions, and economic activities. Too often in the past these aspects have been ignored, and the catalytic effect infrastructure investment could have had on agricultural or industrial development in a region was lost. The shortest or least expensive route may be optimum for the mining project itself, but a judicious rerouting may better serve the total economy without major disadvantage to the mining project. A small thermal power-generating facility may serve the mining venture adequately, but a major hydro development may be better for the total economy, supplying the mine, tying into the national grid, and saving fuel imports. The politics of the venture may become international, particularly for landlocked mineral-producing countries like Bolivia, Rhodesia, and Zambia, where transport facilities cross national boundaries and require international treaties.

The heavy infrastructure demands of the mineral sector have strongly influenced its pattern of development. Base metals and nonmetallics generally have low transfer charges; hence, isolated areas may constitute unattractive exploration targets, except when they contain minerals of high value. Mineral discoveries in such areas may be shelved for the future, awaiting better prices, or be exploited on a very large scale to justify the attending large expenditures for infrastructure. Deposits with good mineral content may be nothing more than worthless rock in such isolated areas. The term isolation need not be considered only in terms of distance. The unavailability of power or water (as well as manpower, for example, in northern Canada) can also make an otherwise good deposit an uneconomic resource. The location of processing facilities, too, is strongly influenced by the availability and costs of the infrastructure. For instance, the availability of low-cost power is a major factor in locating an aluminum smelter and can outweigh the disadvantage of transporting bauxite over large distances. The heavy concentration of aluminum smelters in the United States, Canada, and Europe—far from the bauxite deposits of the Caribbean, Guinea, and Australia—illustrates this point. Low-cost power is also important for zinc, but less so for copper and lead. Lack of water may prohibit processing altogether or call for the use of dry processing technology. In many cases, the infrastructure requires substantially more time to build than the mining and processing facilities. In addition, by raising the investment required, infrastructure—particularly if it is captive to the mine—may increase the project risk, and this in turn may have a twofold affect: it may harden the position of the private party negotiating a concession agreement, and it may increase the cost of financing as well as the security sought by the financiers from the project sponsors.

The mining industry has had a significant influence on infrastructure technology, particularly in transport. For instance, the use of pipelines to pump slurries has become a viable alternative to rail transport, even over considerable distances. The use of very large ore carriers has lowered freight costs considerably, but has also required deep water ports which in some cases can be provided only by anchoring a mooring buoy five, ten, or fifteen kilometers from the shore. Major developments have also taken place in the recent past in loading and unloading techniques.

With the expansion of mineral trade, marine transport has become a major and generally very lucrative business, though extremely sensitive to world economic conditions, and subject to lean years. By 1970, about 2,000 bulk carriers with a deadweight tonnage of 50 million tons were engaged in mineral transport, some only part-time. Over 80 percent of the carriers belonged to developed nations. Many developing countries with large mineral exports have no marine transportation of their own and little or no influence on the operation and rate structure of the world shipping industry.

Concentration of Ownership and Control

The industry shows a major degree of vertical integration and is oligopolistic in nature. Very large mining companies, international in outlook and sophisticated in financial and technical analysis and operations, control the mining cycle from exploration to final marketing of the refined mineral, even to fabrication and production of consumer goods. There has been a significant trend throughout the century toward larger operations and bigger companies through amalgamation and forward integration into semi-manufactures. Well over 90 percent of ore production in the market economy countries is accounted for by operations producing more than 150,000 tons of ore per year. These operations are conducted by no more than 1,250 mines—about 600 underground, 450 open pit, and 200 alluvial—the majority of which are controlled by as few as 150 major mining groups and corporations, many with interlocking directorships. The Canadian industry typifies the industry structure: in 1965 there were 3,860 mining corporations in Canada with total assets of $9,000 million, sales of $3,200 million, and profits of about $650 million; 16 companies, or a mere 4 percent of the total, accounted for 37 percent of total assets, 44 percent of sales, and 46 percent of profits.[13]

In addition to their corporate concentration, the mining groups depend to a large extent on various banks for loans for new projects: for example, Kennecott and Asarco on the Guggenheim–Morgan Bank Group (United States); Amax, Cerro Corporation, and Rhodesian Selection Trust on the Vogelstein–Sussman Bank Group; Union Minière on Société Générale de Belgique; Société le Nickel, Pennaroya, and Mokta on Rothschild (Paris); and Rio Tinto on Rothschild.

When the individual minerals are considered separately, the concentration of control becomes even more apparent. For many years International Nickel Company (INCO) supplied more than 60 percent of world nickel output (excluding the centrally planned countries); it still accounts for some 50 percent, although this dominance is expected to diminish significantly during the 1970s. Other examples of virtual monopoly positions are: American Metal Climax in molybdenum, Rustenburg in platinum, Wa Chang in zirconium, and De Beers in diamonds. Four firms (one each from the United States, France, Australia, and Canada) account for 40 percent of the world's primary refined lead production, eight for 60 percent and twenty for 85 percent. Six firms (one each from Canada, France, and Switzerland, and three from the United States) dominate aluminum production. Furthermore, in 1969 (before nationalization), two U.S. companies produced 90 percent of Chile's copper output; three U.S.-owned companies, again before nationalization, mined and smelted virtually all of Peru's copper; two foreign companies controlled Zambia's copper production before nationalization; half the Malaysian tin output is controlled by European firms; nearly all Caribbean bauxite production is con-

13. The breakdown of the rest was as follows: 198 had assets between $5 million and $99 million and accounted for 46 percent of assets, 40 percent of sales, and 50 percent of profits; 3,646 had assets of less than $5 million and accounted for 17 percent of assets, 15 percent of sales, and 4 percent of profits. (*Statistical Report* tabled in the House of Parliament by Consumer and Corporate Affairs Minister, Government of Canada, 1969.)

trolled by U.S. and Canadian firms; iron ore production in Liberia is controlled by U.S., German, and Swedish interests and that in Latin America is dominated by U.S. firms, although there is a substantial domestic industry. Oligopolistic control is also very evident in zinc and manganese and, to some extent, in potash and phosphate rock.

Overall, forward integration into fabricating is substantial, varying in degree with the particular mineral. Aluminum producers, for instance, dominate the aluminum-fabricating sector, whereas significantly less than half the copper-fabricating facilities are affiliated with copper producers. Forward integration into fabrication for lead, zinc, and tin is minor, whereas in the steel industry the process has been reversed, with substantial backward integration of the steel companies into iron ore, manganese ore, and coking coal production.[14] The emergence of the integrated oligopolistic firm was an inherent and possibly indispensible part of the evolution in the scale of production and demand, the level of technology, and the quantity of capital employed in production. With large capital commitments, firms had to miminimize risks and assure full capacity operation by acquiring not only their own raw material supplies but also their own market outlets. This was particularly important for a newly emerging mineral such as aluminum, since responsibility for promotion and development of new uses lay with the producer and required that all stages of production and marketing be brought under corporate control. By and large, control over marketing outlets is significantly more concentrated than control over production.

The profile of the functions of the multinationals drawn in two extensive studies by the United Nations is typical of the corporations operating in the mining field and need not be resketched

---

14. For an outline of the world aluminum market and the role of the major companies, see United Nations, Committee on Natural Resources, annex, "The Structure of the International Aluminum Industry," in *Problems of Availability and Supply of Natural Resources: The World Mineral Situation* (E/C.7/51) (New York, February 13, 1975). The structure of the iron ore market and the backward integration of steel companies are illustrated in Bension Varon and Jacques Nusbaumer, "The International Market for Iron Ore: Review and Outlook," World Bank Staff Working Paper no. 160 (Washington, D.C., August 1973). An analysis of the structure of the nickel industry and the concentration of ownership and control can be found in George Bonar, *The Nickel Industry: A Reference Study* (Toronto: Canavest House, 1971), and Bension Varon, "Review of the World Nickel Situation," World Bank Staff Working Paper no. 108 (Washington, D.C., July 1971).

here;[15] illustrations and their implications will be provided through-out the book. Additional observations are in order, however:

First, the step of exploration, characteristic of this industry, broadens the already substantial power of the large integrated firms. As discussed earlier, economies of scale in the use of exploration techniques and the concentration of capital among large mining companies increase the probability of success of their exploration programs to a point where these firms are ensured control over a large proportion of resources. The ability to spread losses over a wide variety of operations has considerably reduced the risk of exploration investment for large and integrated mining companies. Even in successful programs by smaller companies, cost considerations have forced many of these to contract the later stages of exploration and the production stage to larger mining companies. Thus, the larger company obtains further reserves with little risk, although at a higher cost. This means that the immediate existence of the large integrated firms does not depend on their probability of success in the exploration sector. Their continued presence in all phases of the sector increases their knowledge and skills through accumulation of experience, and this gives them a further competitive edge over the smaller firm.

Second, aside from the question of outright ownership, which is ultimately a political question, the issue is not the role of the multinational companies as suppliers of, for example, capital, technology, and marketing know-how—that they have a role to play is widely recognized—but rather the way the tasks have been carried out. The international companies' pattern of project selection, investment, location of processing facilities, and revenue-sharing arrangements, while defensible on narrow microeconomic and political grounds, has not always been consistent with the development needs, legitimate interests, aspirations, and sensitivities of the developing countries. The leverage of developing countries over the mining industry has been kept low by the industry's history of guarding closely its knowledge of reserves and resources, technology, and markets, and overstressing its complexity to prevent easy outside intervention. In a number of instances the multinationals have been less than candid with regard to the results of exploration, the parameters of investment and expansion deci-

15. See United Nations, *Multinational Corporations in World Development* (ST/ECA/190) (New York, 1973); and *The Impact of Multinational Corporations on Development and International Relations* (E/5500/Rev.1, ST/ESA/6) (New York, 1974).

sions, processing and marketing properties of the product, technological and economic trends, and market value. Host countries have
thus been deprived of knowledge about their own resources and
of the basic tools with which to evaluate decisions deeply affecting
their interests. That the multinationals have often been the major
source of the information needed for evaluation of their performance has fostered suspicion and placed the multinationals at odds
not only with host countries but also with legislators in their
own countries.

Third, ownership and control do not mean the same thing.
Control of policies can be achieved by less than 50 percent equity
ownership, depending on the distribution of equity holdings, so
that data on the proportion of foreign ownership of firms in a
given country usually understate the proportion of assets controlled
by foreigners. Raymond F. Mikesell reports: "Foreign *ownership*
in terms of book value in the Australian minerals industry in 1970
has been estimated at 55.5 percent, but foreign *control* of Australian mineral firms has been estimated at 67 percent for 1970."[16] In
a broader sense, effective control depends also on domination over
technology and markets, as illustrated by the role of the Japanese
firms in the postwar period. As will be discussed more fully in
chapter 3, the Japanese mineral-processing companies, particularly
the well-known giants of the iron and steel sector, have aggress-
ively sought new sources of supply worldwide. They promote joint
ventures among themselves, with other international mining or
manufacturing companies, and also with Japanese trading companies, often taking only a minority holding which is yet sufficient
to exercise control over operations and policy decisions. This,
coupled with the practice of signing long-term purchase contracts
with the operating companies, and the large volume of finance and
technical assistance made available through the mining, manufacturing, and trading companies (and the Japanese government as
well) increases the leverage of the Japanese companies immensely
and results in a form of backward integration.

Unmistakably, control by multinationals will decrease as host
nations, developed and developing alike, assume more control
themselves. The right of host governments to make basic policy
decisions is indisputable; they will, however, have to continue to
rely on the large companies for execution and basic inputs, such as
capital, technology, and management—for it is there that the experi-

16. "Nonfuel Minerals: U.S. Investment Policies Abroad," *The Washington
Papers*, vol. 3, no. 23 (Beverly Hills and London: Sage Publications, 1975),
p. 5.

ence is concentrated for the time being. Transfer of this experience is a slow process.

The Role of Foreign Investment

During the industrialization of today's developed countries, raw materials were obtained mainly from indigenous sources. But with the accelerating increase in demand—over the past thirty years more minerals have been produced than for all time before—local resources became short, and the search for raw materials extended to the developing countries. This was a logical extension of the process by which the industry became integrated on a national scale. As a consequence, most of the large mining operations in developing countries today originated as foreign investment by the large multinationals. The following factors contribute to the continuation of this situation: First, the principal users of minerals are the industrialized countries; hence the initiative for promoting production originates with them. Second, the large mining firms have acquired a monopoly of the various skills and techniques required to develop and operate the industry. Although engineers, geologists, and other specialists may be hired, the fully integrated teams needed to develop large projects can rarely be obtained without the cooperation of these firms (or, more recently, some government agencies, such as those of the Soviet Union). Managing a mining industry, which involves finding new deposits, evaluating them, and designing new mines, is extremely difficult and few of the developing countries yet have this expertise or can expect to acquire it in the near future. Third, substantial capital is required and the risk involved is great. The large international companies have ready access to capital and are able to spread their risk by carrying out a number of activities and operating in a number of regions. Fourth, access to the world market is dominated by the international firms which have the advantage of an intimate knowledge of the marketing needs in the industrialized countries. Moreover, integration to the marketing stage provides important economies. The integration itself requires major financial resources and an organization generally outside the capacity of domestic producers. With the development of several, sometimes sophisticated, marketing organizations in the developing countries, however, this is becoming less important. Fifth, developing countries themselves have tended, often under pressure from the large companies, to grant concessions to a few large firms rather than encourage the entry of a greater number of companies.

Statistics on the volume and distribution of foreign investment in mining are limited, difficult to interpret, and generally out of date because of the rash of nationalization, especially in Latin America.[17] Only a few indicative figures can be offered as follows: According to a United Nations study, in 1967 foreign investment by countries of the Organisation for Economic Co-operation and Development (OECD) in mining and smelting in the developing countries amounted to about $3,600 million, of which 57 percent was in the Western Hemisphere, 36 percent in Africa, and 7 percent in Asia (investment in the Middle East was negligible).[18] Mikesell estimated that more than half that total, $2,100 million, came from the United States. According to Mikesell again, in 1972 the total amount of direct foreign investment by the United States in mining and smelting amounted to about $7,100 million, of which $4,400 million was in the developed countries (roughly 80 percent of that in Canada alone) and $2,700 million in the developing countries. Between 1968 and 1972 roughly two-thirds of the additional U.S. foreign investment in the sector was in the developed countries.[19] Similar figures for investment by OECD countries in 1972 are not available.

Capital Requirements and Sources of Finance

As has been mentioned, the trend toward massive size has resulted in making investments very large, often above $250 million, with $500 million and even $1,000 million projects not uncommon. A list of mineral projects in the market economy countries either in the process of implementation or at advanced planning stages indicates that while only 25 percent of the projects exceed $100 million in size, these projects absorb more than 75 percent of the funds invested (see appendix B). Many of the small projects are merely expansions of existing plant.

Capital-output ratios vary significantly, from less than 0.2:1 for a simple electrolytic refinery expansion up to 4:1 for a new, fully integrated mine-smelter-refinery with the related infrastructure. Investments of up to $250,000 per operator are becoming common-

---

17. For an account of developments between 1973 and 1975, see United Nations, Committee on Natural Resources, *Permanent Sovereignty over Natural Resources* (E/C.7/53) (New York, 1975).

18. United Nations, *Multinational Corporations in World Development* (ST/ECA/190), p. 150.

19. Mikesell, *Nonfuel Minerals*, p. 4.

place. In the aftermath of the energy crisis these costs have become considerably higher. Some typical capital investment requirements as of 1975 are given in table 1.

TABLE 1 | TYPICAL CAPITAL INVESTMENT
REQUIREMENTS FOR MINING AND
PROCESSING FACILITIES

Mineral and facility	Capital investment per metric ton of annual output (U.S. dollars)
Aluminum	
Bauxite mining	25–30
Aluminum refinery	200–300
Aluminum smelter	1,000–1,500
Copper	
Mining, beneficiating, smelting, and refining	3,000–5,000
Lead	
Smelter expansion	100–500
Nickel	
Mining and smelting	8,000–15,000
Zinc	
Blast furnace and electrolytic refining expansion	300–700

As discussed earlier, mining projects are frequently required to bear a substantial part of the infrastructure costs. This is especially so in developing countries where it is necessary to provide not only water supply, power interconnection, and some community facilities, but often power-generating capacity, townsite, full education and medical facilities, a communications system, rail and road access, and port and shipping facilities as well. For example, between 1960 and 1970, eleven projects were implemented in western Australia at an investment cost of $800 million, of which $515 million (65 percent) was for infrastructure facilities. Aluminum smelting facilities in Costa Rica would require a total investment of close to $1,000 million, of which 60 percent would be for infrastructure facilities, mainly power, but also road, port, and townsite. Numerous other examples could be cited.

As long as it was still on a small scale, the mining industry was virtually self-financing, obtaining less than 10 percent of its capital requirements from external sources. Properties were opened up on a limited scale and progressively expanded out of cash flow. Bank financing, to the extent that it occurred at all, was principally in

the form of unsecured lines of credit for the seasonal needs of manufacturing and fabricating subsidiaries. With the present scale of
operations, however, this approach is no longer possible, and the
industry has been forced to rely increasingly on external debt and
equity financing. While many new projects are financed at least
50 percent, sometimes up to 80 percent, by borrowing, the major
companies have nevertheless retained a very conservative capital
structure, with most companies carrying less than 20 percent of
their total capital in the form of long-term debt; only a few have
allowed their debt-equity ratio to rise as high as 1:1. Reflecting this
conservative approach, the U.S. mining industry in 1969 raised
$1,700 million through new mining securities, 79 percent as equity
and 21 percent in the form of bonds, while the U.S. manufacturing
industry in the same year raised $6,400 million, 30 percent as equity
and 70 percent as debt.

Because of the high cost and risk involved, the availability of
funds for mineral exploration has been restricted to two principal
sources: cash flow of the large mining companies and (to a lesser
extent) speculators. Another minor source in the developed countries is government investment in geological and mineral surveys
and government contributions to domestic exploration funds. In the
context of total worldwide needs, however, government funding is
insignificant. The UN Development Programme (UNDP), with annual
expenditures growing from $5 or $6 million in 1960 to about $20
million in 1970, made a useful contribution to exploration investment until the introduction of country programming of UNDP assistance in 1971.[20] The funds allocated to mineral exploration
projects then dropped considerably as governments gave higher
priority to projects with more readily visible returns. To counteract
this decline in activity, the United Nations has recently established
an exploration fund to assist developing countries in more systematic mineral exploration of their territories. Within its provisions,
mineral operations based on discoveries made by the fund will pay
a royalty to the fund, in the hope that over time the royalty revenues of the fund will match the exploration expenditures and hence
the fund will become revolving (self-sufficient).[21] Financing for the

20. See appendix C for a description of UN activities in the mineral
sector, especially those in the fields of mineral exploration.

21. The royalty, called officially a *replenishment contribution*, is set at
2 percent of the annual value of the commodities produced and will be
payable at this rate for a period of fifteen years from the start of commercial
production or until a ceiling is reached. The ceiling is not firmly set in the

early years of operation will be obtained through voluntary contributions. Commitments and pledges to date (January 1976) amount to $11.2 million, $8.5 million of it from Japan, and have to to be considered disappointing. This and the move toward setting up national exploration funds will help promote exploration in the developing countries to some degree, but the burden of exploration will remain with the private sector for a long time.

The sources of finance for mineral *exploitation,* in addition to the mining companies themselves, include the following. First, consumers and trading companies: in order to control and assure supplies, these have been playing an increasing role in mineral financing and now represent a very important source of finance. Second, financial institutions in the developed countries: they provide a significant amount, but generally make it available only to the large mining companies against the companies' general creditworthiness, although project financing, as opposed to balance sheet financing, is becoming more important. Third, suppliers' credits: these are being increasingly extended for mining projects, but are often available only to the large mining companies, or against a government guarantee. Fourth, speculators, for minor financing directed mainly to projects in the developed countries. Fifth, government participation in equity or provision of infrastructure: this remains a negligible contribution but is expected to increase. Sixth, multilateral and bilateral aid institutions: these have not yet made any significant contribution. Up to 1973, they accounted for less than $750 million altogether or less than $75 million per year. This is less than 1.5 percent of total investment, or 5 percent of the mining investment in the developing countries. The World Bank has made the most important contributions, followed by the United States and Japanese Export-Import Banks, Kreditanstalt für Wiederaufbau in the Federal Republic of Germany, the European Investment Bank, and the Inter-American Development Bank. (The activities of the World Bank are summarized in appendix D.) In most cases mineral sector loans, including infrastructure, made up less than 3 percent of the loan portfolios of these agencies, although in some years they accounted for up to 10 percent.

---

operational procedures, as there is "insufficent experience" to establish the level, but it is suggested that "the ceiling will probably be in the region of a multiple of 15 times the original investment by the Fund, in constant prices." See UN Development Programme, Governing Council, *United Nations Revolving Fund for Natural Resources Exploration: Operational Procedures and Administrative Arrangements* (DP/142) (New York, October 24, 1975).

Mineral Prices and Profitability

Mineral prices are the subject of much controversy and have a major influence on the well-being of many towns, regions, and nations. Wide price fluctuations are the norm rather than the exception for metals such as copper, silver, and zinc. Not only does this volatility of mineral prices have an important bearing on the return on mining investment and the profit margins of mining operations, but it has a major influence on the balance-of-payments position of the mineral-exporting countries, particularly those such as Bolivia, Chile, and Zambia, where minerals make up more than 80 percent of all exports. National economic planning is made very difficult for such countries. In chapter 4 we raise the question of the rationale of the mineral market mechanism and prices. In view of the large degree of vertical integration and concentration of control in the industry, many claim that prices are artifically high, higher than would be required to cover production costs and provide a satisfactory return on capital. On the other hand, until the recent concerted action of the petroleum exporters, there had been no recognition of the inherent value of the untouched mineral in the ground.

These questions of mineral pricing have an important effect on the profitability of the industry. It is commonly believed that the mining industry is one of high or even excessive profits. The data offered to support this claim, however, frequently take account of the larger, more successful projects and companies only and are not representative of the industry as a whole. If all exploration expenditures are included, the industry can probably be said to be one of average-to-above-average profitability, but also one in which numerous entities too small to spread their risk have failed. For example, of the eighty-eight early gold mines founded during the gold boom in western Australia, twenty-four repaid capital plus dividends, twenty-eight repaid capital but showed operating losses, and thirty-six failed to repay capital. The Northern Miner (Toronto) estimates that less than one percent of the mining companies (including venture-capital exploration companies) now incorporated in Canada pay dividends.[22] For the profitable Canadian mines, the average return on investment varied between 2 percent for gold mines (before the increase in gold prices) and 9 to 10 percent for nonmetallic mines; the average profitability of the metallic mines lies somewhere between these levels.

___

22. See appendix E for further details on Canadian experience.

A review of annual reports and the statistics provided for *Fortune Magazine*'s top 1,000 U.S. companies and top 200 non-U.S. companies indicates that the returns of the large mining companies in terms of net profit (after taxes) on equity, while above the total industry average, are below those of some individual industries (pharmaceuticals and tobacco, for instance).[23] The mining corporations included in the *Fortune Magazine* listings showed an average net profit recorded in table 2.

TABLE 2 | PROFITABILITY OF SELECTED GROUPS OF COMPANIES

| | Net profit after taxes as percentage of shareholders equity | | | |
Company grouping	1969	1970	1972	1973
Mining companies in top 1,000 U.S. companies	12–14	7–14	8–10	14–15
Nonmining companies in top 1,000 U.S. companies	11	9–10	9–10	12–13
Mining companies in top 200 non-U.S. companies	n.a.	13–14	n.a.	11
Nonmining companies in top 200 non-U.S. companies	n.a.	8	n.a.	7

n.a. Not available.
Source: Fortune Magazine.

The returns show a wide range from (−10 to 40 percent), as do the earnings of the individual companies from year to year. These figures, of course, refer only to the more successful of the mining companies throughout the world. In periods of economic buoyancy the mining companies generally do better than companies in other industries, but in periods of economic instability and decline the mining industry lags behind the other industries; in other words, it is more susceptible to the state of the world economy than most industries.

There is no doubt that highly profitable projects with capital payback periods of four, three, or two years do exist. These help to attract the large amounts of exploration venture capital required. At the same time, it must be appreciated that the successful projects must cover those unable to repay their capital, as reflected in the operating principles of the UN Revolving Fund, so that the industry as a whole can be viable.

23. For details, see *Fortune Magazine*'s listing for the years 1970 and 1973.

In areas experiencing political instability, mining corporations tend to consider only projects of high profitability. A study conducted for the U.S. Bureau of Mines shows that, while the average annual earnings on total U.S. foreign investment in mining fluctuated between 10 percent and 15 percent over the period 1954–67, this investment returned less than 10 percent in Canada but up to 25 percent in Latin America.[24] Furthermore, income returned to the parent companies, although averaging only 60 percent of earnings from the Canadian investments, was close to 100 percent of the earnings on Latin American investment—a fact which lies at the root of the current controversy over the equitable exploitation of natural resources. There is insufficient information of this sort by country and by commodity. Inadequate disclosure by the multinationals is precisely one of the sore points with the developing countries.

24. See Charles River Associates, Inc., "The Contribution of the Nonfuel Minerals Industry to International Monetary Flows" (Cambridge, Mass., 1968), appendix E.

2 | Mineral Reserves and Resources

BECAUSE MINERAL RESOURCES ARE NONRENEWABLE, buried in the ground and costly to discover, their availability, location, and recoverability have long been a natural concern of the mining industry and the industrialized nations. In recent years, the concern has been shared by development planners in rich and poor countries alike, by politicians, philosophers, social and natural scientists, conservationists, and visionaries. The question of mineral resources is no longer narrowly geological or economic, but a matter of broadest public interest, encompassing the allocation of scarce resources, the economics of waste, the preservation of the environment, and ethical as well as aesthetic considerations. This broadening of perspective has had its price, however: facts have been stretched, grey areas have been arbitrarily painted black or white, and geologists and mineral economists have been brushed aside as narrow specialists, as the debate has become general, fashionable, and heated.

More than by any other single factor, concern over resource scarcity has been triggered by the unprecedented population growth experienced since the Industrial Revolution. World population increased from about 750 million around 1770 to nearly 3,700 million in 1970.[1] Despite attempts at worldwide population control, and eventual reductions in the growth rate, enormously high population levels will have to be supported in the future, putting constant pressure on resources. Beyond this, the idea of equitable consumption of resources, both within individual nations and among nations, has become central to the concern over the relation between resources

1. The number of people added to the world population since the Industrial Revolution is nearly ten times greater than the number added in the preceding 200 years.

and economic growth, adding another dimension to the problem. The development of sophisticated techniques for analyzing and systematizing the interaction of the many forces affecting economic growth—population, food, energy, raw materials, pollution, technology—has brought on a wave of pessimistic predictions; and in nearly all predictions the specter of mineral resource exhaustion has figured prominently.

The role of mineral resources in the growth equation was pushed into prominence by *The Limits to Growth*, a study sponsored by the Club of Rome and conducted by a team of systems analysts from the Massachusetts Institute of Technology, headed by Dennis L. Meadows, which appeared in March 1972 and dramatized the constraints placed by nonrewable resource inventories on unchecked economic growth. The study argued that it is better to establish conscious limits on future growth than to let nature establish them for the world in catastrophic fashion—more specifically, that the salvation of the world lies in moving towards zero growth rates in population and industrial production by 1975.[2] Although the initial excitement generated by the MIT study's zero-growth prescription has subsided, the advent of the energy crisis, food shortages, and confusion about the causes of the current inflation have revived doubts and fostered a feeling of insecurity with regard to all natural resources. Perhaps not surprisingly, the nonfuel minerals industry denied the conclusions on the subject, but with little force, opening itself to accusations of being concerned only with the pursuits of high revenues through reckless exploitation.

No matter how tempting the speculations, the ultimate limits of resource availability cannot be measured; nor are they relevant to the operation of the mining industry in the predictable future. Scenarios that venture beyond fifteen to twenty years have little application to viable planning periods and to mechanisms of management at man's disposal. Moreover, they tend to detract from more pressing problems such as those of narrowing the gap between the rich and poor countries and of averting regional shortages

2. The publication of *The Limits to Growth* was followed by an avalanche of reviews, as well as a series of follow-up projects. Among the earliest ones to question the study's pessimistic assertions on nonrenewable resources was *Report on the Limits to Growth: A Study by a Special Task Force of the World Bank* (Washington, D.C., September 1972), which also summarizes the initial reaction to the MIT study. For a more recent evaluation, see Wilfred Beckerman, *In Defense of Economic Growth* (London: Jonathan Cape, 1974), and "The No-Growth Society," *Daedalus* (Fall 1974).

of food, energy, and key raw materials.[3] Nevertheless, the question of resource availability cannot be left out of an analysis of the mining industry entirely, as it has a bearing not only on the structure of the industry (location, trade pattern, ownership, and control) but also on policy. Mineral development occurs in a continuum, with the resource picture changing all the time. Size of reserves, need for discovery, cost of discovery, and projection of success are key inputs into all major policy decisions at the national and company level. In this chapter, therefore, we examine briefly the raw material base of the mining industry, including ocean mineral resources and the recovery of metals from wastes, which is referred to in the industry as mining above ground.

Concepts, Measurement, and Interpretation

Since minerals are nonrenewable, each deposit is subject to technical and economic depletion. The aggregate supply of mineral resources can generally be considered continuous over foreseeable though ultimately limited time, as technology and capital are allocated to finding new resources and mineral and nonmineral substitutes, as well as to more efficient exploitation and use. But when the aggregate is broken down on the basis of individual industries, commodities, and producing regions, the known resource base is fixed and depletable.

Assessing the quantity and adequacy of mineral resources is a difficult task posing some very real problems. For a mineral occurrence to be classified as a *reserve*, on the one hand, it must be economically exploitable at current prices and with available technology. Reserves are normally classified as proved, probable, possible, measured, indicated, or inferred, according to the degree of measurement or uncertainty. The term *resources*, on the other hand, covers not only reserves but also other mineral deposits that are known but not economically or technologically recoverable at present, or that may be inferred to exist but have not yet been discovered. Resources are classified as recoverable, paramarginal or submarginal, or as conditional, hypothetical, and speculative, on the

3. For a look at the question of ultimate limits in perspective and a discussion of the limits of knowledge about resources, see Bension Varon, "Enough of Everything for Everyone, Forever?" *Finance & Development* (September 1975).

basis of certainty of existence or feasibility of recovery. (See appendix F.) It should be underlined that reserves do not exist to be discovered as such but are developed from resources at a cost and over time, through the application of technology, capital, and know-how, and in response to changes in price (and transport), as illustrated in figure 4.

The nature of the industry—whereby companies only prove up sufficient reserves to assure medium-term production and do not announce their mineral discoveries immediately—together with the confidentiality of information on the strategic minerals, cast doubt on the accuracy of published reserve figures.[4] Quantifying resources is even more difficult, since the concept resource itself is grossly imprecise. In addition to being always highly speculative, estimates of resources are seldom addable; global aggregates combine a collection of estimates which vary in coverage, definition, standards, and accuracy.[5] Furthermore, the interpretation of resource estimates cannot be divorced from the context and specific objective of the inquiry since, given the high cost of mapping and exploration, no entity has ever had the mandate and means to develop complete, standardized, and accurate global data of a nature to satisfy the needs of all inquirers.[6]

Measuring adequacy of resources, either globally or for a given country or region, poses even greater problems. It requires judgments and assumptions on wants and requirements, the pace and structure of growth, income distribution, political climate, vitality

4. Fiscal measures, too, can constitute a disincentive to accurate reporting, since reserves are considered a part of company assets and are subject to property and other taxes in some jurisdictions.

5. Recognizing these shortcomings, the Economic and Social Council of the United Nations has asked the UN Center for Natural Resources, Energy, and Transport to prepare a review of definitions and terminology in use in the field of minerals. Subsequently, the Secretary-General is to convene a group of experts to prepare a report recommending a common set of definitions and terminology for the purpose of reporting to the United Nations on mineral resources. (United Nations, Economic and Social Council, *Resolutions and Decisions*, July 2–31, 1975, Res. 1954 (LIX, B) in E/5740, supp. no. 1.

6. The problems and pitfalls of estimating reserves and resources have been articulated and underlined repeatedly by geologists and mineral economists, but they are not recognized fully or uniformly by users of the results. Many investigators and policymakers treat reserve figures as if they were population census data. For a compact and frank exposition of the problems posed by the many geological and economic indeterminants, see Fernand Blondel and Samuel G. Lasky, "Concepts of Mineral Reserves and Resources," in United Nations, *Survey of World Iron Ore Resources* (ST/ECA/113) (New York, 1970), pp. 53–58.

FIGURE 4 | DEVELOPMENT OF RESERVES

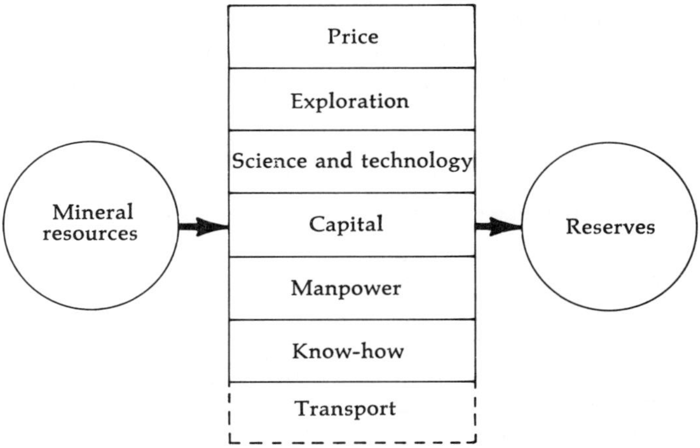

Source: Adapted from Jean-Paul Drolet, "The Demand for Canada's Mineral Resources," paper presented at the International Symposium on Canada's Nonrenewable Resources, Toronto, March 25, 1974.

of institutions, tolerances with regard to a broad range of economic and social costs, technology, and even human ingenuity. Fischman and Landsberg articulated the problem of determining adequacy in the form of twenty-eight questions, leading to the observation that the answers to these questions depend on the establishment of reference standards—ethical, pragmatic, or other—and even different sets of standards for different mineral resources.[7]

Adequacy is commonly measured in terms of the number of years for which available resources can meet exponentially rising demand. Calculating this is a useful first step, but by no means sufficient for a meaningful or definitive assessment of adequacy. After determining that available reserves of a given commodity are adequate to last for X years, it is necessary to ask: Is the commodity essential, to satisfy what needs, and what are the economic and social costs of its depletion? An alternative yardstick which has been attracting

7. For an excellent discussion of the problem of defining "adequacy," see Leonard L. Fischman and Hans H. Landsberg, "Adequacy of Nonfuel Minerals and Forest Resources," in Ronald G. Ridker, ed., Population, Resources and the Environment, U.S. Commission on Population Growth and the American Future (Washington, D.C.: U.S. Government Printing Office, 1972).

some attention is that of production rates. In addition to asking, How much is there? this approach also asks, How much can be produced annually with a twenty- to twenty-four—year perspective? —a question of greater interest to policy planners, but difficult to answer since it involves projecting economic, technological, and political conditions.[8]

Land-Based Reserves

The world mineral reserve position varies significantly from mineral to mineral as shown in appendix H and summarized here: Of the twenty-seven minerals surveyed for this purpose, world reserves for eight (potash, columbium, phosphorus, magnesium, chromium, feldspar, vanadium, and iron, in order of abundance) are more than sufficient to satisfy cumulative requirements for close to, or more than, a century. Most of these minerals are known to form a significant part of the earth's crust; one, magnesium, can be obtained economically in relatively unlimited quantities from the sea.[9] In the case of the most widely used among these, iron, reserves can be doubled with a price increase of 40 percent or less.

Reserves for another nine minerals (cobalt, manganese, nickel, molybdenum, asbestos, titanium, antimony, bauxite, and sulfur) are expected to last for thirty to sixty years. Sulfur and bauxite are borderline cases. Although reserves of standard sources of sulfur are not large, huge quantities of the product can be recovered from gypsum. Moreover, further moves toward the control of air pollution may yield large quantities of marketable sulfur (from smokestacks and elsewhere) which may flood the market. With regard to bauxite, estimates of world reserves vary, and the quantities that can be added to reserves by higher prices are not as great, in relative terms, as in the case of iron ore. Though it is claimed that there are very large undiscovered resources, the need for large amounts of electric power for refining may present a problem.

8. The most articulate proponent of this measure is Jan Zwartendyk of Canada's Department of Energy, Mines, and Resources, who has been working to institutionalize it in Canada. See "The Life Index of Mineral Reserves—A Statistical Mirage," *Canadian Mining and Metallurgical Bulletin* (October 1974); and "Departmental Technology and Definitions of Reserves and Resources: Interim Document," Department of Energy, Mines, and Resources, Ottawa, June 30, 1975.

9. Silicon can be obtained from sand, and its supply, too, is relatively unlimited.

In the case of the remaining ten minerals (copper, tungsten, barite, bismuth, lead, zinc, tin, fluorspar, silver, and mercury), the reserve situation is somewhat tight or even critical, reserves being adequate to meet cumulative demand for thirty years or less. Although its proven reserves are not large, copper is not critically short because it is now mined from the larger reserves of lower-grade ore as a result of technological progress, because the size of minable reserves will definitely be extended through higher prices, and because there is some potential for accelerated recycling. The situation is the same for lead and zinc, the other two minerals with reserve lives of less than thirty years. Among significant minerals, the only ones whose reserves are assuredly tight or critical are silver and tin. Intensified explorations have failed to uncover significant new resources. There are, however, enormous hoards of silver in private hands which can be brought into the market by higher prices. In the case of tin, demand growth has already been forced down to about 1 percent a year through substitution.[9]

For many of the minerals on the tight or critical list (less than thirty years supply) there are a number of mineral and nonmineral substitutes in adequate supply, as shown in table 3. A full exploration of the potential for substitution requires examination of end uses, costs, technology, and the relative quantities in which the minerals are currently consumed. The table is designed simply to show that a number of options are indeed available, and it understates the options at that. For example, since aluminum—one of the most versatile materials—can be produced from widely abundant clays (anorthosite) as well as from bauxite, it could be considered in ample supply.[10]

The Distribution of Resources

On the basis of the value of minerals at the commonly accepted state of transfer in international marketing[11] (for example, blister

9. For a more detailed but gloomier analysis of the world reserves situation see David F. MacInnes, "Estimates of World Metals Depletion: Background for Metals Policy Planning," Firbank Fell, A Center for the Study of Alternative Societies, December 1973.

10. The world mineral reserve situation has been scrutinized by innumerable national and international commissions and institutes recently. Despite individual differences, the basic assessment is the same.

11. Weighted average of all minerals with reserves (valued at the commonly accepted point of transfer) of more than $1,000 million.

TABLE 3 | SUBSTITUTES FOR SELECTED MINERALS

Mineral	Reserves of principle substitute minerals (years of supply)			Other substitute products
	100 or more	30 to 60	Less than 30	
Copper	Steel	Aluminum		Plastics
Lead	Cadmium	Nickel[a]	Mercury Silver Zinc	Plastics
Tin	Steel	Aluminum	Copper Lead	Glass Paper
Tungsten	Tantalum	Cobalt[a] Nickel[a]	Molybdenum Titanium	
Zinc	Cadmium Magnesium Steel	Aluminum		Plastics

a. High concentrations on the seabed may justify classifying as sufficient for 100 years.
Source: Authors' classification, based in part on appendix A.

copper, lead and zinc metal, manganese ore, iron ore, and phosphate rock), mineral reserves are distributed among the economic regions as follows:

Region	Land area (percent)	Estimated mineral reserves (percent of world total, in volume)	Reserves: area
Developed market economies	26	35	1.35:1
Developing market economies	49	38	0.77:1
Centrally planned economies	25	27	1.05:1
Total world	100	100	

The table above indicates that the commonly held opinion that the developing countries possess almost half the world's mineral reserves is not an accurate reflection of the position for the nonfuel minerals. In fact, in aggregate value terms, the developing market countries can barely be credited with more reserves than the developed market countries. Although the reserves of phosphate, tin, sulfur (in petroleum and natural gas reserves), fluorspar, columbium, and cobalt are concentrated in the developing countries, which also account for about 50 percent of the copper, iron, and nickel reserves; the reserves of potash, magnesium, titanium, chromium, manganese, zinc, lead, silver, tungsten, vanadium, bauxite, molybdenum, and mercury are concentrated in the developed market-economy and centrally planned countries (appendix G). Estimates by the U.S. Bureau of Mines indicate that higher mineral prices would not significantly adjust the reserve situation in favor of the developing countries; for many minerals the opposite would be true. Because of conceptual and measurement differences, however, reserve estimates and analyses such as that above must be regarded with caution.

As shown in the table above, mineral reserves in developed market economy countries, in relation to their areas, are substantially higher than in developing or centrally planned countries. To attribute this disparity to the developed countries having squandered the resources of the developing countries is fallacious. Rather, the high ratio of reserves to land in the developed countries and the substantial increases in mineral reserves in Australia and Canada over the past two decades, and more recently in Ireland, are directly related to the extensive exploration activities in these areas, supporting the thesis that reserves are a function of exploration. The implications of this are obvious: since large areas in developing countries are still unmapped, it is quite likely that future explorations will uncover greater reserves in those countries than in the rest of the world. Furthermore, as noted in chapter 1, the cost of finding new reserves in Canada and the United States has been increasing rapidly. (The low reserve position of the centrally planned economies is probably a manifestation of low exploration intensity, incomplete disclosure of the reserve position, and the locational disadvantages of the Siberian resources.) Over the next decade the aggregate value of nonfuel mineral reserves of the developing countries could indeed increase to more than 50 percent of world reserves. Nevertheless, for many of the minor minerals, the distribution of reserves is expected to continue to favor the developed countries.

In appendix G, table G.2 indicates that, for the majority of minerals, reserves are concentrated in present producers; these producers, who include developed as well as developing countries, account for a disproportionately large share of world reserves. Of course, this is not surprising, since large reserves attract development capital first and the establishment of production facilities and infrastructure acts as an incentive to further exploration. Although new discoveries in unpredicted places can never be ruled out, the time required for exploration suggests that for many minerals the geographic structure of production is not likely to change drastically for a number of years.

FIGURE 5 | ENTRY OF SELECTED METALS INTO LARGE-SCALE
PRODUCTION AND CONSUMPTION IN THE UNITED STATES

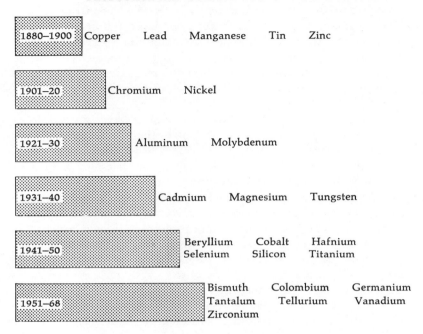

Source: John McHale and Magda Cordell McHale, "The Timetable Project: An Assessment of Projected Relationships between Population and Resources," (Center for Integrative Studies, State University of New York, 1972).

The Dynamism of Resources

The concept resources is itself a dynamic one: as argued eloquently by Zimmermann, many things become resources over time.[12] Many of the metals in use today were not produced commercially or did not enter large-scale production until less than a hundred years ago—some not until the postwar period. (See figure 5.) Before technology was developed to reduce bauxite into aluminum, it was a relatively useless material. Large-scale use of titanium alloys (in the aerospace industry) and of zirconium (in nuclear reactors) is strictly a post-World War II development.

12. W. N. Peach and James A. Constantin, *Zimmermann's World Resources and Industries*, 3d. ed. (New York: Harper & Row, 1972), chap. 1.

As noted in a UN study, estimates of reserves and resources tend to be conservative and are almost always revised upwards, sometimes drastically; "a type of giant leap is frequently involved."[13] (See table 4.) For a number of minerals, reserves have increased stunningly over the last decades, despite massive and accelerating consumption. Reserves of iron ore have risen by twelve times, potash twenty-three times, and chromite six to seven times since the late 1940s. Although reserves of lead and tin are relatively small, their projected reserve lives now are much the same as forty to fifty years ago. Potential resources exceed reserves quite significantly in most cases and reserve inventories have increased also.

TABLE 4 | DYNAMICS OF MINERAL RESERVE ESTIMATES

| Mineral | Published reserves[a] (thousands of metric tons) | | |
	Late 1940s	Late 1960s	Percent change
Bauxite	1,400,000	5,300,000	+279
Chromite	100,000	775,000	+675
Copper	100,000	279,000	+ 179
Iron ore			
Actual	19,000,000	251,000,000	+1,221
Potential	57,000,000	531,000,000	+832
Lead	40,000	86,000	+115
Manganese ore (contained)	500,000	635,000	+27
Potash (K₂O)	5,000,000	118,000,000	+2,360
Tin	6,000	6,600	+10
Tungsten	1,903	1,328	−30
Zinc	70,000	113,000	+61

a. Deep-sea nodules not included.
Source: United Nations, *Projections of Natural Resources Reserves, Supply and Future Demand* (E/C.7/40/add.2) (New York, December 1972).

Even where ore grade has deteriorated, no hard evidence is to be found over an expanded historical span of sharply rising costs. For example, while the metal content of copper ore is estimated to have declined from 8 percent in the sixteenth century to less than one percent (in the United States) at present, copper metal prices have declined from about $10 a pound four centuries ago to roughly 50 cents in recent years.[14] It is also a well-established fact that mineral

13. United Nations, *Projections of Natural Resource Reserves, Supply and Future Demand* (E/C.7/40/add. 2) (New York, December 1972).
14. See T. D. Lowell, "Copper Resources in 1970," *Transactions of the American Society of Mining Engineers*, June 1970; and Orris C. Herfindahl, "The Long-Run Cost of Minerals," in *Three Studies in Mineral Economics* (Washington, D.C.: Resources for the Future, 1961).

grades and mineral resources often have an exponential relation. If the grade of a mineral that can be exploited is halved, that rarely means simply a doubling of reserves; they tend to increase by a factor of ten, a hundred, or more.[15]

Furthermore, because of advances in understanding and altering the molecular structure and composition of minerals, the range of combinations in using metals is ever expanding. Consequently, in terms of use, the aggregate resource base does not have fixed boundaries. Its physical limits, too, are being pushed outward by the exploration and anticipated exploitation of the ocean beds' vast mineral potential.

Ocean Resources

At least thirty common minerals or groups of minerals are known to exist in the sea[16] but only a few are exploited currently in significant quantities. Marine minerals fall into three groups in terms of the physical state in which they occur: those that are dissolved or stand suspended in seawater; those that are associated with bedrock, that is, with geological formations now buried under the sea; and those that are superficial (sediments on the ocean floor) and of relatively recent origin. World production of these marine minerals totaled over $7,000 million in 1969, of which $6,100 million consisted of oil and gas.[17]

Of the fourteen or fifteen minerals most plentiful in seawater only three (salt, magnesium, and bromine) are currently recovered in large amounts. Possibilities for breakthroughs are slim, though technological progress and expanding requirements will undoubtedly raise recovery rates steadily. A major obstacle to large-

15. Recently, this relation has been questioned with regard to porphyry copper deposits. See D. A. Singer and associates, "Grade and Tonnage Relationships Among Copper Deposits," U.S. Geological Survey Professional Paper 907—A,B, 1975.

16. Cement, iron ore, copper, lead, zinc, silver, gold, gypsum, cobalt, nickel, sand and gravel, diamonds, manganese, phosphate, tin, bauxite, salt, potash, platinum metals, fluorspar, magnesium, chromite, tungsten, mercury, bromine, columbium/tantalum, rutile, barite, ilmenite, bismuth, and zircon.

17. The value of offshore production of oil and gas is now more than $40,000 million a year. Up-to-date estimates of the total value of minerals (fuel and nonfuel) from the sea are not available. For a description of ocean resources and recent developments, see United Nations, *Mineral Resources of the Sea* (E/4973) (New York, April 26, 1971); and *Marine Questions: Uses of the Sea* (E/5650) (New York, April 30, 1975).

scale and widespread exploitation is high cost in view of the vast amount of water that has to be processed. Increased production of fresh water from seawater, however, and combined minerals and fresh water production could lead to major reductions in costs and increase the economic importance of this source of minerals.

Commercial exploitation of mineral deposits within bedrock (subsurface deposit) is currently limited to oil and gas and a small group of minerals (among them coal, sulfur, and iron ore) which are mined conventionally, from shafts on land or artificial islands. The earth under the sea is probably mineralized in much the same way as the land and therefore contains a wide variety of minerals in abundance. Costs and physical difficulties, however, are significant deterrents to conventional mining of the ocean bottom. It is also extremely difficult to identify and measure underwater mineral deposits, except those near land and at limited depth. Nevertheless, considering the vast size of the oceans and the great length of the shoreline, even small expansions of the minable boundaries may open up significant resources.

The superficial deposits currently exploited consist of the so-called marine placer deposits found in or near beaches and continental shelf areas, mostly in protected shallow waters and submerged extensions of stream channels. Among deposits of this kind, those that hold the greatest promise from an economic standpoint are: the metalliferous muds recently discovered in association with abnormally hot and saline brines in the Red Sea, which contain extraordinary concentrations of heavy metals (such as iron, zinc, copper, lead, silver, and gold) with a possible total value of at least $2,000 million in 1972 prices;[18] and manganese nodules—the most important of *all* superficial deposits and the seabed's resource of the most immediate commercial significance.[19]

Nodules are metallic objects ranging in size from a pea to a baseball, found scattered over large areas of the ocean floor at depths from roughly 900 to 6,000 meters (3,000 to 20,000 feet). The metallic composition of the nodules varies depending on where they occur. A typical deposit of commercial interest contains 25 to 30 percent manganese, 1.0 to 1.5 percent nickel, 0.5 to 1.0 percent

18. Investigation of the Red Sea muds has already been undertaken by a German group in cooperation with the U.S. Geological Survey. The data suggest that this resource merits economic evaluation and development.

19. The oceans also contain phosphorite nodules which are of secondary importance because of their low phosphate content, compared to land resources, and the abundance of the latter. Hereafter, the word nodule is used to refer exclusively to manganese nodules.

copper, 0.25 percent cobalt, as well as small quantities of several other metals. The remainder of the nodule is made up of water and silica. While all oceans are known to contain nodules, the richest concentrations, in terms of quantity and quality, are found in the central east Pacific.

Although the existence of nodules has been known for about 100 years, widespread interest in them is recent and in part a by-product of growing concern over the possible exhaustion of high-grade conventional resources. At the same time, there has been rapid progress in the technology of nodule mining and metallurgy. The enormous size of the resource has also generated interest in its development. F. L. LaQue has estimated that meeting the world's current needs for manganese and cobalt exclusively from ocean nodules would require mining an area of about 2,850 square kilometers and 620 square kilometers (1,100 and 240 square miles), respectively, equivalent to only 0.0008 percent and 0.00017 percent of the ocean bottom.[20] Furthermore, nodules are renewable, that is, self-regenerating, albeit at a slow pace.[21]

Nodules no longer represent merely an oceanographic curiosity; they offer solid prospects for exploitation. This is amply demonstrated by the fact that today no less than thirty to thirty-five major companies or groups of companies in the United States, Japan, and Western Europe are actively engaged in exploration, development, and equipment construction. Technological breakthroughs have been achieved not only in lifting the nodules through a hydraulic air suction system or a so-called continuous line bucket system, but also in winning the metals from the nodules. Much of the prototype equipment has already been designed, patented, built, and tested. Although unforeseen difficulties may arise, what is already known about the technology, as well as the consensus of professional and technical opinion, indicates that it is almost certainly technically feasible to obtain large quantities of metals from this source. As early as 1972, the UN Secretariat concluded that the problems of

20. "Deep Ocean Mining: Prospects and Anticipated Short-Term Benefits," *Pacem in Maribus*, Center for the Study of Democratic Institutions Occasional Paper, vol. 2, no. 4 (June 1970).

21. Though a great deal remains to be discovered about the genesis of the nodules, most scientists believe that nodules are formed and continuously enlarged by precipitation of elements at a rate of 0.01 to 1.0 millimeters a 1,000 years in the abyssal ocean floor, but probably much faster in continental slope areas. Although the average rate of formation is undoubtedly slow, the vastness of the resource base implies that many metals in the manganese nodules, manganese and cobalt in particular, are accumulating several times faster than they are being consumed by man.

exploitation are "no longer technical but foremost legal and political."[22]

Less is certain about the economic viability of nodule mining, however. The hard facts are a closely guarded secret; besides, as there is no commercial exploitation at present, all estimates are highly speculative. The cost-benefit estimates available differ widely and lead to a variety of views ranging from the assertion that the operation would be totally uneconomic, or at best marginal, to the claim that it would constitute a highly profitable undertaking. This uncertainty is partly the result of the peculiar combination of the minerals found in most nodules in comparison to the present pattern of consumption. The ratio of copper, nickel, and cobalt currently in use is 266:27:1 compared to a ratio of 3:4:1 in nodules of average composition. This discrepancy implies a large potential surplus of manganese, nickel, and cobalt. Once seabed mining gets started even on a fairly modest scale, the price of some of these metals and the output of their present producers may begin to fall sharply. Numerous additional complications arise from uncertainties about the marketability of some of the products, particularly manganese, the interchangeability and joint-product nature (on land) of some of the metals, the ultimate reaction of land-based producers, and the inseparability of technological and economic considerations.[23]

Figure 6 gives the most recent estimates by the UN Secretariat of the entry of firms into nodule mining, based on an assessment of company plans and programs as of mid-1974. They should be considered highly speculative and, on the whole, optimistic, since the resolution of the legal and political problems of who has the right to mine the seabed and under what conditions—a formidable task in itself—is tied to reaching agreement on a number of related issues on, for example, territorial rights, environmental protection, and scientific research. Progress in resolving the seabed mining

22. United Nations, *Projections of Natural Resources Reserves, Supply and Future Demand* (E/C.7/40/add.2) (New York, December 5, 1972), p. 9.

23. For a detailed examination of the factors influencing the economics of nodule mining, the range of estimates of costs, profitability, and prices, and their effects on land-based producers, see United Nations, *Economic Implications of Sea-Bed Mineral Development in the International Area: Report of the Secretary-General* (A/CONF.62/25) (New York, May 22, 1974); and its follow-up report of the same title, (A/CONF. 62/37) (New York, February 18, 1975); UNCTAD, *Implication of the Exploitation of the Mineral Resources of the International Area of the Sea-Bed: Issues of International Commodity Policy* (TD/B/C.1/170) (New York, January 8, 1975) and the UNCTAD case studies on copper, maganese, nickel, and cobalt listed in the annex to the same document.

FIGURE 6 | FORECAST OF ENTRIES INTO NODULE MINING, 1976–85
(millions of metric tons of dry nodules)

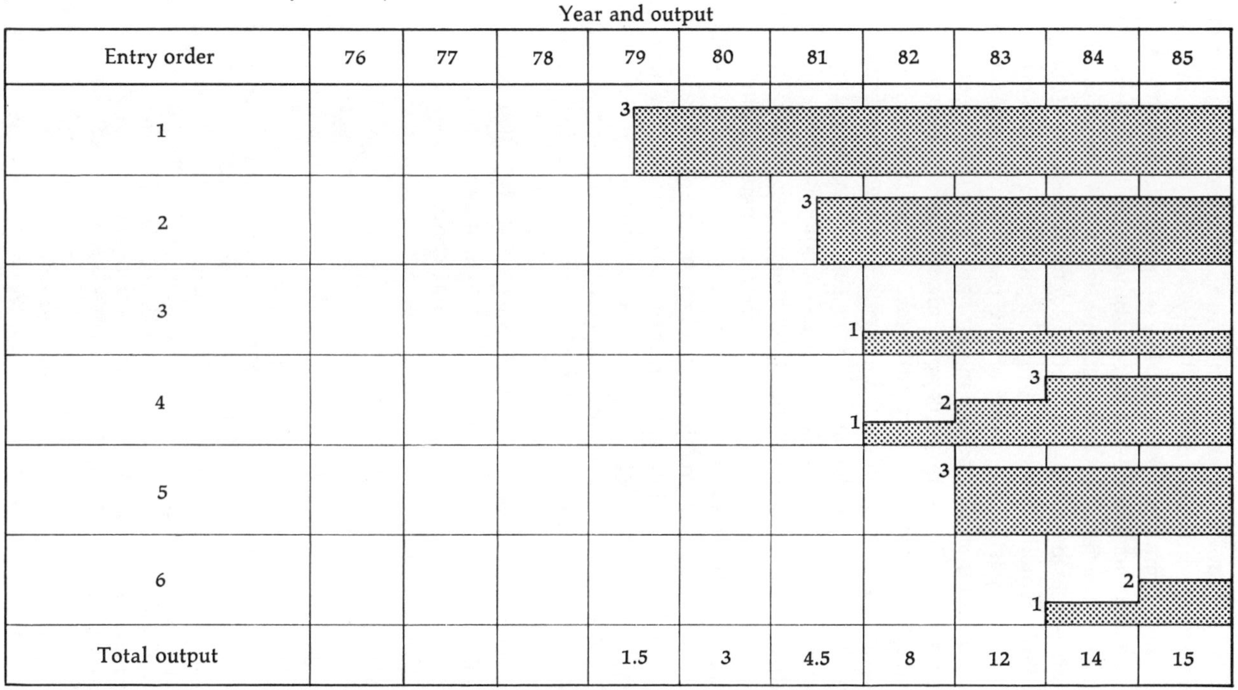

Year and output

Entry order	76	77	78	79	80	81	82	83	84	85
1				3						
2						3				
3							1			
4						1	2	3		
5							3			
6								1	2	
Total output				1.5	3	4.5	8	12	14	15

Source: United Nations, Economic Implications of Sea-Bed Mineral Development in the International Area (A/Conf.62/65) (New York, May 22, 1974).

issue has been slow despite the priority accorded to it at the Third UN Law of the Sea Conference. The conference has already met for four sessions: June to August 1974 in Caracas, March to May 1975 in Geneva, and March to April and August to September 1976 in New York. A fifth session is scheduled to take place in New York in May to July 1977.[24]

The race among rich countries to harvest the mineral wealth of the seabed is spurred by the following considerations: manganese, copper, nickel, and cobalt are important industrial raw materials, some of them indispensable to industrial societies; most of the industrialized countries are deficient in these metals and rely on imports for the bulk of their requirements; a nonpolitical source of supply which cannot spring surprises in the OPEC style ranks high among their priorities. Developing countries, on their part, feel they cannot afford to remain passive because many of them are large suppliers of the minerals found in the oceans. Some, such as Zaïre and Zambia, are large exporters of two or more of these minerals and are heavily dependent on them; many have large and in some cases newly discovered reserves of these minerals and, particularly the least developed, cannot afford to lose the opportunity to develop them. They fear quite justly that large-scale seabed mining may lead to revenue lost as well as revenue forgone.[25] While the principle of sharing in the revenue from the exploitation of the common heritage of mankind through the payment of a royalty to a central international authority is attractive to the developing countries, especially the landlocked countries, it is by no means certain that the net income of the proposed authority will be sufficient to compensate them for the potential export earnings they might forgo as a result of the introduction of seabed mining.[26]

It should be emphasized that land-based resources of the four

24. The Third Law of the Sea Conference has probably generated more reporting and analysis than any other conference in recent memory. For a brief review of the issues and an evaluation of the progress made in the first two sessions, see Bension Varon, "Slow Sailing at Law of the Sea: the Implications for the Future," *Finance & Development* (March 1975); and Bension Varon, "Ocean Issues on the International Agenda," in Guy F. Erb and Valeriana Kallab (eds.), *Beyond Dependency: The Developing World Speaks Out* (Washington, D.C.: Overseas Development Council, 1975).

25. A recent UN report concluded: "The question is not *whether* mineral markets will be affected by competition from nodules, but *how soon*, to *what extent* and by *how much.*" *Economic Implications of Seabed Mineral Development* (A/CONF.62/37), p. 34.

26. UNCTAD, *Implication of the Exploitation of the Mineral Resources* (TD/B/C.1/170), p. 7.

minerals found in the nodules are ample. There is no evidence that obtaining these minerals at lower prices from the oceans would increase the economic well-being of the developed countries measurably in the immediate future, nor that, even if this were so, the benefits of such improvement would spill over to the developing countries. Since there are no demonstrable immediate large benefits from seabed mining, there is no demonstrable urgency to institute arrangements that are less than acceptable to all parties concerned and equitable in design.[27]

In the very long run, the question takes on an entirely different perspective. If technological obstacles to large-scale nodule mining are overcome (or no new obstacles arise), ocean resources can offer strong cost advantages. Nodules are expected to have a horizontal cost curve (long-run supply curve) for a great many decades (since grade does not deteriorate rapidly, as resources are abundant and the mining ship is not tied to one location), thus offering a distinct advantage over the steeply rising cost curve of land-based resources. (Figure 7.) Technological advances may find new uses for metals obtained from nodules in excess of their projected requirements and at prices lower than those for land-based minerals. For example, if manganese metal could be substituted for steel, or nickel for copper in some uses, this could radically change the relative importance of this new source. "In that case nodule mining could increase spectacularly and the industry would become a major supplier as well as the largest source of cobalt, manganese, nickel, molybdenum, vanadium, and possibly other metals."[28] In that case, too, but only in the very long run, developing countries might be among the beneficiaries of nodule mining as consumers.

Recovery and Recycling

If the recovery of metals from wastes can be viewed as mining above ground, it is largely because many of the metals so won (copper, lead, and aluminum, for example) are equal in quality to their virgin counterparts. But the parallel does not stop there. Solid

27. Not surprisingly, the developing countries have strong allies within some of the developed countries, the United States in particular, in resisting moves to start seabed mining unilaterally, without awaiting the resolution of the issues in an international framework.

28. United Nations, *Economic Implications of Seabed Mineral Development* (A/CONF.62/65), p. 44.

FIGURE 7 | COMPARATIVE LONG-RANGE SUPPLY
CURVES FOR LAND-BASED AND
OCEAN RESOURCES

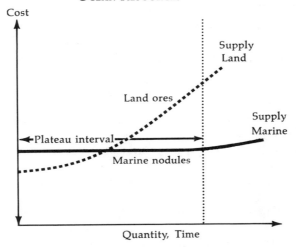

Source: Miller B. Spangler, "Deep Sea Nodules as a
Source of Copper, Nickel, Cobalt, and Manganese," in
New Technology and Marine Resources Development, © 1970
by Praeger Publishers.

wastes are a pool of potentially usable material, much like unmined
resources, their transformation into exploitable reserves depending
on technology, investment, infrastructure, quality, and prices.
There are significant differences, however. First, while recycling is
basically an economic process (relative prices influencing the
extent to which consuming industries dig into the reserve), environmental objectives—which are increasingly subject to public
influence everywhere—play a key role. Second, the success of setting and meeting waste recovery objectives depends, above all, on
the institutional organization of a society; administration and management are as important as technology and economic incentives.
Third, the volume of ultimately recyclable material is fixed more
rigidly than that of virgin resources and its distribution strongly
favors the industrialized nations. Fourth, the cost of energy has
a direct and varying influence on the incentive for waste recovery
and use.

There are many kinds of exploitable wastes, each with different
problems and prospects, depending on its origin and the recoverability of minerals and metals. Mineral wastes resulting from the
activity of mining itself (including washing and milling) consist

mostly of piles (sometimes mountains several hundred feet high) of residual, low-grade waste material. Beneficiation and chemical treatment of low-grade copper, lead, zinc, phosphate rock, and other ores and nonmetallic minerals produce vast accumulations of finely ground tailings. It is estimated that more than 1,500 million tons of mining, washing, and milling residuals (exclusive of overburden deposits) accumulated in the United States between 1942 and 1965.[29]

Industrial waste includes the waste products of processing and fabricating which either do not leave the plant and are immediately recovered for reprocessing as home scrap, or come back to the mill from fabricating plants or dealers as prompt or runabout scrap. Examples of industrial waste recovery are the remelting of mill-generated scrap in steel mills, the recovery of aluminum from the so-called red mud residuals of certain bauxite processing plants, and the recovery of zinc or sulfur from refinery fumes—although some of these activities can be considered by-product recovery rather than recycling.

Postuser or obsolete scrap refers to products discarded by consumers, which revert back to the mills for recycling. While this is the category most readily identified as scrap in the public's mind, it is not always the major source of metals recovery, home scrap or industrial scrap being more important in a number of cases, for example, in aluminum. Recently, municipal solid wastes have been included among the potential sources for recovering metals.

Societies have not been oblivious to the potential for saving through the reuse or reprocessing of products. For most key metals, a rising long-term trend in recovery can be inferred from the historical figures. For example, whereas world pig iron consumption increased ten to eleven times between 1900 and 1970, steel production expanded by a factor of roughly twenty, reflecting the increased use of scrap. Similarly, world consumption of new copper rose fourteen times, but use of copper metal increased twenty times as the proportion of secondary copper expanded from about 10 percent at the turn of the century to 35 percent in 1970. The growth factor for primary zinc was 11.4, while that for primary lead was only 4.5, partially as a result of expanded use of scrap lead, which rose in the United States from 8 percent in 1910 to over 40 percent

---

29. Frank Austin Smith, "Waste Material Recovery and Reuse," in Ronald G. Ridker, ed., *Population Resources and the Environment*, U.S. Commission on Population Growth and the American Future (Washington, D.C.: U.S. Government Printing Office, 1972), p. 63.

at present. There is, however, some evidence that the rate of post-user scrap recovery in some metals declined in the United States in the 1960s, despite the continued expansion of the recyclable base during this period. This underlines the importance of management and incentives.[30]

Mineral wastes, especially submarginal tailings dumped near mining sites, are likely to increase even more in the future since, as several studies have pointed out, the progressive depletion of high-grade ore deposits has tied production in industrialized countries to extractive technologies which generate more mine tailings.[31] The potential for saving through home scrap recovery is small, as over 90 percent of such scrap is already reprocessed. The prospects for fabricating and especially postuser scrap are better, although they vary from metal to metal, particularly in the medium term, depending on current recovery rates, technological constraints, the life cycles of their end products, and the limits of recovery. (Obviously not all the virgin metal can be recovered since some of it goes into such dissipative uses as lead in gasoline and titanium in paints.) Table 5 gives some estimate of the proportion of U.S. production met from secondary sources and the proportion of recoverable material currently recycled.

Unlike the exploitation of nodules, recycling does not involve conquering a new frontier; the reservoir and experience are there. It is clear, however, from the simple arithmetic of scrap generation and metal recovery (the leakage through dissipation and the lag due to the durability of products) that recycling—no matter how efficient or extensive—cannot provide indefinite relief to a society whose resource needs are growing at an exponential rate. Yet it can impart a considerable element of flexibility to long-term resource management, especially if coupled with measures to dampen demand through conservation. Fischman and Landsberg found that though considerable potential for conservation in the United States exists in aluminum and zinc through an active recycling policy, such a policy would add only a few more years' worth of U.S. reserves, far less than could normally be expected to be added by technological evolution or a modest price rise. They went on to conclude, however, that the importance of recycling goes beyond the matter of U.S. reserves; the potential recycling increase in aluminum, as one

30. See National Commission on Materials Policy, *Material Needs and the Environment Today and Tomorrow*, final report (Washington, D.C., June 1973), pp. 4D–6.

31. Ibid., pp. 4D–8.

TABLE 5 | SELECTED ESTIMATES OF SCRAP RECOVERY IN THE UNITED STATES

| | Scrap recovery as percentage of production or consumption | | | | | | Recoverable material (percent)[a] |
| | | | | | Fischman and Landsberg[f] | | |
Metal	USBM[b] 1968	NASMI[c] 1970	Smith[d] 1968	EPA[e] 1967	Current	Possible[g]	Battelle NASMI
Aluminum	17	30	17.5	18.3	17.3	42.6	48
Chromium	10						
Copper	45	45	39.8	49.7	44.0	54.4	61
Gold	17						
Iron	30			31.2			
Ferrous metals			21.3		47.3	48.9	
Steel							26
Stainless steel							88
Lead	38	52	40.8	49.6	43.6	47.2	42
Magnesium	14						

Mercury	17				40
Nickel	15				
Platinum group	24				
Precious metals					75
Silver	50				
Tin	28	28.3			
Titanium	1				
Tungsten	3				
Zinc	20	12.6	16.5	34.6	14

Note: Differences in the estimates are due to differences in the definition of "scrap," year, and method of calculation. The various estimates are reproduced to underline that, despite differences, most of them are quite comparable and fall within a narrow range.

a. Estimates by Battelle Memorial Institute quoted by NASMI in source given in footnote c below, referring to scrap recovery as a percentage of recoverable material.

b. U.S. Bureau of Mines, *Mineral Facts and Problems*, 1970.

c. Presentation by the National Association of Secondary Material Industries (NASMI) in *The Economics of Recycling Waste Materials*, Hearings before the Subcommittee on Fiscal Policy of the Joint Economic Committee, 92 Cong. 1 sess. (1971), p. 34.

d. Frank Austin Smith "Waste Material Recovery and Reuse," p. 67.

e. Environmental Protection Agency estimates quoted in National Commission on Materials Policy, *Material Needs and the Environment Today and Tomorrow*, final report (Washington, D.C., June, 1973), pp. 4D–6D.

f. Fischman and Landsberg, *Resources in America's Future*, p. 98.

g. Under an active recycling policy.

example, while not making the United States self-sufficient, would over a period of fifty years save 20 percent of the world's bauxite reserves and 40 percent of its zinc reserevs.[32]

Above all, recycling is seen as an attractive alternative by highly industrialized nations sensitive to charges of reckless resource gobbling. It underlines a crucial difference between fuel and nonfuel minerals. Finally, whereas stipulated limits to growth are unacceptable to policymakers in industrialized countries, limits to waste are attractive on both ethical and economic grounds, since recycling can serve to reduce dependence on imports of virgin materials.

32. Leonard L. Fischman and Hans H. Landsberg, "Adequacy of Nonfuel Minerals and Forest Resources," in *Population, Resources and the Environment*, p. 98.

3 | Production, Processing, Consumption, and Trade

CONSUMPTION OF MINERAL RAW MATERIALS on a large scale started with the Industrial Revolution and has continued to grow at an extraordinary rate.[1] World consumption of all mineral commodities combined increased tenfold between 1750 and 1900, whereas, over the same period, population expanded by a factor of 2.2 and per capita consumption by 4.5. During the last seventy years, mineral consumption has grown by a factor of 12.7, population by 2.4, and per capita consumption by 5.3. Before the Industrial Revolution, around 1700, world production of pig iron was about 25,000 tons—less than one ten-thousandth of today's output. In 1800, world production of copper, one of the time-honored metals, was still only 16,000 tons, 0.5 percent of current production; aluminum, world consumption of which amounts to more than 10 million tons today, was not known; tin production was less than 10,000 tons (under 5 percent of current output), and zinc production was about 1,000 tons, compared to its present level of about 5 million tons. For most minerals, large production levels (on the order of 5 to 10 percent of current levels) were not achieved until the second half of the nineteenth century. The rate of expansion accelerated in the post-World War II period, as illustrated in figure 8. Growth rates have been highest in the new metals, especially aluminum, and in alloying metals, such as nickel, chromite, molybdenum, and titanium, which are used to improve the properties of iron and steel.

1. The historical data given here are based on Alexander Sutulov, *Minerals in World Affairs* (Salt Lake City: University of Utah Printing Services, 1972); P. Lamartine Yates, *Forty Years of Foreign Trade* (London: George Allen and Unwin, 1959); and Metallgesellschaft, *Metal Statistics* (various issues).

FIGURE 8 | GROWTH OF POPULATION AND VALUE OF WORLD
MINERAL OUTPUT IN CONSTANT (1972) PRICES,
1900–70

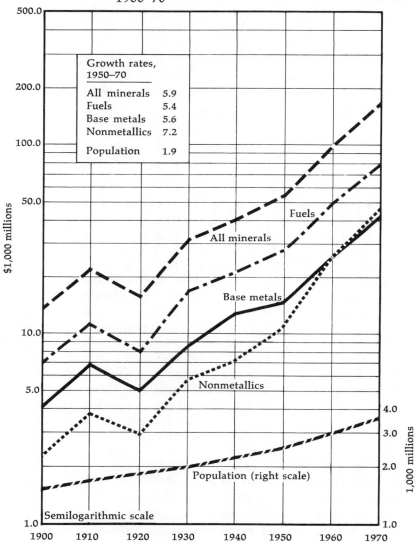

Growth rates,
1950–70

All minerals	5.9
Fuels	5.4
Base metals	5.6
Nonmetallics	7.2
Population	1.9

Source: Alexander Sutulov, *Minerals in World Affairs,* (Salt Lake City; University of Utah Printing Services, 1972).

The pattern of world production, consumption, and trade has undergone significant changes in the last fifty to sixty years as a result of shifts in industrial centers, progressive depletion of high-grade reserves in consuming regions, technological change, and cost-saving advances in transportation. Industrialized countries have become more and more dependent on imports. The United States, for example, shifted from being a net exporter of copper, lead, and zinc, and nearly self-sufficient in iron ore at the beginning of the century to a net importer position by the early 1950s.

TABLE 6 | SELECTED ORES, UNITED STATES AND WESTERN EUROPE: PRODUCTION AS A PERCENTAGE OF CONSUMPTION

	United States			Western Europe		
Ore	1909–13	1954–55	1972	1909–13	1954–55	1972
Copper	160	80	83	10	5	7
Iron	99	62	68	99	89	63
Lead	104	42	25	52	21	25
Zinc	118	50	45	65	38	39

Source: P. Lamartine Yates, Forty Years of Foreign Trade (London: George Allen and Unwin, 1959), and national statistics.

The shift illustrated in table 6 started much earlier in the United Kingdom than in the other industrialized countries, although she remained a major producer of mineral raw materials for a long time after the Industrial Revolution. From 1700 to 1850, she mined over 50 percent of the world's lead; from 1820 to 1840, she produced 45 percent of the world's copper; and from 1850 to 1890, she increased her iron ore production from one-third to one-half of the world output. But the United Kingdom reached her peak of production for lead in 1856, for copper in 1863, for tin in 1871, and for iron ore in 1882.[2] France, however, produced fully one-fourth of the world's iron ore and 30 percent of the world's bauxite as late as 1929, while Hungary supplied another 18 percent of the bauxite output. The postwar period has witnessed a number of significant changes in both the exports and imports of minerals, the most important being the emergence of Japan as the world's leading importer of mineral raw materials.

2. T. S. Lovering, Minerals in World Affairs (New York: Prentice Hall, 1943), p. 61.

Statistical Problems and Adjustments

Published figures on production, consumption, and trade of mineral commodities have a number of shortcomings and should be used with caution. These stem not so much from misreporting as from the fact that mineral commodities are marketed in varying degrees of processing (ore, concentrate, ingot, and so on). Because each intermediary product is an input for the next stage, it is difficult to determine in standardized fashion for all minerals which stage constitutes final consumption. Statistical sources do not record production, consumption, and trade at uniform stages of processing. Therefore, unless properly adjusted, published statistics do not permit aggregation nor assessment of the degree of processing taking place in different regions.

In order to present a composite picture, we developed two separate detailed sets of production, consumption, and trade estimates for selected minerals in 1950, 1960, and 1970—one set at minehead value, the other at the final product (metal ingot) stage—using unit prices applicable to each stage. Since uniform price assumptions were used for each period, the estimates thus obtained do not distort the trend, resulting, in fact, in a comparison of the value of production, consumption, and trade in constant prices. The prices used were those judged to reflect the dominant long-term trend around 1970, not necessarily those actually experienced in any one year. The purpose of the exercise was to compare relations (interregional, intercommodity, and by-processing stage) rather than to measure actual market values. The method of adjustment is explained further in appendix H, which also contains the two sets of estimates.

The exercise was carried out for the nine major minerals which account for more than 85 percent of the minehead value of all nonfuel minerals. (Other minerals were also reviewed when the major minerals did not appear to be fully representative of the whole industry.) Listed in order of importance at their commonly accepted production values, the nine minerals (and their share in the production value of all minerals) are: copper, blister or matte, 32 to 35 percent; iron ore, 28 to 31 percent; zinc metal, 6 to 7 percent; nickel metal, 4 to 5 percent; phosphate rock, 3 to 4 percent; lead metal, 3 to 4 percent; tin metal, 3 to 3.5 percent; manganese ore, 2 pecent; and bauxite, 1 to 1.5 percent.

The relevance of the adjustment undertaken can be illustrated as follows: Published production and consumption values indicate that nonfuel mineral output in the early 1970s has been on the order of $25,000 to $30,000 million a year. Production at minehead value has been on the order of $2,000 million. If all mineral values are converted to the common denominator of finished metal ingot, however, the value increases to $60,000 to $70,000 million a year. Under this method of valuation, the share of the nine minerals rises from 85 percent to 95 percent and the order of importance of the individual minerals changes significantly: steel ingot takes first place, with 60 to 70 percent; copper falls from first place to second place with a significantly smaller share (10 to 12 percent); and aluminum ingot rises to third place with 7 to 8 percent, compared to the ninth place and 1 to 1.5 percent share of bauxite in the earlier ranking.

Global Trends

The growth in global production (including centrally planned economies) of the nine major minerals over the period 1950 to 1970 is shown in table 7. World mineral production (and therefore, apart from inventory changes, consumption) has been increasing at annual rates of 5 to 6 percent over the past decade, although increases have varied substantially across the range of minerals. For example, uranium, nickel, and aluminum have all shown above-average growth rates of 7 percent or more a year; copper, lead, and zinc have been growing at 3 to 5 percent; and tin at less than one percent.

Comparable estimates (in standardized value terms) are not available for more recent years. The selected output figures for 1971 to 1975 shown in table 8 indicate that after a bad year in 1971 world mineral output recovered rapidly in 1972 and in 1973, exhibiting above-average growth rates for most minerals in response to bullish demand associated with a rare simultaneous business expansion in all industrialized countries. As will be argued more fully in chapter 4, this contributed significantly to the price boom of 1973 and 1974.

As might be expected, consumption and production have not expanded evenly in all three economic regions. The following conclusions can be drawn from the combined experience of the nine major minerals which is summarized in table 9 (for commodity detail, see appendix H).

First, developing market economies have increased their mineral production faster than developed market economies. This trend is expected to continue; by 1980 the value of mineral production is likely to be about equal in the two regions, representing 35 to 40 percent of world mineral output in each case.

TABLE 7 | ESTIMATED RAW MATERIAL VALUE OF WORLD PRODUCTION
OF NINE MAJOR MINERALS, 1950–70

Mineral	Value (millions of dollars)			Distribution (percent)			Growth of value 1950–70	
	1950	1960	1970	1950	1960	1970	Total (1950=100)	Per year (percent)
Bauxite and Alumina	63	253	726	1.1	2.4	4.3	1,152	13.0
Copper	2,415	4,056	6,080	41.6	38.9	35.7	252	4.7
Iron	1,537	3,337	5,655	26.5	32.0	33.2	368	6.7
Lead	333	469	677	5.7	4.5	4.0	203	3.6
Manganese	184	345	483	3.2	3.3	2.8	262	4.9
Nickel	214	492	960	3.7	4.7	5.6	448	7.8
Phosphorus	225	407	804	3.9	3.9	4.7	357	6.6
Tin	403	431	540	6.9	4.1	3.1	134	1.5
Zinc	432	648	1,122	7.4	6.2	6.6	260	4.9
Total	5,806	10,438	17,047	100.0	100.0	100.0	294	5.5

Source: Appendix H, Table H2.

TABLE 8 | SELECTED WORLD MINERAL OUTPUT STATISTICS, 1971–75

Item	1971	1972	1973	1974	1975
Index numbers			*(1970=100)*		
Industrial production	104	112	122	126	126
Mining	103	107	114	116	114
Metallic minerals	101	102	107	109	106
Manufacturing	104	112	122	127	126
Basic metals	99	107	118	121	114
Metal products	104	113	126	133	133
Volume of output			*(millions of metric tons)*		
Crude steel[a]	557	602	666	674	667
Pig iron and ferro-alloys[a]	407	431	477	489	485
Iron ore[a]	403	411	453	472	483
			(thousands of metric tons)		
Copper[a]	6,225	6,956	7,473	7,754	7,644
Lead[a]	3,060	3,210	3,353	3,273	3,226
Zinc[a]	4,544	4,904	5,017	5,189	5,252
Tin[b]	186	191	185	179	178
Aluminium[a]	10,114	10,797	11,905	12,534	12,545
Nickel	619	633	684	746	723

a. Excluding the People's Republic of China.
b. Excluding the German Democratic Republic, Democratic People's Republic of Korea, and Soviet Union.
Source: United Nations, *Monthly Bulletin of Statistics* (May 1976) and (June 1976); World Bureau of Metal Statistics, *World Metal Statistics* (March 1976).

Second, centrally planned economies have increased their mineral output even faster than developing market economies, accounting for about 26 percent of total mineral output in 1970 compared to 14 percent in 1950.

Third, most of the growth in world mineral consumption has occurred in the developed market economies, with substantial growth in the centrally planned economies as well. In 1970, developing market economies which in that year produced about one-third of the world's mineral output (in value) accounted for less than 6 percent of world mineral consumption. This picture is not expected to change much in the next five to ten years; the developing countries will probably still consume under 10 percent of world mineral output, compared to 65 percent or more for the developed market economies and about 25 percent for the centrally planned countries.

Fourth, per capita consumption has varied widely among the three economic regions. In 1970 developed market economies consumed roughly thirty times more mineral raw materials (in value) per capita than developing countries and 3.5 times more than the centrally planned economies. Consumption per unit of GNP

TABLE 9 | PRODUCTION, CONSUMPTION, AND NET TRADE OF
NINE MAJOR MINERALS, BY REGION, 1950–70

Item	Value ($1,000 millions of dollars)			Distribution (percent)		
	1950	1960	1970	1950	1960	1970
Production						
Developed market economies	3.1	4.4	7.3	54	43	41
Developing market economies	1.8	3.5	5.3	32	33	33
Centrally planned economies	0.8	2.5	4.4	14	24	26
Total	5.7	10.4	17.0	100	100	100
Consumption						
Developed market economies	4.6	7.0	11.6	80	70	68
Developing market economies	0.2	0.5	0.8	4	5	6
Centrally planned economies	0.9	2.6	4.6	16	25	26
Total	5.7	10.1	17.0	100	100	100
Net trade[a]						
Developed market economies	−1.5	−2.6	−4.3	(−33)	(−39)	(−39)
Developing market economies	+1.6	+3.0	+4.5	(+87)	(+86)	(+83)
Centrally planned economies	−0.1	−0.1	−0.2	(−9)	(−6)	(−2)
Total		+0.3				

Note: The nine minerals are bauxite, copper, iron, lead, manganese, nickel, phosphorus, tin, and zinc.
a. Net exports (+), net imports (−). Figures in parentheses refer to net imports as percentage of consumption and net exports as percentage of production.
Source: Appendix H, table H1.

did not vary as widely, since low mineral consumption is generally a sign of underdevelopment, that is to say, the level of development and mineral consumption are related.

Fifth, there is virtually no stable trade in minerals between centrally planned economies and the rest of the world, with the exception of trade in minor minerals such as tungsten and antimony. Production in the centrally planned economies just about equals consumption. Most of the world mineral trade takes place between developing and developed market economies, although the situation may change progressively. Both market economy and centrally planned countries have expressed interest in larger and more stable two-way trade in minerals.

Sixth, for the developed market economies as a whole, the ratio of mineral imports to mineral consumption has increased from about 33 percent in 1950 to 39 percent in 1970, and the figure is expected to rise further. Whereas North America has been able to reduce its import requirements during the past two decades (mainly because of major increases in Canada's mineral output) and Australia and South Africa have become major mineral exporters, Western Europe and Japan have become highly dependent on mineral imports. This trend is expected to continue, so that by 1980 Western Europe may import more than 80 percent of its mineral needs and Japan about 95 percent.

Finally, the developing countries produced more than half the output (excluding that of the centrally planned economies) of only three of the nine major minerals—bauxite, manganese, and tin.

Since each mineral has special applications, minerals other than the nine discussed above can be of key importance in meeting specific needs, even though their production value may be relatively small. This is true of antimony, asbestos, feldspar, magnesium, mercury, molybdenum, platinum, potash, titanium, tungsten, and vanadium, most of which are produced mainly in developed market economies.

Comparison of the relative shares of production and reserves during the late 1960s reveals that developed market and centrally planned economies have depleted their presently known reserves more rapidly than the developing countries with respect to only nine minerals (asbestos, feldspar, fluorspar, iron, molybdenum, nickel, phosphate, sulfur, and tin). Ten minerals (antimony, barite, copper, lead, magnesium, mercury, potash, titanium, tungsten, and vanadium) are being depleted in both groups of countries at about the same rate. Reserves of eight minerals (bauxite, bismuth, chromium, cobalt, columbium, manganese, silver, and zinc) are being depleted in the developing countries more rapidly than in the rest of the world. These facts run counter to the often repeated observation that the developed countries are rapidly depleting their supplies and will have to place increasing reliance on supplies from developing countries. No doubt, over the medium-to-longer term, with the projected increase in reserves in the developing nations, supply will tend to shift to those countries, but this is likely to be a gradual process that will not significantly alter the geographic pattern of supply in the next five to ten years.

The Concentration of Production and Processing

Mineral production capacity shows extreme geographic concentration as indicated in table 10. This is a manifestation not only of the uneven geographic ditstribution of mineral resources but also, to some extent, of the concentration of ownership and control. Not enough data are available, however, to establish a clear correlation between geographic and ownership concentration. It is significant, nevertheless, that 70 to 75 percent of the world mineral output is produced in only a dozen countries, half of which are developing market economies, namely: the Soviet Union (18.7 percent), United

TABLE 10 | CONCENTRATION OF MINERAL PRODUCTION CAPACITY FOR
SELECTED MINERALS IN PRINCIPAL PRODUCING COUNTRIES

| | Degree of concentration | | |
Mineral	Percent	Number of countries	Principal producing countries in order of importance
Columbium	90	2	Brazil, Canada
Titanium	90	2	United States, Japan
Molybdenum	91	2	United States, Canada
Magnesium	73	3	United States, Soviet Union, Norway
Asbestos	88	3	Canada, Soviet Union, South Africa
Vanadium	87	3	United States, South Africa, Finland
Nickel	81	3	Canada, Soviet Union, New Caledonia
Phosphate	79	3	United States, Soviet Union, Morocco
Barite	61	2	United States, Iran
Sulfur	60	2	United States, Soviet Union
Cobalt	72	3	Zaïre, Zambia, Canada
Manganese	71	4	Soviet Union, South Africa, Brazil, India
Antimony	73	4	South Africa, People's Republic of China, Bolivia, Soviet Union
Tin	66	4	Malaysia, Bolivia, Soviet Union, Thailand
Silver	69	5	Mexico, Canada, United States, Sovet Union, Peru
Tungsten	70	5	People's Republic of China, Soviet Union, United States, Democratic People's Republic of Korea, Republic of Korea
Copper	71	5	United States, Soviet Union, Zambia, Chile, Canada
Bauxite	63	5	Jamaica, Australia, Surinam, Soviet Union, Guyana
Zinc	59	5	Canada, Soviet Union, Australia, United States, Peru
Lead	51	4	United States, Australia, Soviet Union, Canada
Iron Ore	67	5	Soviet Union, Western Europe, United States, Australia, Canada

Source: Appendix G, Table G2.

States (15.9 percent), Canada (11.5 percent), Chile (4.6 percent), Zambia (4.1 percent), Australia (3.4 percent), China (3.2 percent), Zaïre (2.4 percent), Peru (2.3 percent), South Africa (1.9 percent), Mexico (1.8 percent), and Brazil (1.6 percent).[3]

3. The figures are based on 1968 data and understate the share of Australia and Brazil, whose output has expanded greatly since then.

Historically, most processing of minerals beyond the concentrate stage has been done in the industrialized economies. As indicated in table 11, only about 30 percent of the minerals mined in the developing countries are processed there. This ratio has remained relatively constant over the past two decades, suggesting that increases in processing facilities in these countries have merely met increases in mine capacity. In the industrialized countries (except Australia and South Africa), increases in processing capacity have outstripped increases in mining capacity, particularly in Japan. In both Australia and South Africa, mining capacity has expanded much more rapidly than processing facilities, with a resultant increase in the quantities of ores and concentrates shipped. Within the centrally planned economies, processing capacity has been maintained commensurate with mining capacity.

TABLE 11 | DEGREE OF PROCESSING CONDUCTED IN DIFFERENT REGIONS

Region	Minerals processed as a percentage of total minerals mined in each region[a]		
	1950	1960	1970
United States and Canada	146	179	179
Western Europe	250	250	295
Japan	235	381	1,046
Australia and South Africa	89	72	38
Developing market economies	30	28	29
Centrally planned economies	99	102	108
Total	100	100	100

a. Computed as the value produced by mining and processing operations as a percentage of total value produced, had all ore mined been processed to metal ingot stage, except for iron ore, manganese ore, and phosphate rock for which pelletized or sinterized iron ore, ferromanganese, and superphosphate fertilizer were taken as representing the processed product.
Source: Authors' computations, based on data in appendix H.

As shown in figure 9, the degree of processing within the supplying country varies significantly from mineral to mineral. The relevant factors are the extent of concentration of control and vertical integration within the industry, the technology required and the need for energy inputs, as well as the distance between source of supply and markets.

Although facilities to produce aluminum from bauxite are being established to a significantly greater extent in the producing nations, only 10 percent of the bauxite mined in those countries is processed right through to aluminum there. On the other hand, more than 75 percent of copper mined is processed to copper metal

FIGURE 9 | PERCENTAGE OF PROCESSING CONDUCTED FOR NINE
MINERALS IN DEVELOPING MARKET ECONOMIES, 1970
(weighted average)

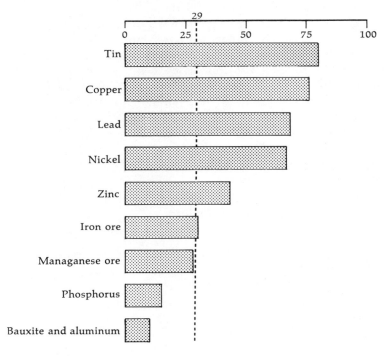

Note: See footnote a., table 11.
Source: Data in Appendix H.

in the supplying countries. There has been a marked trend toward
conducting more tin processing in the developing countries; but in
iron ore the bulk of the new supplies of high-grade ore from the
developing countries has been flowing to consuming countries with
little or no processing, although the situation is changing.

Both developing and developed countries recognize that there is
great scope for increasing value added through processing in the
developing countries, although this has yet to be translated into
an action program with this as a specific, high-priority objective.[4]

4. UNCTAD has a number of case studies under preparation which may
provide commodity-by-commodity estimates. Varon has tentatively concluded: "High profits (and external economies) come from processing, since
value can be increased by as much as four times through semiprocessing

The insistence on processing is not limited to the developing countries; it forms a key component of the current resource policies of both Canada and Australia. How rapidly the shift occurs will depend on the nature of the future partnership between producing and consuming countries, particularly as it affects transfer of capital and technology and control of markets and marketing. It can be argued that tariff restrictions are of secondary importance, given the current location of processing facilities. Tariffs on ores and concentrates are negligible for all major minerals in industrialized countries but they rise—sharply in some cases—with degree of processing; in some developed countries, absolute import restrictions are imposed and subsidies are made available to domestic producers. While these no doubt inhibit the expansion of processing in developing countries, in today's market, they are designed primarily to guard against competition from other industrialized countries, as the bulk of processing capacity is located there. Limited access to processing equipment and technology is probably a bigger impediment to the further processing of minerals in developing countries than import restrictions in consuming countries.[5]

The Structure of Trade

As noted earlier, most international trade in mineral commodities takes place between the developed and developing regions. Appendix H indicates that in 1970 the net imports of developed

---

and by as much as 20 times through full processing up to the metal bar stage. If the entire current mineral output of developing countries were to be processed up to this stage, the value of their aggregate output could be as much as $10–$12 billion higher. This is not to suggest that no progress has been made toward the local processing of minerals, nor that processing should be pursued without regard to comparative advantage or investment priorities. This illustration does portray the difficulties that arise when only one or two sectors of an economy grow, having little feedback effect on the economy as a whole which lacks enough internal strength or external support to respond quickly to the initial stimulus. And it symbolizes the difference in the stages of development between the developing and developed countries, which, in turn, affects their trade relationship." See "Enough of Everything for Everyone, Forever?" *Finance & Development* (September 1975), p. 20. Some experts believe that the $10,000 to $12,000 million estimate is too high.

5. For a brief survey of the technological and financial factors affecting the location of processing facilities, see UN Interregional Workshop on Negotiation and Drafting of Mining Development Agreements, *Processing*, prepared by the United Nations Secretariat (ESA/RT/AC.7/12) (New York, October 3, 1973).

market economies were in the order of $4,300 million; the net exports of developing market economies came to $4,500 million; and the small balance ($200 million) represented net imports by the centrally planned countries. These figures grossly understate the value of world mineral trade and oversimplify the structure of trade, since intraregional trade is quite significant. For example, in 1972, trade between developed countries (in value) accounted for nearly 60 percent of world trade in nonferrous metals. (In comparison, trade between developing countries is unimportant— no more than 2 to 3 percent of the world total in nonferrous metals.)

The distribution of gross exports and imports by region is shown in table 12. It shows that developed countries as a group account for 90 to 95 percent of world imports, as expected, but supply, in return, roughly 60 percent of world exports.

TABLE 12 | GROSS EXPORTS AND IMPORTS OF SELECTED MINERALS, BY REGION, 1970

	Total value (1,000 millions of dollars)	Distribution (percent)			
		World	Developed	Developing	Centrally planned
Exports (f.o.b.)					
Ores and concentrates[a]	4,179	100	58	41	1
Metals[b]	10,470	100	65	31	4
Total exports	14,649	100	63	33	4
Imports (c.i.f.)					
Ores and concentrates[a]	6,084	100	94	2	2
Metals[b]	10,513	100	90	8	2
Total imports	16,597	100	91	6	3

a. Iron ore, bauxite, copper ore, nickel ore, manganese ore, zinc ore, chrome ore, lead ore, tin ore.
b. Copper, tin, nickel, lead, zinc, aluminum.
Source: United Nations, The Significance of Basic Commodities in World Trade in 1970 (A9544/add.1) (New York, April 4, 1974).

Since developed countries dominate world imports so overwhelmingly, the structure of mineral trade can be examined fruitfully from this side. In 1970, the three major industrialized regions, the United States, Japan, and Western Europe, imported roughly 60 percent of their requirements of the nine major minerals, compared to 55 percent in 1960 and 44 percent in 1950. Roughly 12 percent of their aggregate net imports come from Australia and South Africa, 16 percent from Canada, and 72 percent from the

FIGURE 10 | IMPORT DEPENDENCE AND SOURCE OF NET IMPORTS
FOR NINE MAJOR MINERALS, UNITED STATES,
WESTERN EUROPE, AND JAPAN, 1950 AND 1970

Imports as percentage of consumption

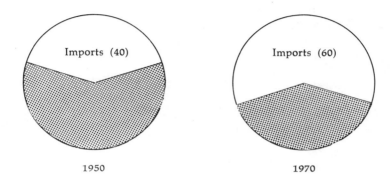

1950

1970

Source of imports (percentages)

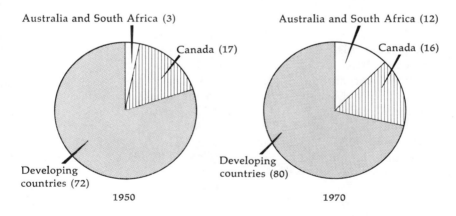

1950

1970

Source: U.S. Department of the Interior, Bureau of Mines, *Mineral Facts and Problems*, 1970.

developing countries. While the share of Canada has remained stable, that of developing countries has declined in the last twenty years as a result of the recent emergence of Australia as a major new supplier. (Figure 10.)

Import dependence and source of imports vary by commodity and by country. For example, at one extreme, the United States imports only 25 to 30 percent of its aggregate requirements of nine minerals; it is a net exporter of one (phosphate rock) and depends heavily on imports only in the case of four (tin, manganese, bauxite, and nickel). A large proportion of its imports comes from its two mineral-rich neighbors, Canada and Mexico, as illustrated in table 13.

TABLE 13 | PERCENTAGE OF 1973 U.S. IMPORTS
SUPPLIED BY CANADA AND MEXICO

Mineral	Canada	Mexico
Nickel	82	
Fluorspar		77
Tungsten	61	9
Zinc	60	24
Mercury	59	17
Iron ore	50	
Copper	31	
Lead	29	17

Source: Council on International Economic Policy, *Critical Imported Materials* (Washington, D.C., December 1974).

Although economies in transportation have been a major factor in shaping this pattern, the political stability of the two suppliers and the history of horizontal and vertical integration of the multinational corporations have also been influential. It is significant that the Soviet Union has become a major supplier of some minerals in recent years. In 1973, it supplied 32 percent of U.S. imports of chromium, 32 percent of its imports of the platinum group, and 19 percent of its imports of titanium. The first two are metals traditionally supplied by South Africa and Rhodesia; all three are considered strategic raw materials.

At the other extreme, Japan obtains about 90 percent of its mineral requirements from abroad. It depends on imports for almost 100 percent of its needs of five major minerals (bauxite, nickel, phosphorus, tin, and iron ore) and for about 95 percent of copper and manganese ore. This makes Japan the world's largest importer of minerals and a powerful force in the market. With less than 3 percent of world population and about 6 percent of world GDP, it accounts for approximately 15 percent of world mineral imports —more than 35 percent in the case of iron ore and 20 to 25 percent in chrome and manganese ore, as shown in table 14. (Though its share of world copper and nickel *metal* imports is about 15

TABLE 14 | JAPANESE MINERAL IMPORTS, 1970, AS PERCENTAGE
OF WORLD IMPORTS AND DOMESTIC CONSUMPTION

Mineral	World imports	Domestic consumption
Aluminum	6	23
Bauxite and alumina	10	100
Chrome ore	26	100
Copper ore and metal	16	90
Iron ore	36	94
Lead ore and metal	5	76
Manganese ore	23	90
Nickel ore and metal	14	100
Phosphate rock	13	100
Tin ore and metal	14	97
Tungsten ore	9	100
Zinc ore and metal	12	80

Source: United Nations, *The Significance of Basic Commodities in World Trade in 1970* (A/9544/add.1) (New York, April 4, 1974); and Council on International Economic Policy, *Critical Imported Materials* (Washington, D.C., December 1974).

percent, it absorbs over 70 percent of world copper *ore* exports and over 25 percent of nickel *ore* exports.)

It should be underlined that a large portion of Japan's raw material consumption goes into manufactured products destined for other markets. Japanese import demand, therefore, depends on economic conditions (and market access regulations) in third markets—largely, but not exclusively, other industrialized nations.

The changes in world mineral trade brought about by Japan go far beyond the reorientation of exports in terms of destination and merit special attention. Greater participation by Japan in world mineral trade has played a key role in increasing competition among importers, altering the pattern of resource development and procurement, diversifying the source of exports, and providing new oppotunities for suppliers in Asia and Oceania, such as the Philippines, Indonesia, India, and, of course, Australia. Japan's aggressive strategy of securing supply through long-term contracts has provided a model for other importers and exerted a stabilizing influence on the market. Through innovations in transport and marketing, Japan played a key role in widening the geography of the world mineral market, as witnessed by the fact that its imports originate in five continents: roughly 40 percent in North and South America, 15 to 20 percent in Europe and Africa, 20 to 25 percent in Asia, and 15 to 20 percent in Oceania.

The changes fostered by Japan benefited all mineral-producing countries, developed and developing, and some had an especially favorable impact on resource development in the developing countries. For example, Japan's vast and expanding need for raw materials and her policy of diversifying the sources of supply induced her not to overlook small projects and benefited many small countries in Africa. The pressure of Japanese competition jolted the generally conservative European investors into action and shortened project appraisal and investment decision time in some cases. The relative security of markets provided through long-term contracts was instrumental in attracting co-investors. That these benefits resulted from policies based on self-interest—to gain markets for her own products and to avoid the opprobrium of neocolonialism—does not detract from their importance. The pragmatism of Japanese foreign resource development policy emanated from the totality of her import dependence and confidence in the international resource supply system it helped to forge.[6] In retrospect, Japanese resource policy can be seen to have had some unfortunate side effects for the developing countries: It favored the import of mineral ore and maximum processing at home; it made producers excessively dependent on one economy alone;[7] and it led to some exaggeration of the security provided by long-term contracts. It would not be surprising, however, if the totality of her import dependence induced Japan in the future to take initiatives to respond better to the needs of the developing countries, for example by encouraging local processing in the producing countries, as advocated by some influential Japanese experts.[8]

Although in the last two decades world minerals trade has become geographically more diversified, exports of most individual minerals continue to be heavily concentrated in a few countries. With few exceptions, however, no single economic region—developed, developing, or centrally planned—dominates the export picture. The recent experience with oil has generated interest in the share of the market in other commodities controlled by developing countries. The market power of developing countries and its impli-

6. See Saburo Okita, "Natural Resource Dependency and Japanese Foreign Policy," *Foreign Affairs* (July 1974); and Philip Connelly, "Resources: The Choices for Importers," *International Affairs* (October 1974).

7. It is surprising that the usually alert research community has not yet fully studied the implications of a severe slowdown of the Japanese economy for the developing countries. Long-term forecasts of the Japanese economy coming out of Japan recently have been lower than those of outside experts; the implications of these forecasts for mineral-exporting developing countries are potentially very serious.

8. Okita, "Natural Resource Dependency," p. 131.

cations will be discussed in chapter 4. It suffices to note here that while developing countries' mineral exports exhibit great geographic concentration, this of itself is not a measure of market power, since their share of world exports or of industrialized countries' gross requirements (domestic consumption) varies. For example, although the five largest exporters of individual minerals among developing countries account for more than 90 percent of aggregate developing-country exports in five minerals (copper, tin, zinc, manganese, and phosphate rock) and 75 to 90 percent in four others, their share of world exports is under 30 percent in three (iron ore, zinc, and lead), about half in another three, and 60 to 80 percent only in two (tin and bauxite), as shown below. (For the identity of the individual exporters see appendix I.) In 1972 the percentage export share of the five largest developing country exporters was as follows:

Mineral	Total developing country exports	World exports
Copper	96.4	52.2
Tin	93.6	79.7
Zinc	92.1	20.3
Manganese ore	91.5	51.2
Phosphate rock	91.1	48.9
Bauxite	87.6	63.7
Lead	83.7	17.7
Iron ore	75.8	28.3

For most of these minerals the major competitors of the developing countries are Canada, Australia, and South Africa. In 1970, for example, these three countries accounted for over 40 percent of world exports of iron ore, copper ore, zinc ore, and lead ore.

Some producing countries enjoy competitive advantages in certain markets because of geographic location and the tailoring of processing capacity in these markets to the grade and processing characteristics of the minerals they produce. Examples of such captive market situations are Morocco in phosphate rock exports to Western Europe, Caribbean countries in bauxite exports to the United States, Australia in a number of exports (iron ore and coking coal, in particular) to Japan, and Canada in nickel and iron ore exports to the United States. While these factors undoubtedly give producing countries a bargaining advantage, the advantage is not always onesided. Proximity of supplier and user and the gearing of processing technology to the product's processing properties also mean that the supplier is captive to the importer. Iron ore sales by Sweden to continental Europe and bauxite shipments from Jamaica to the United States are examples of such mutual dependence.

The Contribution to National Economies

The contribution of the mineral sector to civilization and material progress is immeasurable; it is so easily understood that it is unnecessary to give a detailed account of the historical sequence—painting the cumulative effect in a few broad strokes suffices.

All major advances in meeting human needs in the past—for food, housing, health care, education, jobs, and transport—have been predicated on the use of additional minerals, more efficient use of minerals, or use of better minerals—indeed, very often a combination of all three. Throughout history, the discovery of a new mineral, or a new alloy, or a new method of extracting or processing a mineral, or a new orebody has had a major impact on industrial growth as well as on life style. The mineral sector provided the foundation on which the Industrial Revolution was built, completely reorganizing modes of living and revolutionizing goods, foods, transport, and modes of construction as well as destruction (arms). If this crucial role is not revealed in the orders of magnitude we cite below, it is because available statistics stop showing the contribution of minerals once the resources move from the mining sector to the manufacturing sector. The problem is one of categories (as defined in the present system) which vanishes with historical perspective.

What is the significance of the mineral sector globally and for individual countries today? The answer depends on the yardstick used (quantitative or qualitative; economic, social, or political), the degree of disaggregation attempted in the analysis, and how far one carries out the measurement of the multiplier effects and external economies of mineral development. Data on a country basis are skimpy and lack comparability. Therefore, the question can be answered quantitatively only in broad terms and with regard to the situation in selected large producers.

Although the mineral sector plays a crucial role in the economies of several countries—Australia and Canada, Chile and Jamaica, Peru and Bolivia, Zaïre and Zambia, Liberia and the Republic of South Africa—on a global or regional basis, its contribution to GNP, industrial production, or employment is not significant.

In the developed market economies the nonfuel minerals sector contributes 0.66 percent of GNP, less than the 0.72 percent of a decade ago. Even in the developing countries its contribution is only 1.2 percent of GNP, slightly up from 1.1 percent ten years earlier. In the centrally planned economies, the figure falls somewhere in between. The contribution of the sector to industrial production[9] comes to 1.9 percent in developed market economies, 5.4 percent in developing countries, and 2.9 percent in centrally planned economies. On a regional basis, the ratio varies from 7.0 percent in Oceania to 1.4 percent in the European Economic Community. Globally, the work force employed by the nonfuel minerals sector amounts to only 3 percent of that employed by the manufacturing sector, or about 0.2 percent of population. The figures are, respectively, 2 percent and 0.3 percent for the developed market economies, 3 percent and 0.1 percent for developing countries, and 3 percent and 0.35 percent for the centrally planned economies.

While the foregoing suggests that the impact of the mineral sector is greatest in the developing economies, in terms of value added per capita, the reverse is true, largely because of the concentration of processing facilities in the industrialized nations.

The value added per capita by the nonfuel mineral industry in dollars is as follows:[10]

Region	Value added
Developed market economies	12
Developing market economies	2
Centrally planned economies	16

The mineral sector can nevertheless make a very important contribution to the economies of individual developing countries. For example, in four developing countries, all of them in Africa, the sector accounts for more than 30 percent of GDP, in another eight (half in Africa, half in Latin America) for more than 10 percent, and in another six for more than 5 percent.[11] In nearly half of forty developing countries surveyed, estimates of mining employment are not available. Available statistics indicate, however, that the mining sector accounts for as much as 15 percent of total employment in three countries (Zaïre, Zambia, and Liberia). The mining industry of the Republic of South Africa provides employment for large numbers of migrant workers from neighboring countries. In some countries, such as Malaysia and Bolivia, employment in small-scale mining represents a significant proportion of

9. Value added in mining, manufacturing, electricity, and water. Value added defined as gross value of output less cost of materials, supplies, fuels and electricity consumed, services purchased, and work contracted out. Based on UN estimates for 1970, generally at factor cost.

10. Derived from UN *Monthly Bulletin of Statistics*.

11. These statistics are based on the situation in 1971–72 in most cases and do not reflect the opening of new mines since then in Papua New Guinea, Botswana, and the Dominican Republic, for example, which are likely to have a major impact on national economies.

total employment. Even in the industrialized countries, mining and on-site processing of minerals provide needed employment opportunities in depressed areas. Coal mining in the Appalachian Mountains region of the United States is an example.

The contribution of the nonfuel minerals industry is most readily measurable and appears to be greatest with regard to export earnings. Approximately 16 percent of the current exports of the developing countries consist of nonfuel minerals, compared to 12 percent in the mid 1950s. The mining sector accounts for up to 95 percent of total exports in some developing countries, for more than 50 percent of exports in eight to ten countries, and for 20 to 50 percent in a dozen countries. In the developed supplier nations of Australia, Canada, and South Africa, nonfuel minerals make up approximately 12 percent, 25 percent, and 30 percent, respectively, of total exports and, except in Canada, these exports are growing in importance.

Substantial benefits can accrue to a country from a properly structured and administered mineral industry. Mining activity earns foreign exchange and produces additional revenue through taxes and royalties; it may stimulate development of depressed regions, improve the professional and technical skills of nationals, and provide a nucleus for economic development. In the past two decades, mining has become a major source of public and private revenue for many newly emerging nations. Most mineral projects are by and large independent of the size of the local market. With proper policies and assistance, the industry can be competitive in any country suitably endowed with natural resources. Consequently, once a mineral resource has been discovered, internal political pressures to develop it tend to be great, especially in countries not endowed with much else or facing a steep uphill struggle to become competitive in other sectors.

Quantitative measures such as the share of mining in GDP can often overstate the contribution of the mining industry to the economic well-being of a country (although in some cases the beneficial economic and social impact may in fact be greater than is revealed by such measures). There is no doubt that the mining industry can have adverse effects, directly or indirectly, on the economy of a developing country. By their very nature, mineral export projects have remained enclaves, better integrated with the outside world than with the host economies, and have allowed little backward integration. The capital intensiveness of the industry results in the employment of a relatively small labor force and a small wage bill. Furthermore, to bid for the scarce resource of skilled labor and to counter the disadvantage of remote location of operation, the companies pay relatively high wages and establish quasi-urban areas. These steps encourage wage increases in other sectors, as well as a move to more capital-intensive methods. They may lead to a deterioration of the competitiveness of domestic industrial and agricultural products in regional and world markets. They also tend to create a labor elite or middle working class, which leads to increased imports of food and other consumer goods and directs industry toward the production of middle class goods which usually have a high import content. This creates problems for the host government not only in achieving its mineral sector objectives but also in planning its overall economic development.

In reacting to this situation, however, governments and concerned observers fail to give sufficient credit to: the establishment of company towns (which, despite their shortcomings, are on the whole socially beneficial) and the related upgrading of education and health; the cadre of trained workers created at considerable cost; and the establishment of economic activities which justify infrastructure development and thus contribute to the opening up of remote areas. Furthermore, there is reluctance to recognize that disappointment of expectations from mineral sector development can in many cases be attributed to the government's failure to use the industry's tax contribution effectively to diversify the economic base of the country. This reinforces the economy's dependence on the mineral export sector for its imports of consumer goods, and the standard of living and growth of national income become even more tied to the performance of the mineral sector.

The basic questions concerning the mineral sector's negative contribution to national economies can be reduced to three, none of which lend themselves to generalized answers. They are: First, to what extent are the adverse effects offset by real benefits? Second, are the adverse effects intrinsic to the mining industry? And third, do these effects vary with the degree of foreign ownership or control of the sector? There is no reason to assume that mining activity, even when foreign owned or controlled, is bound to have net adverse effects on the economy. Unequivocal answers to any of the three questions require empirical study of specific circumstances case by case. One such case study has recently been completed by Mikesell and suggests some partial answers.[12]

---

12. Raymond F. Mikesell, *Foreign Investment in Copper Mining: Case Studies and Mines in Peru and Papua-New Guinea* (Baltimore and London: Johns Hopkins University Press for Resources for the Future, 1975), pp. 100–21. The analysis of the contribution of the second project covered in the book (the Toquepala Copper Mine in Peru) is not as detailed.

Mikesell's evaluation and analysis of the Bougainville copper mine in Papua New Guinea concludes that the project has had both positive and negative effects but that, especially when these are projected over the next fifteen years, the benefits more than offset the adverse effects. To mention some of the usually overlooked benefits, the project's contribution to employment has already been substantial and will continue to be far in excess of the 3,600 workers currently employed directly by the mine. At the peak of the construction period the total work force of the project amounted to over 10,000 workers, the majority of whom were formerly unemployed urban and rural dwellers, not wage and salary earners leaving previous employment. "It seems likely that the withdrawal of skilled and experienced workers from other sectors of the economy (during the construction phase) was more than compensated for by the training and experience of the workers returned to the economy."[13] In the exploitation stage, too, the project will result in the training of large numbers of workers far greater than the normal work force of the mine because of the high rate of turnover. Between 700 and 800 trained and experienced workers have already left the mine "many of whom will eventually employ their skills in other sectors of the PNG economy [Papua New Guinea]. Even the nonskilled labourers will have acquired an understanding of the disciplines of a modern industrial society. It seems likely, therefore, that over the years BCL[14] will make a significant contribution to the supply of mechanics, electricians, machinists, welders, heavy-equipment operators, carpenters, and supervisors in the PNG economy."[15]

In the area of agriculture, although the construction of the mine resulted initially in a significant loss of cash crop production and the withdrawal of labor previously available for agriculture, the increased demand for fruits and vegetables generated by the mining communities is expected to more than compensate for the initial loss. The region's major crops, cacao and copra, have already gained from increased access to markets and ports provided by the trans-island road built by the company, and by the creation or upgrading of other roads in the region.

According to Mikesell's analysis, the Papua New Guinea project conforms to our profile with regard to the creation of a labor elite, since the average indigenous worker employed by the mine received wages over four times those of the average worker in this

13. Mikesell, *Foreign Investment*, p. 102.
14. Bougainville Copper Limited.
15. Mikesell, *Foreign Investment*, p. 119.

sector and the import content of personal consumption of the workers at the mine was higher than the average for the region. Mikesell's analysis also highlights the way the contribution of the mine to the economy depends on measures to improve output in other sectors. Mikesell concludes:

> The ultimate contribution of the Bougainville mine to both the national product and to the PNG balance of payments will depend upon an increase in the domestic value-added content of market expenditures. For there to be a substantial rise in real national income beyond the direct contribution, there must be an increase in investment in agriculture and industry together with an increase in productivity. Increased investment should be induced by the increased demand for local goods and services and the new investment financed by the additional savings generated by the larger incomes and by the availability of foreign exchange for imported equipment, materials, and technology. . . . If nothing is done to increase productive capacity and productivity the vast bulk of the domestic income generated by the mine may simply be used to purchase additional inputs for consumption. On the other hand, if investment and productivity rise as a consequence of the stimulus provided by the increase in domestic purchasing power, the rise in national income could be substantial—perhaps 50–100 percent of BCL's direct contribution to national income.[16]

To summarize, the enclave industry label is well deserved. But this should not be used to argue that mining is bound to have gross adverse effects in the developing countries and therefore should be given low priority on a development plan. This would prevent the establishment of a properly operated, regulated, and economically integrated mining industry—the only model we advocate on the basis of the unacceptibility of the current experience. To offer a cliché of our own, it would be like throwing out the baby with the bathwater.

Unfortunately, the enclave character is but one of several negative features of the mining industry as it now exists. Many segments of the industry show insufficient concern for environmental damages, tolerate poor working conditions for miners, and exhibit a skewed income distribution. To be sure, these are not characteristic of the mining industry alone (its skewed income distribution is all

16. Ibid., p. 111.

but dwarfed by that existing in agriculture as a result of the un-equal distribution of landholdings) but they are more glaring in an integrated industry dependent on host countries, where a responsi-ble and responsive company ethic should be the order of the day. Yet in imagining the ideal contribution of the industry and the multinationals in particular, one can easily fall into the trap of asking them to fill a role beyond their purview. It is one thing to ask an industry not to aggravate the maldistribution of income—indeed to assist in its correction—quite another to look to it for a model. That would imply quasigovernmental powers on the part of the mining company and the spread of its influence over other sectors. Income redistribution is the responsibility of governments. In short, it is inconsistent to complain about the power of the companies while deriding their lack of initiative in areas which are government prerogative.

4 | Mineral Price Behavior

THE DEVELOPING WORLD's current call for a new international economic order stems in part from gross dissatisfaction with the pattern of mineral production, processing, consumption, and trade outlined in the preceding chapter. The most direct expression of this is found in "The Dakar Declaration and Action Programme of the Conference of Developing Countries on Raw Materials" which states: "Primary commodities form an area of the world economy in which structural changes are necessary and inevitable."[1] Many of the specific demands accompanying this view concern prices—prices in relation to, for example, production costs, prices of imported inputs or food, prices of the final products, prices of manufactures, and prices of investment goods. The demands, however, reflect considerable confusion about structural (market) and price changes: which is means and which is end? To some extent, the confusion is intentional and understandable. Developing countries feel they cannot afford to wait for systematic structural change (moving from the production base up) to yield the desired changes, nor do they trust the developed countries to set the process in motion with sufficient speed and determination. In our view, the confusion of means and ends has its origin also in confusion on a broader scale, concerning mineral price behavior in general and the forces affecting market power in particular. In this chapter, therefore, we begin with a review of the role and determinants of mineral prices and, after summarizing the price trends, we focus on attempts to influence prices unilaterally.

1. Guy F. Erb and Valeriana Kallab (eds.), *Beyond Dependency: The Developing World Speaks Out* (Washington, D.C.: Overseas Development Council, 1975), p. 219; the Declaration is also reproduced in United Nations, (E/AC.62/6) (New York, April 15, 1975).

The Role of Mineral Prices

The concept of price and its measurement has a number of limitations in the case of minerals that must be understood before proceeding with an examination of mineral price behavior.

In the market system, the role of price is to balance demand and supply by allocating scarce goods among competing end uses. As noted in a recent study, in theory at least, the balancing of demand and supply deals with three allocation problems at once: which goods will be produced, how (with what combination of inputs) they will be produced, and to whom (which users) they shall be distributed.[2] In the case of minerals, optimally, prices have two other allocation functions: allocating consumption between the present generation and future generations, and distributing the economic benefits of exploitation among host countries, foreign investors, and consumers. The first deals with the tradeoffs between conservation and income; the second deals with the distribution of income among countries. Both defy optimal solution, in each case because of the imperfections of the market and the limits of knowledge.

In microeconomics it is assumed that in the absence of structural change production of a good can go on indefinitely. Production of mineral resources is fundamentally different, however, because of the possibility that supplies will someday be exhausted and production will stop. This raises the question of rationing consumption among generations. The issue is not too germane to this book, as we are dealing here with nonfuel minerals which are recyclable: use by one generation does not preclude use by future generations. Since, however, the popular notion of scarcity makes no distinction between recyclable and nonrecyclable minerals, its implications for pricing merit attention here.

In the context of strict economic theory, the problem of allocating scarce resources among generations is insoluble. The market process is conceived of as a bargaining process, with the number of participants and their knowledge about the market determining the degree of imperfection of the market. As it is physically impossible for future generations to be present at contemporary bargaining, there is no way for their preferences to be expressed. Moreover, the future is a continuum inhabited by an infinite num-

2. U.S. Congress, House, Committee on Banking and Currency, *Meeting America's Resource Needs: Problems and Policies, Report of Ad Hoc Committee on the Domestic and International Monetary Effects of Energy and Other Natural Resource Pricing*, 93d Cong., 2d sess., November 1974, chap. 3.

ber of variables; controlling one—resource availabilities—does not enable the analyst to predict the total picture. The question then can be asked, Why bother at all? In answer, it can be assumed that nations will not consider the possibility of nonsurvival and will make their political and economic decisions with a view to the future. It can be argued, however, that past generations have not left us the present mineral riches because of their concern for this generation's welfare, but because they did not know how to exploit them for themselves. Furthermore, as each generation tends to be materially better off than its predecessor, transfer of wealth between generations amounts to redistribution from the poor to the rich and for this reason may be viewed with disfavor. Obviously, this order of generalizaiton involves gross oversimplification. What is underlined here is that prices cannot perform the function of rationing exploitation optimally among generations. Economics deals with alternatives in which philosophical or very long-term considerations do not play a role; therefore, the tools are inadequate to deal with such concerns.

It should be clear from the discussion in the preceding chapters that mineral exploitation is based on imperfect knowledge of the extent, availability, and grade of the deposit. The theory of the second best suggests that there are no criteria for choosing among suboptimal solutions. It should not therefore be surprising that there is not yet any universally accepted theory about the pricing of minerals. What consensus has emerged points toward the maximization of the present value of the future output of the mine.[3] Even such a generalization requires difficult assumptions about the physical attributes of the mine as well as about the general performance of the economy in determining the proper rate of discount.

Perceptions of the determinants and role of mineral prices are in the process of reevaluation and are undergoing fundamental transformation, though without commensurate refinement of the analytical tools required to evaluate and assist in that transformation. Historically, under assumptions of competition, prices have been viewed as a function of demand and supply in the short run

3. See Harold Hotelling, "The Economics of Exhaustive Resources," *Journal of Political Economy* (April 1931); Robert M. Solow, "The Economics of Resources or the Resources of Economics," *American Economic Review* (May 1974); and Raymond F. Mikesell, "Rate of Exploitation of Exhaustible Resources: The Case of an Export Economy" (presented at the Second Trans-Pacific Seminar, Minerals Across the Pacific: Bridge or Barrier? sponsored by the Australian Society for Latin American Studies, Melbourne, Australia, June 20–22, 1975; mimeographed).

and cost determined in the long run. The magnitude and conditions of recent changes in oil prices have drawn attention to the idea of availability and cost of substitutes as a benchmark for pricing. More important, persisting inequality in the global distribution of income and a sense that international economic developments are working against them have induced many developing countries to reexamine the determination and function of prices, moving away from the market clearance concept toward a resource transfer concept. Though this new view implicit in the demands of many raw-material–producing nations has strong economic and moral underpinnings, economic theory is unable to provide a means of optimizing prices by this method. The problems of the industry with the already high degree of uncertainty and risk of operation are thus compounded. A recent investigation by the U.S. House of Representatives notes:

> In an era of declining validity in limiting assumptions (holding certain factors constant) the tenuous art of price forecasting has become all the more difficult. Theories calling for all other factors to be held constant have frequently proved limited, fallacious, and unworkable in light of current developments in the world economy and natural resources market; the speed at which the outside variables such as market control, the nature of market concessions, the stability of foreign investment, and the cost of energy inputs and environmental protection change has exacerbated the difficulty of prediction.[4]

What characterizes the present scene is the certainty of fundamental change—in the very rules of the game, with prices as a major target—but unpredictability as to the nature, degree, and extent of the change and the adjustment required, since the outcome depends on bargaining among political bodies, namely, governments. This situation can put severe strains on an industry such as mining which is capital intensive and where project preparation and lead times are very extended and require large preinvestment programs. It is, therefore, in the interest of both consumers and producers to reach accommodation soon and to make the change smooth so as to avoid costly paralysis of investment decisions.

4. House Committee on Banking and Currency, *Meeting America's Resource Needs*, p. 62.

The Nature of Price Information

In view of the international character of this age-old, multibillion dollar industry, it may come as a surprise to the nonspecialist that international or market prices are difficult to determine in mining. The reasons are to be found in the structure of the market and the complexity of the product.

The markets for minerals range from "free commodity markets" (insofar as that term implies a system of transactions between independent buyers and sellers on the basis of day-to-day prices) to highly horizontally and vertically integrated markets.[5] In the first, measuring market prices poses no major problem, except for difficulties associated with quality or grade; in the second, however, a market price for a mineral may be almost impossible to determine. The markets for most minerals fall between these two extremes. Typical is the case of iron ore: it has been estimated that in the late 1960s roughly 40 percent of world iron ore trade took place between importers (steel companies) and captive mines abroad, another 40 percent was transacted under long-term contracts of up to twenty years, and only 20 percent occurred under conditions approximating a "free market"—in this case, mostly under short-term (one-year) contracts between Western Europe and Swedish suppliers. The composition of iron ore trade in this respect is changing continuously and varies from importer to importer (see figure 11).

Two points are important in this connection: one, international trade in most minerals combines each of the three importer-exporter relationship categories typical of iron ore; two, change is in the direction of long-term contracts, with the "free market" shrinking and, in effect, becoming a residual market. Under these conditions, the analyst is faced with the problem of weighing prices by the quantities traded in each submarket; frequently he also faces the problem of finding prices which are representative of each submarket. The vulnerability of published price estimates

---

5. Completely free markets, where 100 percent of the output is sold under conditions of perfect competition, are rare in minerals. However, to claim that no mineral is sold under nearly free market conditions or does not have large pockets of free market is to ignore the existence of the London Metal Exchange and the notorious price fluctuations in commodities such as copper which provoke demands for stabilization. Nevertheless, as we are dealing with minerals in general, putting the term *free market* in quotation marks throughout the chapter is justified.

FIGURE 11 | DISTRIBUTION OF IRON IMPORTS BY TYPE OF IMPORTER–
EXPORTER RELATION, FOR WORLD (1960 AND 1968) AND FOR
MAJOR IMPORTERS (MOST RECENT ESTIMATES CIRCA 1968)

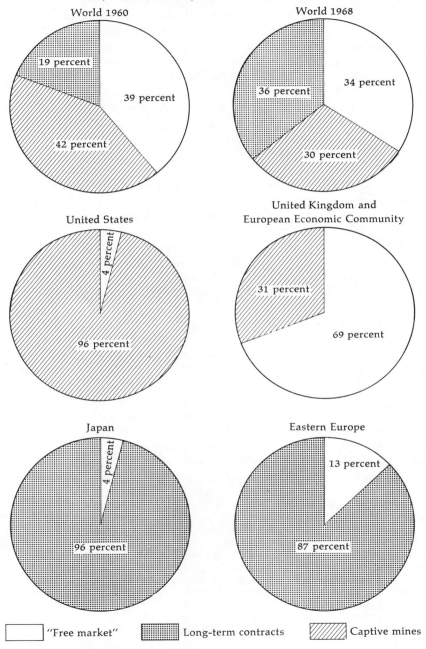

Source: Bension Varon, Jacques Nusbaumer, and others, "The International Market
for Iron Ore: Review and Outlooks," World Bank Staff Working Paper, no. 160
(Washington, D.C., August 1973).

to transfer pricing practices is well appreciated. It is less frequently realized that long-term contract prices, unless carefully scrutinized, do not provide the basis for building a consistent price series. Prices depend on the complex provisions of each contract; contracts cover not only the terms of marketing but also the terms of investment and processing, and the mutual concessions agreed upon are reflected in the agreement on prices.

In practice, for metals such as copper, lead, and tin traded on a futures market like the London Metal Exchange, quotations based on this market provide good reference prices. Other metals which are not traded on a futures market may be so dominated by one producer that that producer's published selling price is accepted as the reference price for that metal, even though a small "free market" may exist alongside. Nickel and molybdenum illustrate this practice. There are a number of metals, however, which have neither a futures market nor a producer price, and for these the prices quoted in such reputable trade periodicals as *Metal Bulletin* are commonly used as reference prices. But with many minerals variations in grade and degree of beneficiation, and especially the trend toward trading in concentrates, are a major source of difficulty and confusion. *Metal Bulletin*, which has wide experience in this field, has noted: "The pricing of such concentrates has become so complicated lately that it might need a book to explain all the details. However, such a book would almost be out of date as soon as written because practice is changing so rapidly."[6]

The techniques developed over the years for providing reasonably accurate information on prices are of little help where the mineral is not traded as such because of vertical integration. Very often minerals leave the host countries as ore or concentrate for further processing within the same corporate complex. Since there is no international market for these intermediate products, except in the case of iron and manganese ores, the real question is how accurately the intracompany transfer prices reflect costs in the host countries, and to what extent they are being manipulated to shift profit centers within the corporation to more favorable tax or risk areas. Sufficient information is not available for an adequate answer to this question, but there is strong evidence of price distortion within the industry. The aluminum industry is a case in point. An evaluation of this industry indicated that in 1969 and 1970 bauxite prices, f.o.b. host country, varied between $5.3 and $17.6 a long dry ton, and alumina prices between $51.5 and $74.3 a short

---

6. "The Problem of Reference Prices," *Metal Bulletin Monthly* (August 1974), p. 30.

ton f.o.b. This considerable variance cannot be accounted for by production and freight cost differences or by product characteristics. It thus implies some arbitrary assignment of prices.

The problems highlighted above are not unique to minerals—they are encountered in determining the international or market prices of many other products, especially manufactured and semi-manufactured goods—but they are particularly serious in this case for a number of reasons. First, prices are perhaps the most important factor in determining the economic benefit to a host country from the exploitation of its resources; imperfect knowledge and access to knowledge on price is a source of potential conflict and an obstacle to planning. Second, the structural imperfections of the market which account for the imperfection of information on prices have distorting influences on the movements of prices themselves. For example, in cases where quotations are based on a major producer's selling price or even on reports from multiple traders, information may be manipulated to influence the market. The shrinking of the "free market" results in accentuating price fluctuations in that market and may give wrong signals to both consumers and producers. Finally, although long-term trends can be deduced, despite shortcomings in the measurement of price, the difficulty of estimating current market value objectively makes it difficult to evaluate projects and to arbitrate conflict. It is therefore in the interest of both parties, exporters and importers, to work toward the improvement of information on prices.

Determinants of Prices and Elasticities

Today, mineral prices are influenced by a wide array of factors. The basic magnitudes of demand and supply, the general economic climate, and economic growth rates are of primary importance. Inflation rates play an important role which goes beyond determining the course of nominal prices: sustained inflation tends to have a cumulative effect on producer and consumer expectations and is built into the cost structure. The intensity of use, the extent of exploration, the growth of productive capacity, and technological innovation in industries which produce, process, or transport minerals affect prices through either demand or supply. Also important are trends in production costs—labor, capital, energy, transportation, and environmental control. The degree of competition among suppliers, specifically the type and degree of market control by major producers, can determine both the availability of the mineral and its price. Changes in protective measures in the market—subsidies, tariffs, price controls—have ramifications for pricing. Finally, fluctuations in exchange rates affect the prices of internationally traded resources.[7]

The economic complexity of the factors enumerated above is compounded when they become subject to manipulation and sensitive to political considerations, either domestic or foreign. Furthermore, the very variables generally held constant in making long-term demand, supply, and price projections in the past—changes in taste, changes in technology, changes in the organization of the market, hypothesized rates of economic growth, regulation of the market through international agreements and the absence of economic or political conflict—may themselves be affected by price developments and expectations. Oil prices, for example, can have a bearing on the rates of growth of the world economy, while those, in turn, are at least partial determinants of prices. Although individual nonfuel minerals cannot have such power, they can do so together if price movements are sharp, sustained, and synchronized. It is not farfetched to suggest that mineral prices are potentially sensitive even to the world food situation and outlook inasmuch as the latter has a bearing on the volume of savings, the allocation of investment, the volume and distribution of aid, and, through changes in relative prices, on the pattern of consumption as well. The growing complexity of mineral price formation calls for caution in analysis and projection, and restraint in claiming that one can neatly sort out all the elements of the problem.

Raw material prices have become planning variables more crucial and more difficult to project than ever before. This is reflected in the growing interest in elasticities (which measure, for example, the ratio between the extent of a price change and the ensuing change in demand or supply). These are no longer obscure measures of interest to, and understood by, statisticians and economists alone; they are measures increasingly relevant to policymaking at the highest level.

The price elasticities of minerals have peculiar characteristics associated with the facts that demand for nonfuel minerals is a derived demand, and expanding supply requires a long time. Both contribute to making price elasticities low in the short run (relative to those for other goods and compared to long-term elasticities),

---

7. U.S. Congress, *Meeting America's Resource Needs*, p. 49. See same source for a recent, systematic review of the importance and operation of these factors.

depending on such factors as whether new demand is apt to be met from the exploitation of already developed resources, the exploitation of known but undeveloped resources, the discovery of new resources, or substitutes (with similar questions on their state of development).[8]

Three questions dominate the determination of price elasticities in the current situation and for the future: the level of prices, technology, and policy. In principle, estimates of past elasticities are poor guides to the future when prices reach levels far outside those observed in the past. Under these conditions, technological change gains in importance; while its results are inherently unpredictable, efforts to bring about change are a function of resources and incentive. Policy measures can have a direct role in moderating elasticities. On the supply side, lead times may be cut or output regulated; on the demand side, both the level and pattern of consumption may be influenced through a variety of measures. It may, however, be wrong to view consumers as an amorphous mass reacting in predictable fashion to prices. For example, if traditional end uses of minerals are in conflict with perceived environmental or social and moral values, price incentives alone might not overcome their conscious resistance. On the other hand, if consumers do not perceive the nature of the problem, they may not respond to high prices resulting from government policies by curbing their consumption.

While it would be cynical to suggest that the above considerations justify throwing all estimates of past elasticities out of the window, it is appropriate to remember that consumers, producers, and governments—acting individually or in concert—have made fools of forecasters in the past and may do so again in the future. In the rest of this chapter, therefore, we dwell on past trends briefly and concentrate on attempts to influence prices.

---

8. Although the econometric measurement of price elasticity is a tricky process leading to different estimates in individual cases, there is little disagreement on the broad point of short-term and long-term price elasticity. One finds that while the short-run elasticity of world demand for tin has been in the neighborhood of 0.55, the long-run elasticity is estimated at about 1.25; and whereas the short-run price elasticity of U.S. demand for aluminum or copper has been about 0.20, the long-run elasticities are around 1.35 in the case of aluminum and above 2.50 in the case of copper (all figures are, of course, minus). See, for example, F. E. Banks, "An Econometric Model of the World Tin Economy: A Comment," *Econometrica*, vol. 40, no. 4 (July 1972); Charles River Associates, Inc., *Economic Analysis of the Copper Industry* (U.S. Department of Commerce Publication, PB 189 927, March 1970); and Charles River Associates, Inc., *An Economic Analysis of the Aluminum Industry* (Cambridge, Mass., March 1971).

Price Trends

The behavior of mineral prices in the past century is illustrated in the following four charts. Figure 12 depicts the trends in the deflated prices of minerals as a group and of selected metals from 1870 to 1957; figure 13 presents the unit values of exports of minerals and metals from developing countries between 1962 and 1974; figure 14 shows the deflated prices of selected minerals and

FIGURE 12 | DEFLATED PRICE INDEXES FOR ALL MINERALS, AND FOR COPPER, LEAD, AND PIG IRON

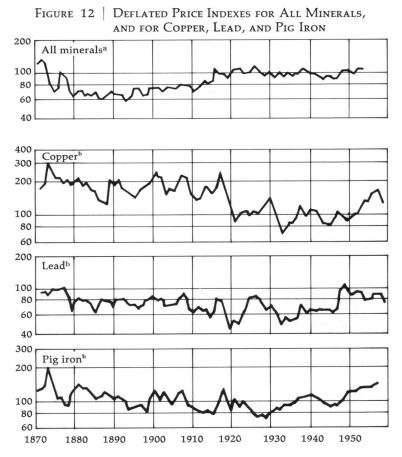

a. Bureau of Labor Statistics Wholesale Price Index (1954 output weights, 1947–49 = 100).

b. Bureau of Labor Statistics Wholesale Price Index (1947–49 = 100).

Source: Orris C. Herfindahl, "The Long-Run Cost of Minerals," in *Three Studies in Mineral Economics* (Washington, D.C.: Resources for the Future, 1961).

FIGURE 13 | INDEX NUMBERS OF PRICES OF EXPORTS OF MINERALS AND METALS AND ALL PRIMARY PRODUCTS FROM DEVELOPING COUNTRIES, AND UN UNIT VALUE INDEX OF EXPORTED MANUFACTURED GOODS (1963 = 100)

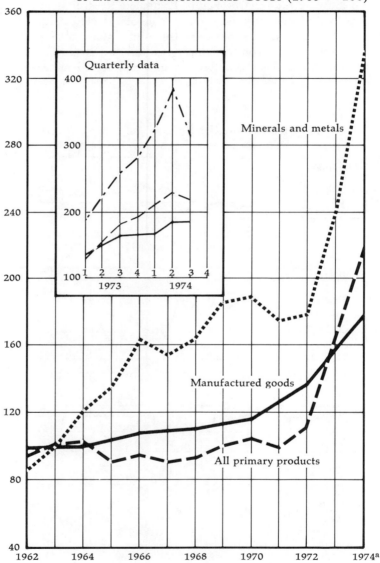

a. January to September.
Source: National Institute Economic Review (London), and United Nations, *Monthly Bulletin of Statistics.*

metals, 1963 to 1973, and the average (*A*), high (*H*), and low (*L*) for each product in calender 1974; and figure 15 traces the month-by-month movement of copper prices and London Metal Exchange stocks in 1973 to 1974. In this chapter, indeed in this study, we are not concerned with short-term year-to-year changes; our concern is with problems and developments of a secular or structural nature affecting rate of return calculation and investment decisions. However, the price changes of 1973 to 1974 fall in a special category, first, because of their special turbulence—sharp rises followed by sharp declines—and, second, because of the special global context (hinting at a change in rules of the game) in which they occurred. In the midst of the current dynamic situation it is difficult to ascertain which elements of the 1974 experience—the highs, the lows, or the average—are most relevant to reading the future, especially in light of the fact that neither producers nor consumers were pleased with 1974; consequently, we expose the reader to the range of price changes in figure 14 and to the special experience of copper in figure 15.

The major trends illustrated in the charts can be summarized as follows:

According to the pioneering analysis by Herfindahl (see figure 12), the long-term trend in mineral prices (in constant dollars) spanning the last quarter of the last century and the first half of this century has been either more or less stationary or sloping gently downward. Under sufficiently competitive conditions the long-term price trend can be expected to approximate the long-run cost trend. Although some mineral industries have strong and sometimes persistent elements of monopoly, for most minerals the marketing bases are sufficiently diversified to bring about meaningful competition and provide reasonable assurance of a price which may be termed competitive. Furthermore, the fact that for a fair number of minerals there are known resources or substitutes which can be developed if persistent profits appear reinforces the view that, on the whole, minerals have been competitively priced. (This, however, applies more to finished products, such as refined metal, than to intermediate products.) If the above assessment is correct, the charts in figure 12 support the conclusion that the trend toward mining lower-grade ore has not been reflected in increased costs—at least, not until the late 1950s and for the commodities shown—having been offset by advances in technology. The major minerals have been produced on a large scale for many decades and are probably now being mined as efficiently as possible. Since the 1960s, however, there have been signs that the cost trend for most

FIGURE 14 | DEFLATED PRICES OF SELECTED MINERALS AND METALS,
1963–73, AND AVERAGE (A), HIGH (H), AND LOW (L)
FOR 1974 (1973–74 ENLARGED)

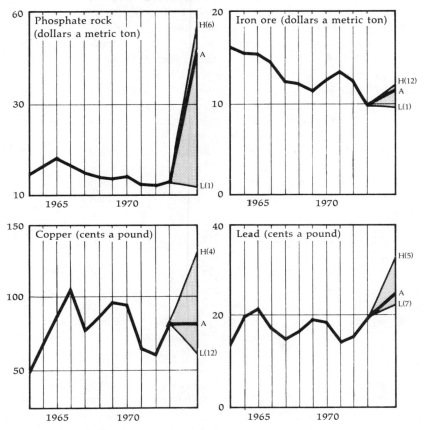

Note: Prices deflated by UN unit value index of exported manufactured goods (1973 = 100). Figures in parentheses refer to month in which high or low was recorded: January (1), February (2), and so on.

Source: UNCTAD, "An Integrated Programme for Commodities: The Role of International Commodity Stocks," (TD/B/C1/166/supp.1/add.1) (New York, December 13, 1974); and Monthly Commodity Price Bulletin.

minerals has turned upward and is likely to persist in that direction, as discussed in chapter 7.

In the last ten to twelve years, even stopping short of the 1973 boom year, the unit value of exports of minerals and metals from developing countries has risen considerably, and faster than the prices of primary products or the unit value of exports of manufactured goods from the developed countries. While prices of min-

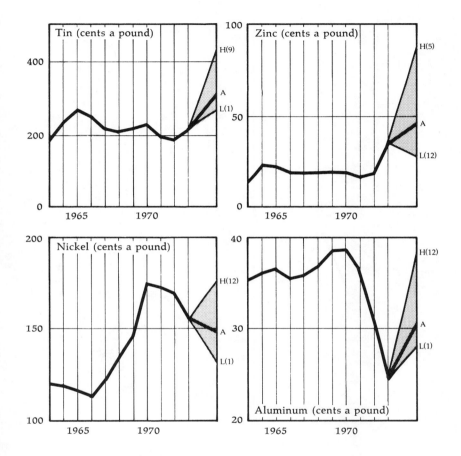

erals and metals did better than other product groups and improved in real terms, experience has been mixed and mineral-exporting countries did not benefit uniformly. The unit value of developing countries' exports of minerals and metals is heavily weighted by copper which pushed the index up during most of the 1960s. Real prices of iron ore and manganese ore weakened throughout the 1960s and prices of tin and phosphate rock in the second half of the decade. On the whole, more developing countries faced declining real prices, and for longer periods, than those benefiting from stronger prices.

All minerals reacted to the conditions setting off the worldwide commodity boom of 1973 and the first half of 1974, since mineral

FIGURE 15 | MONTHLY AVERAGE COPPER PRICES AND
LONDON METAL EXCHANGE STOCKS ON THE
LAST FRIDAY OF THE MONTH, 1973–74

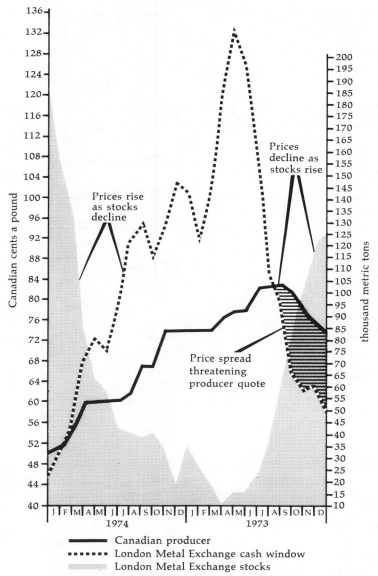

Source: Adapted with permission from *The Northern Miner* (February 6, 1975).

prices are notoriously sensitive to the business cycle. In a number of metals, price increases were bolstered by special factors, notably supply problems and bottlenecks associated with strikes, mine accidents, pollution control problems in the nonferrous metal smelting industry, and maladjustment of mining and processing capacity. The upward trend in prices was reversed in the third quarter of 1974. While the downturn had been anticipated, prices contracted abnormally fast, with potentially serious consequences for the developing countries. The weakening of metal prices reflects, in addition to the business cycle, the elimination of the temporary supply bottlenecks mentioned above; the fulfilling of capacity expansion plans initiated in response to previous high prices; and the inclination of certain countries, particularly those heavily dependent on exports of a given mineral, to produce for export at high capacity levels in order to cover ever-expanding import and debt-service costs. Relative prices have changed in the worst possible combination for the majority of developing countries: the commodity scene in late 1974 to early 1975 was characterized by rapidly deteriorating raw material prices, weakening values for many of the beverage crops and fats and oils, unrelenting increases in cereal prices, elevated oil and fertilizer prices, and continously rising costs of manufacturers.[9] Even in those ores and metals where producer prices rose through the commodity cycle, or in those where the decline in price was arrested before the recession bottomed out, price levels during 1975 were not sufficient to compensate for the decline in export volume. Besides, price discounts were common, and these developments took place against a backdrop of increases in the cost of production of 10 to 15 percent at least. In short, producers of all major minerals suffered.

Figure 14 shows the highs and lows reached by mineral prices during 1974 and, in parentheses, the month in which each was achieved. It thus permits reading at what level each mineral price series ended the year. It is apparent that those metals for which supplies and prices are closely controlled by a few major producers did best and were not harassed by the changed market conditions. The price of copper illustrates the experience of metals not in this category. The copper shortages of 1973 gave way quickly to considerable surpluses as recessionary factors cut down consumption for housing, automobiles, and other uses in the industrialized

9. For a more detailed review of the recent commodity cycle, see Kenji Takeuchi and Bension Varon, "Commodity Shortages and Changes in World Trade," *Annals of the American Academy of Political and Social Science*, vol. 420 (July 1975).

countries. Overstocked refiners in certain industrialized countries, committed to purchases of concentrates under long-term contracts, Japan in particular, were unable to finance large stockholdings of refined metal and had to offload surplus stocks on the open market. Copper production in some developing countries also increased greatly. The result was a halving of the copper price within six months from its all-time peak early in 1974. (Figure 15.)[10]

Despite the economic recovery currently in progress in the major industrialized countrties, mineral markets remain depressed or sluggish, first, because the recovery itself has been slow to gather force and to spread and, second, because the stocks accumulated during the recession are still overhanging the market. In fact, prices, though on the upswing at last, are in many cases below their 1971 levels in real terms. The trend has been reversed, but the pace and strength of the recovery are yet to be revealed.

The turbulence since 1973 has led to the realization that the old rules of the game are no longer acceptable and the time has come to change them. In the current atmosphere of heightened sensitivities, more attention has been paid to the means for changing them than to the nature and degree of the correction sought. While the new concerns find strongest expression in the controversy over prices and pricing, clearly they go beyond prices, indeed beyond economic issues, into the realm of politics. It makes little sense to seek solutions by belaboring the issue of whether recent prices have been too high or too low when all traditional yardsticks are being questioned, when the whole development problem has been blown wide open, and when action on multiple fronts has been recognized as a necessity. Even though the final destination and conditions of the journey are not clear, the course has been set and it points toward the not yet fully explored waters of harnessed price fluctuations and a massive readjustment of relative prices, if need be through unilateral action.

Past Attempts to Influence Prices

The power of major companies to influence or control prices unilaterally was noted in chapter 1. Attempts to achieve this through coordinated action, which have received wide attention

10. See also United Nations, Committee on Natural Resources, *Survey of Current Problems in the Fields of Energy and Minerals: The World Mineral Situation* (E/C.7/51) (New York, 1975).

recently, are not new, nor are they limited to initiatives by producers, and one does not have to go far back in history to find illustrations. The aluminum industry provides many examples of interindustry, multicountry cooperation in the form of swap operations among major producers, primarily for logistic reasons, to realize savings on freight and tariffs. The so-called Gentlemen's Agreement made in 1957 by the major aluminum companies supplying the Western European market to absorb the aluminum exports of the Eastern European countries effectively prevented a weakening in the price of aluminum, as was intended. Consuming countries have at various times set up special mechanisms for the control of supplies and prices of copper on their internal markets, a notable example being the Groupement d'Importation et de Repartition des Métaux (Mutual Import and Distribution Pool), generally refered to as GIRM, in France. Steel companies, well aware of their relatively strong bargaining position in the international market, have long been acting together in relation to their raw material suppliers. The British steel industry used to acquire overseas supplies through a single body even before the nationalization of the industry. In the Federal Republic of Germany, two central purchasing bodies (Rohstoffhandel Gmbh. and Erzkontor Gmbh.) centralize purchases and negotiate agreements with iron ore producers as well as shipowners.[11] Similar arrangements exist in Belgium, France, Italy, and, of course, Japan, where interindustry cooperation extends to multiple raw materials. These practices at the national level are further developed within the framework of regional or international associations which act, at the very least, as forums for the exchange of views and possibly for the working out of common attitudes and policies.[12]

An example of cooperation, indeed cartelization, on the export side is provided by Malmexport, a joint sales company entrusted with selling iron ore on behalf of three different enterprises, the Swedish state-owned LKAB, the Swedish privately owned Grangeberg, and LAMCO, a Liberian company with sizable Swedish participation. Mikdashi concluded in 1971:

11. Another German company, Exploraton und Bergbau Gmbh., acquires participation in and operates iron ore, coal, and other mines overseas for all major German and some Dutch, Italian, and Austrian iron and steel producers.

12. Analysis of these cases can be found in the voluminous writings of Zuhayr Mikdashi of the American University of Beirut, especially in "A Comparative Analysis of Selected Metal Exporting Industries" (Vienna, March 1971; mimeographed).

In its 12 years of existence, Malmexport seems to have successfully designed a sales strategy convenient to the three competing companies. It has managed to maintain Sweden's position as the most important single supplier of iron ore to Western Europe, despite the severe price competition of ores coming from overseas. Malmexport has also achieved effective regional cooperation, though on an informal basis, with the Norwegian state-owned iron ore company (Sydvaranger) with a view to averting major ore importers playing off one Scandinavian country against the other.[13]

Governments have often sanctioned or assisted such action in a variety of ways, most directly through stockpiling policies. While not necessarily or deliberately designed to manipulate prices or to serve the interests of specific industry groups, government stockpiles, especially those of the United States, have been a potent factor in the market for many minerals for a number of years.

Although developing countries have been among the major producers of minerals for many decades, their interest in producer alliances and the developed countries' concern over the implications of "the new mood, urge, need, or weapon" are relatively recent. Until the so-called energy crisis, only the copper-producing developing countries attempted to establish a base for cooperation among themselves and succeeded in doing so.[14] Partly prompted by copper price weaknesses obtaining in 1966 and the first half of 1967, the four major copper-producing countries of the developing world—Chile, Congo (now Zaïre), Peru, and Zambia—formed in June 1967 the Intergovernmental Council of Copper Exporting Countries (CIPEC, after its French name), which remains in existence. While informal consultations on other minerals were held by developing countries from time to time, these fell short of real producers' cooperation.

The remarkable success of the Organization of Petroleum Exporting Countries (OPEC) in negotiating contract terms raising oil revenues dramatically, beginning in 1971, generated the developing countries' interest in producers' alliances for other minerals or major agricultural commodities. The link between the energy crisis and the new mood in nonfuel minerals, however, goes beyond setting an example. For developing countries hurting from high oil import bills, the incentive to seek better returns from their traditional exports is no doubt greater. Similarly, for developed countries

13. Mikdashi, *A Comparative Analysis*, p. 80.
14. The International Tin Agreement, in existence since 1956, includes as members both consumer-importers and producer-exporters.

facing huge oil import bills, the specter of higher raw material prices weighs heavier than in the days of cheap oil. The role of OPEC members in spearheading the demands for better terms of trade for the developing countries as a group suggests a new era for primary commodity prices in connection with the energy crisis. Last, but not least, energy is an important input in the extraction and processing of minerals, as well as a key determinant of the pattern of consumption into which metals fit. The new energy prices may begin a long series of complex technological and economic relationships, prompting aggressive and defensive action by nonfuel mineral exporters and importers, respectively.

The new awareness of the threat and rewards of producers' alliances, especially in mineral raw materials, has causes more basic than the recent energy crisis. On the consumers' side, it follows from growing realization of the heavy dependence of modern economic growth on nonrenewable mineral raw materials and the increasing import dependence of industrialized countries in minerals. On the exporters' side, it mirrors not only their continuing dependence on exports of primary commodities, in view of the slow progress in expanding and diversifying their production base, but also painful disappointment in their efforts to reach international commodity agreements and accelerate the flow of assistance. To these, of course, must be added the trend toward national political and economic independence. True appreciation of the root causes of the present situation requires tracing the course of international economic and political relations in postwar history, which is beyond the scope of our inquiry.

Following the energy crisis, steps have been taken by the developing countries to express their concerns and assert their will, either through general statement (under the auspices of the United Nations or in special forums improvised for this purpose) or through specific action. In the field of nonfuel minerals, specific action to March 1976 included the following: In March 1974, seven major bauxite exporters formed the International Bauxite Association (IBA).[15] Subsequently, Jamaica, a leading member of the IBA, succeeded in quintupling government revenues from its bauxite and alumina industry by increasing royalties and taxes on bauxite. Other members have begun to follow suit. So far, actions have been taken on an individual basis but the foundation is being laid for concerted action.

Morocco, the world's largest phosphate exporter (with a share of

15. Australia, Guinea, Guyana, Jamaica, Sierra Leone, Surinam, and Yugoslavia. Haiti, the Dominican Republic, and Ghana joined later.

about 35 percent in recent years), started raising its phosphate rock price in 1973. By October 1974 the price had reached $70 a ton, representing an overall increase of over 400 percent. Major U.S. prosphate producers also adjusted their prices upward very sharply, and other producers followed. These moves, however, have not taken place under any formal agreement.

Four major copper-exporting developing countries decided through CIPEC to cut back their exports by 10 percent, beginning in December 1974, in the face of collapsing copper prices. Indonesia joined CIPEC in 1975 as a full member and Australia and Papua New Guinea joined as associate members.

In April 1975, concerned over the unfavorable trend in terms of trade and anxious to assure remunerative returns, eleven iron ore-producing countries drew up the Association of Iron Exporting Countries (AIEC). The association became formally established in September 1975 with the signature of the agreement by seven countries.[16] The objectives of the association include cooperation and consultation on prices and markets.

In April 1975 several mercury-producing *companies* from five countries[17] formed the International Association of Mercury Producers (ASSIMER) with the object of curbing wide price fluctuations and promoting the use of mercury as well as providing technical assistance to members.[18]

What does all this mean for the world mining industry, not just for one group or another, and what does it augur for the future? Only tentative answers can be provided in the present fluid situation, and only by way of adding perspective rather than offering firm predictions.

Issues and Directions

From the very beginning, the question of producers' alliances has been politicized by both sides. In developed countries the issue was not seen as one of the relative market strength of consumers and

16. Algeria, Venezuela, Australia, India, Mauritania, Chile, and Peru.
17. Algeria, Italy, Mexico, Spain, and Turkey.
18. Intergovernmental or intercompany discussions also took place on a number of commodities such as lead and zinc, manganese and tungsten, prompted by concern over extremely unfavorable market conditions. To give the impression that these have already resulted in cartels, as in the title of a recent publication [Kenneth W. Clarfield and Associates, "Eight Mineral Cartels: The New Challenge to Industrialized Nations" (New York: McGraw Hill, 1975)] is untruthful packaging and analogous to claiming that one who studies philosophy is automatically a philosopher.

sellers, but rather as one of a newly emerging political and economic force ominously aligned against the consumers, the industrialized nations.[19] Their feeling of beleaguerment has apparently
caused the industrialized countries to add to their anxiety over the
availability of raw materials a concern for the ideology of those who
control them. Some developing countries, in fact, have recognized
the political possibilities of this tool and have thus reinforced the
power play aspects of the resource control issue. For the most part,
however, developing countries tend to regard arrangements of the
OPEC kind enviously on economic grounds. Both sides have been
guilty of exaggerated negative or positive expectations which hinder
their seeing the issue in a measured historical and economic
perspective.

In the past, bargaining power has been disproportionately with
consuming industrialized nations, which have enjoyed control over
capital, technology, processing, marketing, and shipping. In some
ways, this power has been increasing, through growing vertical and
horizontal integration, technological advances, regional economic
arrangements, and so on. What appears to be at issue today, at least
in the eyes of developing countries, is not so much the merits of
competition versus other forms of market organization in the abstract, as the need to counterbalance the substantial power of consuming countries over the exploitation of the world's scarce natural
resources. Producers' alliances are not necessarily the optimal or
only answer; theoretically, the same results could be achieved by
breaking up consumers' alliances where these exist, although this
might be difficult and therefore unrealistic. One thing is certain: A
market situation where competing and unorganized sellers confront
a strong buyer favors sellers least among all possible forms of
market configuration. In light of this, and given the successive disappointments of the developing countries with aid flows, transfer
of know-how, trade liberalization, and attempts to draw up international commodity agreements, it is neither an historical anomaly
nor an economic violation for the developing countries to seek
more equitable returns from the exploitation of their scarce natural
resources through producers' alliances. While the word *cartel* has
come to carry a connotation of hostility, it must be remembered that
supply management is a respectable tool of modern economics. No
one can argue that copper-producing developing countries ought

19. The first to sound the warning and the most articulate exponent of
the view that cartels are the wave of the future is Fred Bergsten of the
Brookings Institution. See his "The Threat from the Third World," *Foreign
Policy* (Summer 1973); "The Threat Is Real," *Foreign Policy* (Spring 1974); and
"The New Era in Commodity Cartels," *Challenge* (September–October 1974).

to keep operating at full capacity in the face of declining prices, or have a greater obligation to ignore revenue maximization opportunities than firms in the industrialized countries.

The issue, then, is not whether developing countries can or cannot or should or should not act in concert, but rather whether and to what extent and at what cost they can benefit from such action, individually and collectively, and over what time frame, and what this means in terms of the global efficiency of resource use. While one can highlight the parameters and speculate on their values, one cannot predict events so dependent on national decisions—decisions not purely economic in content and shaped by each country's reading of the future.

The prerequisites for successful action in the OPEC manner in nonfuel minerals can be usefully grouped into three categories: minimum and essential requirements, factors facilitating successful action, and elements contributing to the net benefits derivable by the producing countries.

In the first category of minimum and essential requirements, there is really only one precondition: namely, that demand be price inelastic (the more inelastic, the better) which, in practical terms, means that the mineral be an essential input for the manufacture of an essential good and that neither have a close substitute.

Conditions facilitating successful action include that few countries (the fewer the better) control a large portion of world production (the larger the better) and preferably of reserves and resources as well; that supply outside the members of the alliance be high cost and inelastic; that members enjoy political compatibility, communality of interest, and protection from retaliation, that is, that their economies and economic prospects not be linked inextricably with the markets and fortunes of the consuming nations.

To benefit from such action both individually and collectively, developing countries must not be large importers of the commodities in question or depend heavily on them for employment. Their initial bargaining strength and the stream of benefits will be greater the larger the annual-production-to-reserves ratio. Either strong demand growth or scarcity of resources will tend to enhance the power of the producing countries.

While none of the above factors need exist at peak force, each of them must figure considerably in the combination.

These hypotheses, however, are subject to a number of qualifications: First, the relative values of short-run and long-run price elasticities can influence both the size and the duration of benefits; second, simultaneous action on minerals which are close or potential substitutes can reinforce the position of each; third, in several minerals, participation in the alliance by industrialized country producers can enhance the chances and degree of success; fourth, significant changes may be achieved short of concerted action through price leadership, as by Morocco in phosphates, and, fifth, the availability of financial support to producing countries can be an important factor.

The prospects for alliances of producers in nonfuel minerals have been the subject of much attention and contention recently. While the flow of opinion and studies (the distinction is intentional, since there has been a dearth of opinion based on systematic study) gives the impression that assessment falls into two neatly divisible camps, this is not the case; there are no antagonists and protagonists as such. Some analysts, chief among them Bergsten, have concentrated on whether alliances of producers are feasible and likely and have concluded that they are. The determination of some countries, who see this as the only way to rectify wrongs, lends support to this view. Others have focused on the possible achievements of such alliances and have concluded that they will vary from mineral to mineral and are not likely to measure up to OPEC in benefits to developing countries or hardships to consumers. Among the obstacles are: small share of the market; small share of reserves, and in some cases even smaller share of potential resources; possibilities for substitution and recycling; the new mineral frontiers of the oceans; and the onus of existing stockpiles.[20]

In the final analysis, only future developments in the marketplace will prove or disprove the validity of the current speculation on these complex issues. The final question revolves around the risks of acting or reacting without further homework. We feel there are risks, especially risks of exaggeration, although we are painfully aware that for some of the developing countries these are dwarfed by the risks of starvation and continuing poverty. It is prudent, nevertheless, to underline that, on the producers' side, the failure of one cartel may result in strengthening the hand of the consumers on a broad plane for years to come. There are also risks in failing to recognize that while controlling supply in pursuit of higher prices is a legitimate tool of revenue maximization, it can serve the developing countries well only if it is undertaken without shortshifting the attainment of their overall development goals, which transcends revenue maximization in one commodity or sector. On the consumers' side, there is the risk that exaggerated fears of alliances of producers will be used by diverse interest groups to

20. See Bension Varon and Kenji Takeuchi, "Developing Countries and Non-Fuel Minerals," *Foreign Affairs* (April 1974); Raymond F. Mikesell, "More Third World Cartels?" *Challenge* (November–December 1974); and Stephen D. Krasner, "Oil Is the Exception," *Foreign Policy* (Spring 1974).

urge governments to adopt inward-oriented policies—eventually costly to them—resulting in regressive steps in aid, transfer of technology, or trade liberalization. There are also risks for third parties and in terms of global welfare. For example, we are impressed by the fact that the current debate deals with the current structure of production as frozen, ignoring the possibility that developing countries where truly large and low-cost resources might be discovered will and should enter the market for reasons of national interest and global efficiency.

The debate on alliances of producers has recently been frustrated by the lack of real prospects and has been superseded by wide-ranging discussion of commodity agreements as a vehicle for balancing the needs and interests of the producing and consuming countries. At the center of the discussion is UNCTAD's so-called integrated commodity program, proposed in 1974, which aims to stabilize prices through a network of buffer stocks financed through a common fund, and contains provisions for improving the terms of trade as well as the gains from trade of the developing countries.[21] The program encompasses twenty-one commodities of major export interest to the developing countries, ten of which have been designated as core commodities suitable for buffer stocks. Of the twenty-one commodities, six are minerals (copper, iron ore, tin, bauxite, zinc, and lead) but only two of these—tin and copper—are included in the short list recommended for stocking. Tin, of course, has already been subject to stocking for twenty years under the International Tin Agreement. So the only truly new element, as far as nonfuel minerals are concerned, is the proposal to stock copper.

Developed and developing countries now recognize more than ever before their mutual interest in stabilizing primary commodity prices, especially in averting the wide swings characteristic of copper prices. Even on the part of the industry there is a sincere desire to work toward a solution acceptable to all parties and, if not a consensus, wide recognition that commodity agreements can play a useful role in this endeavor. This of course is most encouraging. But the pros and cons of stabilization are not at issue in this chapter. The question is rather, What role can commodity agreements play in achieving the new goal of ultimate income redistribution through a massive upward readjustment of price levels? For after all this is what the call for a new international economic order—the major impetus to the integrated commodity program—is all about.

---

21. See UNCTAD, *An Integrated Programme for Commodities: Measures for Individual Commodities* (TD/B/L.1/194) (New York, October 1, 1974).

There is serious doubt in our minds that the present climate is conducive to achieving the above goal through commodity agreements. For commodity agreements to be reached, both negotiators must have a reasonable reading of future trends and developments by which they can assess their interests and possible confluence of interests. When one cannot read the future well—and present conditions do not permit a clear reading—one is likely to commit very little and hedge against very much. The climate of uncertainty is further compounded by the fact that national governments in developed and developing countries alike have accepted the possibility of instituting radical new courses of action affecting import dependence and export strategy, and have thereby expanded the number of variables at play in assessing one another. Against this backdrop, the postulated commodity agreement would ask for assured stability of demand and security of supply at prices agreeable to producers and consumers over the long term—an object rarely realized even under conditions of relative political and economic stability and with limited commodities and trading partners.

In pointing up the difficulties attending commodity agreements, we do not mean to write them off. On the contrary, we favor them on the ground that they can have a positive influence on the lifeline of the mining industry, namely investment. They can also assist economic planning in the developing countries and help to make trade more equitable. But we do wish to make the point that they are a conventional vehicle insufficient for the radical new goal of redistribution of wealth. If too much reliance is placed on commodity agreements—indeed, on trade—as an equalizer, there is danger that the anticipation of exaggerated results may enter the projections prematurely and obscure the real distance from the goal.[22]

A new element affecting the outlook for commodity agreements is the apparent community of interest between oil-exporting countries and other primary commodity producers in insisting that the problem of oil be discussed simultaneously with the problem of nonoil primary commodities, implying that concessions on oil by OPEC countries ought to be linked to counter-concessions by the developed countries on raw materials. This no doubt strengthens the

22. "Trade, though imperfect, is still the best vehicle we have to work through toward this goal. However, to strain it to the point of breakdown by treating it as the only means for correcting all inequalities among nations—in terms of capital, technology, resources and standard of living—and all inequalities arising from relative positions of strength, is to obscure the need to attack the development problem on a broad front." See Takeuchi and Varon, "Commodty Shortages and Changes in World Trade," p. 57.

hand of the developing countries as a group and would have a major influence on the commodity negotiations if these were held today. Assuming, however, that commodity by commodity discussions do not take place for one or two years, the outcome becomes more sensitive to unpredictable developments affecting the world economy and international political relations. Besides, the linking of oil and raw materials will at some point open up the complex question of the distribution of income among nonindustrialized countries, since neither the oil-importing developing countries' need for changes in raw material prices nor developed countries' ability or disposition to respond to them are independent of OPEC strategies on oil.

Perhaps, however, the question has been asked the wrong way. In nonfuel minerals, at least, the objective ought not be to raise prices for the sake of raising them, but to allow them to rise to ensure a much needed expanded flow of investment, to keep ahead of costs and inflation, and to permit, for example, the improvement of working conditions and adoption of environmental safeguards. Since the structure of the industry has not permitted this in the past, attacking it promises greater and more lasting success to the developing countries. While price-related issues are important, one should not lose sight of the fact that what needs to be assured is a bigger share of the ever-expanding market for the developing countries. The benefits of this will have multiplying effects and outweigh those obtained only through higher prices. Developing countries need both better prices and a bigger share; but the demands on prices should not be such as to deter the developed countries from relying more on the developing countries.

Looking ahead and sticking strictly to prices, four observations are in order. First, the trend toward aggressive attempts to influence prices seems irreversible. Mineral prices are likely to ascend in the foreseeable future, depending on the stance of the producing countries, but as much, if not more, on global economic trends, cost factors, technology, and policy decisions affecting the pace, distribution, and productivity of global investment in exploration, mining, and processing.

Second, the view that alliances of producers cannot go too far in achieving increases of the OPEC kind in mineral prices has much support.[23] However, this does not preclude the possibility of some

23. This support is sometimes covert. The weight given by the developing countries and their spokesmen to the integrated commodity program is the best proof of their skepticism about the feasibility and prospects of producers' alliances. In the aftermath of OPEC's action in 1973, much was made of the

developing countries benefiting from such action—or some sub-sectors in the consuming countries being hurt by it. While the values of absolute or relative impact may not be large compared to the figures we have become accustomed to since OPEC, they may be significant for individual parties.

Third, stable prices are important for the smooth functioning and steady expansion of the mining industry, and commodity agreements can perform a useful role in this respect, especially for countries heavily dependent on mineral production.

Fourth, it is in the long-term interests of both the developed and developing countries not to interrupt the flow of investment into the mining industry. While some of the acts may need changing, the show must go on. We therefore turn to an examination of the problems of mineral development in the developing countries and to a survey of mineral development objectives and policies in the next two chapters.

---

possibility that OPEC members might assist in the formation of other cartels, for example, through financial assistance. This has not been borne out by experience. In fact, whatever evidence there is suggests that OPEC members, through their domestic and foreign investments, might add to rather than help to curtail or control production capacity for nonfuel primary commodities. This is not a matter of joint policy but the outcome of individual members' priorities and programs.

5 | Problems of Mineral Development in Developing Countries

THE MOST CONTROVERSIAL PROBLEMS of mineral development in the developing countries have to do with their relation to the developed countries as providers of capital and technology and as consumers of the minerals produced. In this chapter we consider the growing interdependence of developed and developing countries and the problems and conflicts to which this gives rise.

Interdependence of Developing and Developed Countries

We have suggested that during the next decade developed economies may rely increasingly on the supply of minerals from developing economies and, as we discussed in chapter 4, this may make an important contribution to the future foreign exchange earnings of the developing economies. Modern mining and processing methods have become so capital intensive, however, and the capital requirements of modern mines and their attendant infrastructure so large that few of the developing countries can expect to bring a sizable project into operation on their own. Up to now, the large mining companies have provided most of the funds, technical know-how, and marketing outlets, although with the recent trend toward national autonomy, the situation has been changing. Some developing countries have already managed to produce a cadre of experts in this field, working through the public and private sectors. Nevertheless, the remaining gap in skills, finance, and technology will require continued participation of the large integrated producers in mining development in the developing countries. Whatever the form of future cooperative arrangements, if they are to be workable, they must be acceptable to both importing and supplying nations, reflecting their common interest in an expanded flow of resources to the world markets.

In the long run the stake of the developing nations in resource development may be greater than that of developed countries, since for a number of important minerals technology is providing a broad array of options in the form of synthetics, abundant natural substitutes, and processes for extracting minerals from internationally available raw materials. The past advantages of suppliers with rich ore reserves have been further reduced because even low-grade ores can now be made competitive through advanced technology and large-scale extraction. Despite increased reliance on mineral supplies from developing countries, industrialized nations do not face an immediately critical supply situation. Over the long run, however, developing countries will be able to negotiate their more abundant supply situation into better leverage over, and larger benefits from, joint exploration and production ventures. While the position of the industrialized nations may weaken, developing countries' revolution of expectations and growing absorptive capacity will intensify the pressure on the development of their resources. Thus, the interests of the two parties will again interlock, intersect, and interrelate.

Divergent Objectives of Investors and Host Governments

Because of the major role the large multinational mining companies have played and must continue to play in the development of mineral resources in the developing countries—though under different rules—their conditions of operation, position in the developing countries, and relationship with the various parties in the host countries warrant brief review.

It is unlikely that the objectives established for the exploitation of any particular mineral deposit by a multinational firm will coincide with those of the host government; in fact, these objectives may diverge considerably. The multinational company will act to maximize profits and spread the risks of the company as a whole, not necessarily those of the affiliate in a particular producing country alone. In determining the distribution of production between subsidiaries located in different countries, a mining company will take into account the relative costs (including taxes) of the different subsidiaries, the preferential access to some markets of various suppliers, the need to maintain minimum production levels as specified by contracts, and the degree of political risk in each country. Furthermore, intrafirm transfer prices may not be based on world prices (often a world price does not exist), but may reflect a concentration of profit in a particular affiliate in order to minimize taxes or avoid restrictions on transfer of profits.

On the marketing side, companies tend to specialize in commodities experiencing high growth rates and to shift incremental resources from a commodity whose growth rate has fallen off to one with a higher growth rate. In the copper industry, for example, the shift has been to a competing commodity, aluminum (as with Anaconda, Revere, and Kennecott). Countries with marginal deposits and an uncertain investment climate may not fare as well as those with better mineral resources and more favorable investment conditions. Moreover, the companies themselves are deeply involved in influencing the growth and displacement of commodities through their large research and development establishments, which are constantly putting forward new products and promoting product uses based on their mineral resources. Perhaps most notable is the demand for aluminum, which has been very significantly influenced by the aluminum companies themselves.

A government, on the other hand, is concerned with maximizing total revenues of the subsidiaries operating within its territory, and especially its share of revenues, with little interest in overall corporate profits. Governments also seek to influence the level and geographic pattern of resource development; encourage backward and forward linkages in the economy; and expand the processing, refining, and fabrication of raw materials, both for domestic use and for export.

The Sources of Conflict

The divergence of objectives can lead to serious conflict and some form of nationalization or confiscation, as evidenced in the recent past in Algeria, Bolivia, Burma, Chile, Ghana, Guyana, Tunisia, Peru, Zaïre, and Zambia. In his recent investigation of two copper mining projects, Raymond F. Mikesell concluded: "The two case studies confirm the generalization that conflicts between the host government and the foreign investor tend to be more or less continuous, and the greater the profitability of the mine the more intense will be the demand for renegotiation of the contract on the part of the host government."[1]

1. *Foreign Investment in Copper Mining* (Baltimore and London: Johns Hopkins University Press, 1975), p. xxii. See also Mikesell's earlier, authoritative work on the subject, *Foreign Investment in the Petroleum and Mineral*

A vast confidence gap characterizes the relations between host government and foreign company from the very beginning. Alun G. Davies of the Overseas Mining Association, London, described the problem as follows:

> From the point of view of the host country, the mining company negotiators represent a hard-faced, profit-dominated negotiator entirely motivated by the capitalistic urge to maximize advantages and ignore whatever arguments may appeal to the other party. To the third world, moreover, these negotiators appear as diabolically clever, fully apprised about all the technicalities of the subject, and prepared to take the other side for a ride at any time. . . . From the point of the negotiating mining company, the other side often seems so suspicious of motive that it is unable to make up its mind on most subjects, and unable to comprehend the factors which govern competitive business in this world. Moreover, there is a difference in time factors, and the important significance which is attached to prompt decision making. Above all, there is sometimes a complete lack of mutual confidence, or even of a recognition that Western world mining companies have a capacity for objective consideration and a conscientious regard for the rights of others. . . . Given the desperate needs of developing countries for outside capital for resource development, the existence of a psychological abyss between the two parties is a tragedy, both from the point of view of development in the third world, and from the point of view of encouragement of international trade in essential raw materials.[2]

John Carman of the United Nations lists among the "inhibiters of investment" in mining, especially in the developing countries, "suspicion on the part of governments of the motives, ethics and methods of the large international mining houses; a suspicion, incidentally which is more than amply reciprocated when said

---

Industries (Baltimore and London: Johns Hopkins University Press for Resources for the Future, 1971). With regard to the Bougainville project in Papua New Guinea, the remarkably high profitability of the early years which brought about this pressure was largely due to the outstanding engineering and administrative performance of the company. A less satisfactory or even average performance by the company would have resulted in the mine's coming on stream with a long delay, missing the abnormally high copper prices of recent years, turning in average returns, and reducing government reaction.

2. Alun G. Davies, *Taxation and Incentives* (paper prepared for the UN Interregional Workshop on Negotiation and Drafting of Mining Development Agreements, Buenos Aires, November 2–18, 1973) (ESA/RT/AC.7/9) (New York, September 27, 1973), p. 2.

houses size up governments." He then adds, "Neither party lacks justification."[3]

The power and spread of the multinational allow it to influence, directly or indirectly, the policies and actions of home and host countries, and can at times place countries in interdependent or dependent positions. Multinational corporations have been known to cause jurisdictional disputes among governments and some-times—when they succeed in drawing their home countries into their own disputes with host countries—bring about political confrontations. Traditionally, host countries, and recently some home countries also, have found that the global context in which corporations operate and the many options open to them can restrict the effectiveness of government policies. Social and cultural conflict can also arise when nationalistic or reformist forces in the host country perceive the operations of the corporation as a threat to the country's traditions and heritage.

Foreign companies sometimes enter the host country under a concession agreement covering ownership and control of the project, including production levels, marketing and export pricing, exploration requirements, and degree of processing. Alternatively, they may acquire the mineral rights of domestic enterprises. Conflict may arise if either party violates the terms of the concession or if the government changes legislation, fails to acknowledge agreements of previous governments, or imposes additional taxes and conditions.

On an even broader plane, the multinational mining company, together with the nonmining multinationals, can have a disruptive influence on the functioning of the international monetary and trade system. The recent currency crises have focused attention on hot money movements; the predominance of intracorporation transactions in trade may, at the very least, render adjustment mechanisms less sensitive and limit free market operations. In addition to raising questions relating to the prospects and implications of nationalization, taxation of multinational corporations creates a number of difficult problems. The complexities of inter-country differences in tax rates, definitions of taxable income, and taxation principles regarding income accruing abroad are compounded by transfer pricing practices which affect income allocation and government schemes of compensation for taxes paid abroad. Bilateral tax treaties, mainly among developed market

3. John S. Carman, "Notes on Impediments to Mining Investments in the Developing World" (prepared for the Meeting of the Association of Geoscientists for International Development, Bagauda, Nigeria, September 1975; processed), p. 18.

economies, have provided a partial solution, but alternatives need to be explored, especially with respect to operations in the developing countries.

An issue central to the conflict between the host country and the foreign investor is the split of revenues. The arrangements agreed upon will depend largely on the bargaining strengths of the two parties at the time of establishing the frame of reference for the foreign company's activities. The configuration of bargaining power can vary considerably depending upon the level of development of the mineral sector, the extent to which the existence and economic value of mineral resources are known, the alternative economic opportunities available to the country, and the changing relationship between the foreign investor and the host country from exploration through exploitation. Following is a brief description of the relative negotiating positions of the parties at different stages of mineral resource development, preexploration, preexploitation, and postimplementation.

Preexploration

At the preexploration stage, there is frequently little or no geological information available on the basis of which to evaluate the mineral potential of a region. Investment must therefore be made strictly with risk capital. Governments of developing countries have little or no surplus resources available for such investment. Because of the worldwide scarcity of exploration capital and the number of different areas competing for it, the private firm, particularly the large multinational firm, enjoys a strong bargaining position. This position is further strengthened by the firm's ability to offer scarce exploration know-how.

The major strengths of the host government in this situation lie in its power to solicit bids from different firms and in the attractiveness of its terms and conditions relative to other countries. The exploration booms of Canada, Australia, South Africa, and Ireland in the past are attributable not only to the terms and conditions available there but to the unfavorable terms and conditions of other countries. The recent hardening of the terms imposed by some of the provincial governments in Canada has already caused a flight of exploration capital, a slowdown of the exploration effort, and the cancellation of several concessions. A similar slowdown was experienced in Australia around 1974 and 1975 with the hardening of investment laws, and the cancellation of the twenty-year tax-exempt period in Ireland has stemmed the flow of risk capital into that country.

As there is no return on exploration activities alone, the multinational firms will invariably try to negotiate as many of the exploitation terms as possible before exploration. Given the high-risk element of exploration, they must, under the basic rules of corporate survival, negotiate terms which provide returns sufficiently high to cover not only the successful exploration expenditure, but also unsuccessful exploration activities in the same country and elsewhere. Most host governments are reluctant to accept the argument that successful mineral operations within their territories should subsidize exploration in another country. At the same time, they fail to recognize that the very exploration expenditures which located their mineral reserves were subsidized by other successful operations, possibly in other countries.

Preexploitation

The bargaining position of the government becomes stronger if exploration conducted by or for it has succeeded in finding and delineating economic mineral reserves. Although the multinational firm is still needed for its expertise, marketing outlets and in most cases capital, its bargaining position is weaker, for the government will be in a position to invite competitive bidding for the project by a number of firms. It is even possible (though only in a few countries) that the government might proceed without foreign participation. On the other hand, since the risk of investment at this stage is considerably lower, the cost of capital is also significantly lower; consequently, foreign firms may be willing to soften their negotiating position and agree to enter into joint ventures with nationals.

This raises the question of whether the economic and social benefits which may be realized by a country through a better bargaining position are greater than the cost of upgrading the country's knowledge of its mineral potential and, if so, the extent to which it should itself undertake exploration, and by what method. The spread and hardening of nationalistic sentiments over the past decade will force the mining firms to soften their terms. (Many companies have already become more cautious in the exercise of their power and more sensitive to their social responsibilities.) But it may also stem the flow of exploration funds and make firms more selective in their choice of areas. This trend has already been apparent over the past decade, as evidenced by the concentration of exploration in countries such as Canada and Australia, although these countries are now following the developing countries in demanding greater national control over the exploitation of their natural resources. The reduction in exploration funds also means that the developing countries, particularly those in which there has been little development of the mineral sector, will have to participate more actively in exploration if they expect to improve their position in the world mineral markets.

Of perhaps greater importance than physical (geological) risk is political risk. The high returns sought by foreign companies coming in at a low level of geological information increase the risk of potential confiscation and of legislative action designed to reduce their share of benefits at some later stage. Where, because of better geological knowledge, a lower return is acceptable to the foreign corporation, political risk is reduced and the development of the mineral sector is facilitated. On these grounds alone, therefore, it seems desirable for a country to increase the level of its geological information.

Postimplementation

After investment has been made and a mine is in production, the bargaining power of the foreign investor diminishes considerably. Some governments become oblivious to the risks under which the capital was first invested, may ignore expenditures on unsuccessful ventures, and are prone to look only at the level of company earnings from successful operations. Often they request renegotiation without taking into account the potential adverse effects of such action over the long term—for example, the possibility that it may discourage new foreign investment. The position of the government is strengthened with the growth of the mining sector, its increased geological and marketing knowledge, and its expanding cadre of trained local personnel. The options open to the foreign investors in the event of conflict at this stage are to refuse to provide capital or managerial, technical, and marketing services; to withdraw; or to call for support from their own government in the form of guarantees or economic pressure. A number of governments in developed countries insure their private investors against political risks. The United States, Japan, and the Federal Republic of Germany have offered such insurance for some years. Eleven other countries (Australia, Belgium, Canada, Denmark, France, Japan, the Netherlands, Norway, Sweden, Switzerland, and the United Kingdom) have recently established insurance systems. Austria and Portugal have limited schemes. With the increasing tension between host governments and foreign investors, there has been a surge of interest in such programs. Perhaps the strongest weapon is the control of foreign corporations over markets. For some minerals, this control is absolute, giving the country no alternative outlet for its product, although this situation is rapidly changing. Because nearly all developing countries are heavily dependent on external aid, however, their governments operate within severe constraints, though the widespread sensitivity to accusations of political or economic imperialism has made the threat of reprisals less significant than previously. The new sources of finance from the recently enlarged oil revenues may significantly move the balance of power in the direction of the developing countries and away from the multinationals.

The Division of Benefits

The division of benefits between the host nation and the foreign investor varies widely from country to country, mineral to mineral, and project to project. The arrangements in any given case depend on the relative bargaining strength of the two parties at the time of negotiation, subsequent changes, and the attitude of the host government towards private, particularly foreign, investment within its territory. The early investors in mining in the developing countries managed to secure very favorable terms and conditions because investment opportunities were plentiful and pressure to develop resources was low, so that the foreign investor could be attracted only by very high potential returns. Consequently, a large portion of the profits and revenues went to the foreign companies and little to the host government. In the 1920s, for example, the Chilean government's share of pretax profits was only 16 percent. Furthermore, virtually all supplies were purchased from foreign sources; a high proportion of the employees were foreign and received salaries paid in foreign currency; and much of the output was shipped as low value-added concentrate.

Over time, countries have sought to increase their revenues. The first step has often been a change in tax laws, which could frequently be achieved without violating the original concession agreement. Increased taxes and retroactive taxation tend to create a climate of uncertainty, however, which reduces the level of production and the volume of investment. The copper industry in Chile offers a good example: the government share of pretax profits increased from 16 percent in 1930 to 28 percent in 1940, 58 percent in 1950, and 69 percent in 1965. During the period 1944 to 1955, Chilean copper production dropped from 540,000 tons per year to 400,000 tons per year, while over the same period world copper production increased by 20 percent. In constant prices, government receipts declined, although they rose in current values because of the increase in copper prices. Virtually all profits from the U.S. affiliates in Chile and other Latin American countries were repatriated in the late 1960s, whereas in Canada, where a high degree of tax certainty and political stability prevailed, almost 50 percent of earnings were reinvested. Greater tax certainty is frequently a condition for increased investment, as illustrated in Chile by the Frei government agreement with the copper companies in the 1960s which provided a twenty-year guarantee on tax rates as one of the conditions for considerable additional investment by the companies. Long-term tax agreements (later abrogated) in Ireland resulted in a major influx of mineral exploration and investment capital.

There is a limit to how far a government can use taxes to increase its share of revenues without becoming involved in the control of heretofore corporate prerogatives, since the variables determining the net profits to which the tax is applied are largely under the control of the corporation itself. The corporation normally starts out with considerable leeway over the size of depreciation, depletion, and amortization allowances; the option of either expensing or capitalizing exploration and development expenditures; and significant control over the price used to value the production, which is often an accounting item used for tax manipulation purposes. The problems of taxation will be dealt with in greater detail in chapter 6.

Government Intervention in Foreign-owned Companies

Most governments are aware that changes in accounting procedures and prices have a significant impact on tax receipts. Hence, they seek to participate in decisions on production levels, accounting practices, pricing, and marketing. In some cases governments have established an artificial exchange rate for the mineral sector, which has the effect of imposing an additional tax on the companies. Furthermore, governments may insist on posted prices for valuing exports and taxes, and require that additional processing of the raw material be carried out within their territory. Added to these restrictions on the companies' freedom of operation (as they perceive it) has been the increasing frequency of labor disruption, sometimes political in nature.

To reduce investment risks in the developing countries and sometimes to comply with legislation requiring varying degrees of domestic participation in resource projects, an increasing number of mining companies have been promoting private domestic participation or joint ventures with the government or government agencies. The object is to facilitate the conclusion of agreements with governments and to help assure their continued effectiveness over the long run. An even more recent approach—one that is particularly designed to minimize friction and disputes over the split of benefits—is the phaseout investment under which ownership and control by the foreign partner are phased out or substantially reduced in accordance with an agreed timetable. Mining companies are adapting to the situation and have recently indicated their willingness to provide technical and managerial assistance, principally in return for assured supplies.

The long-term contract approach pioneered by Japan has already gained wide acceptance; it is attractive to both sides, since it provides both security of supply and security of demand. Though seductive in its simplicity, however, the approach delivers less than it promises, for the security is neither long-term nor of equal value to the partners. It is unlikely that in a dynamic world the terms and conditions agreed upon at the time of signature will remain satisfactory to both sides for the duration of the contract— which, in Japanese contracts, can run up to twenty years. For this reason, long-term contracts have been described as "no more than gentlemen's agreements to do business together;"[4] both sides must understand that renegotiation of terms cannot be avoided. Furthermore, experience with such arrangements is limited; although the current recession has put them to a severe test,[5] the big test is still to come. It remains to be seen how changed secular trends or structural adjustments—for instance, a significant downward revision of the growth rate of the Japanese economy, or the urgent desire to increase processing in the producing countries—will be reflected in renegotiation of existing contracts. Finally, while the security provided by long-term contracts goes a long way to reduce conflict and to accelerate the flow of technology and funds (as governments are more willing to make or guarantee loans), it does not address the problem of finding equity participation fully and directly. This problem and the attendant questions of, for example,

4. Bension Varon, "Coke and Coking Coal Availabilities: A Potential Problem or Not?" World Bank Staff Working Paper, no. 124 (Washington D.C., January 1972), p. 21.

5. Japan's difficulty in taking delivery of contracted quantities, especially of copper, in the recessionary conditions of 1974–75—despite its sincerity and vested interest in respecting the agreement—led it to renege on its iron ore contracts with Australia and to sanction the export of copper metal, which depressed world copper prices even further.

equitable return on investment, security of investment, and transfer of earnings have to be addressed and solved simultaneously. Even achieving the limited objectives of long-term contracts requires prior and explicit agreement on a schedule for renegotiation and the areas open to renegotiation. It requires, above all, the narrowing of the confidence gap and the psychological abyss referred to earlier in the chapter.

In the longer run, joint venture and phaseout agreements and management contracts may become more common as the only effective and feasible solutions acceptable to both sides. However, they require that developing countries accept a much greater share of the responsibility and risks and contribute more of their own resources than they have in the past. A substantial degree of caution will also be required if the benefits hoped for are to outweigh the additional economic costs. Additional funds must be made available to host countries for private and public mineral investment, and the host country must know well in advance that it can count on these funds when it needs them. The source of these funds can be multilateral or bilateral aid agencies; the oil revenues of the OPEC countries could be used to this end if suitable channels can be established; and the banking and financial institutions may be willing to provide funds given satisfactory returns and guarantees. The policies of all these parties are not yet clear and need to be ascertained. Some compromises definitely need to be worked out in altering past policies, which attached greater importance to the financial strength of the multinational sponsor than to the viability of the project or the creditworthiness of the host government. This would strengthen the domestic bargaining position of developing countries and should result in agreements fair to both parties, not only at the time of negotiation but over the life of the agreement.

The Importance of Exploration

An important conclusion to be drawn from an analysis of the split of benefits and the terms of concession agreements is that geological knowledge of the country and the deposit is crucial. Improved geological knowledge reduces the technical uncertainties and provides the parties with a better basis for negotiating a fair and long lasting agreement. Though the desirability of helping the developing countries improve their knowledge of their mineral resource base is clear, the flow of exploration funds to many of the developing countries has been blocked by the hardening of nationalist sentiments over the past decade. From 1970 to 1973 more than 70 percent of exploration expenditure in the market economies was concentrated in four countries: Australia, Canada, South Africa, and the United States. With the accentuation of nationalism and the increasingly onerous tax legislation introduced in Australia, Canada, and Ireland, however, there has been a noticeable drop in exploration expenditure in these countries between 1971 and 1974. The only countries with increased expenditure appear to be Brazil, the Philippines, and South Africa, and the consensus is that total exploration expenditure in the non-communist world has dropped since 1970, despite the increased demand for minerals and the near certainty that additional demand in the next decades can be met only by substantial new discoveries. A large number of these discoveries will have to be made in the developing countries and these countries, particularly those in which there has been little development of the mineral sector, will have to *participate much more actively* in exploration if they expect to improve their position in the world mineral markets.

How does a country go about doing this? If it has a well-developed mineral sector, it can perhaps stimulate exploration by the domestic private sector through a government share in the exploration risk, perhaps through establishment of an exploration fund which makes finance available to operating companies, getting repaid in successful exploration projects and absorbing the loss in others. Some countries with well-developed mineral sectors, such as the United States, Canada, Australia, and Brazil, have already made use of such funds; so have other countries where the sector is developing rapidly, such as Morocco and the Philippines. Bolivia, Iran, and Thailand have been considering setting up such funds. These national funds have different objectives: some are designed primarily for the benefit of the small local prospector or company; some conduct their own exploration; and others facilitate exploration by large domestic and foreign mining companies. The technique has met with varied success but, if carefully planned, it can be a direct and workable vehicle for encouraging exploration in developing and developed countries alike. One approach is to start from the exploration fund concept and expand into full-fledged production operations. Alternatively, countries with national operating entities can direct revenues into exploration activities, or the government may allocate revenues obtained from the sector to the funding of its own exploration program.

One of the more successful exploration promotion efforts is that of the Quebec provincial government. After reviewing the various alternative practices elsewhere in the world, the government of

Quebec established the Quebec Mining Exploration Company (Société Quebecoise d'Exploration Minière, or SOQUEM) as a joint stock company intended to promote mineral exploration and development through direct participation in exploration activities on its own account, for others, and in joint ventures. SOQUEM is a state entity with full autonomy, operating in full competition with and under the same legislation as the private mining companies. In the ten years between 1966 and 1975, SOQUEM participated in more than 200 exploration ventures, privately and in joint venture, making four significant discoveries and acquiring three other prospective properties. It should become a self-sufficient, revenue-generating entity by early to mid-1980s. Additional details on the experience of SOQUEM are presented in appendix J.

In addition to increasing the exploration effort, a national exploration fund in a developing country will serve to introduce new technology and know-how in exploration and in developing mining operations, spur interest in exploration by local and foreign companies, familiarize local mining companies with new management techniques, and provide some coordination of the exploration effort and assist in establishing a long-term development philosophy for the sector.

A lesson to be learned from this and other experience is that an aggressive approach to promoting exploration and follow-up development through a fund of this kind may be superior to the use of government subsidies. A program that operates jointly and in competition with bona fide mining companies provides better results than a government monopoly, and it is essential that the entity be fully autonomous, with the ability to engage staff under conditions fully competitive in the industry. A major problem, however, is that in the majority of cases the developing country has neither the funds nor the expertise to conduct its own exploration program. It is important to point out that Can$45 million was allocated from the government budget to SOQUEM. This points to the need for financial institutions, bilateral and multilateral, to provide assistance, including assistance in establishing adequate institutional arrangements to monitor the sector. Governments should be aware, however, that unless they can carry out the exploration as efficiently as private entities, their direct participation at this early stage may result in lower returns to the country. There are many pitfalls in the use of foreign aid for promoting mineral exploration.

A novel approach now used in Peru and Bolivia for petroleum exploration and in Indonesia and Iran for mineral exploration is exploration by private parties, often the large multinationals, under contract to the government. The mining companies have indicated a willingness to do this. One company offered to undertake the full exploration and feasibility work on a deposit at its own expense in return for assurances of a management contract (if a project results) and a portion of the mineral output. More and more concessions are negotiated in two stages: the first for exploration only, with broad guidelines for the terms of exploitation; and the second for exploitation of any deposit discovered, negotiated with full knowledge of the mineral resource, often only after completion of a detailed feasibility study. But the approach is only applicable to countries with a well-established mineral sector or considerable geological information. Countries with little geological data and an undeveloped mineral sector have considerable difficulty in interesting foreign private capital in exploration of their territories. The basic geological mapping (infrastructure geology), and grass roots exploration will remain the responsibility of the state.

In most of the poorer developing countries and those with little mineral sector development, there has been little or no exploration activity. These countries, given their limited financial resources and the competing demands upon these resources, cannot afford to invest in the risky business of mineral exploration. Revenues from mineral production could enable some of these countries to make a quantum jump in economic growth. Yet the present state of knowledge of their mineral resources is limited; foreign mining companies will not go in without some indication of the existence of significant occurrences of minerals of special interest to them; and the governments themselves are unable to take the necessary first steps.

Some assistance has been extended to these countries since the war through bilateral programs and, since 1961, from the United Nations through the UN Development Programme. The latest attempt to supplement this assistance is the creation of a UN Natural Resources Exploration Fund, mentioned in chapter 1, which should help accelerate the exploration effort of the developing countries. However, the ultimate efficacy of the fund is very uncertain. It still has not been possible to solicit significant financial support, and even if the targeted level of expenditure of $20 million a year were achieved, this program and the present levels of bilateral assistance will fall far short of meeting the future exploration needs in the developing countries. Their needs are estimated to be considerably more than $100 million a year (for the nonfuel minerals) and will require significant increases not only in multinational, bilateral, and national expenditures but also in private risk capital expenditures of the foreign and domestic mining companies. Mineral policy, both national and international, as well as the attitudes of consuming countries, must be directed toward this end.

The Pitfalls of Foreign Aid

Expanded aid programs are clearly required because of the major exploration gap in the developing countries. While there are many examples of excellent past or ongoing aid programs by multilateral and bilateral agencies, however, some of the aid now provided is inefficient and ineffective. Some of it is poorly designed and planned and even more poorly implemented; lack of coordination between the various aid agencies is common, duplication of effort noticeable, and costs frequently unnecessarily high.

The shortcomings of aid programs have been the subject of regular attention by the UN Committee on Natural Resources which has had "the coordination of programs within the United Nations system in the field of natural resource development" as a permanent item on its agenda for several sessions. While considerable progress in this area is reported, "drawing a comprehensive plan of action" for this purpose—a long-standing objective—has eluded the committee so far.[6] There are encouraging signs that the problems are becoming widely recognized by technical experts from both donor and recipient countries and, equally important, that the experts are willing to talk about them candidly. A recent example is provided by the International Workshop on Earth Science Aid to Developing Countries held at Memorial University, St. John's, Newfoundland, in May 1974.[7]

Many experts at the workshop pointed out that response to requests for assistance is generally not as rapid as it should be because of red tape in donor and recipient organizations. Delays of several years between initial requests and inception of programs are far too common. Many of the aid programs are being handled by agencies "locked into the format of their own paperwork." The earth scientists who work with them should be constantly trying to adapt to

6. See United Nations, Committee on Natural Resources, *Report on the Fourth Session* (March 24–April 4, 1975) (E/5663, E/C.7/56) (ESCOR, 59th sess., supp. no. 3), p. 32.

7. For the proceedings, see A. R. Berger (ed.), *Geoscientists and the Third World: A Collective Critique of Existing Aid Programs*, Geological Survey of Canada, Paper 34–57, 1975.

new changes in Third World conditions "otherwise we are trying to solve what are really tomorrow's problems with yesterday's tools, and worse yet with yesterday's paperwork!"[8]

Effectiveness of the aid is sometimes diluted by actions of the recipient. The use of counterparts to supplement the foreign experts, frequently required for external or internal reasons, can have a major influence. Equipment may be badly treated and operated, geologists may introduce ploys to avoid going to the field, misinterpret data, and do substandard work. The reason generally is not laziness, as is often claimed, but lack of motivation (because of inadequate pay which forces professionals to hold down two or more jobs), lack of opportunity to gain experience and competence, lack of equipment and facilities, and especially the social norms of some host countries. A clean hands attitude in many countries makes the job of sweating up a ladder as a shift boss or braving the elements as a field geologist unattractive. This is a major problem, since efficient exploration requires highly qualified and experienced geologists in the field; a good geologist can make the difference between a discovery and an unsuccessful exploration program. Furthermore, the selection of counterpart staff may be based more on political than technical grounds.

The training part of the aid is often overplayed and misdirected. Too often it provides fellowships for graduate study by professionals, most of whom would be better served with practical on-the-job training. Many fellows do not return home, and those countries with the greatest need for a cadre of experts have no candidates qualified for the fellowship programs as designed. Restructuring the training to serve the long-term needs of the sector rather than the immediate project requirements would ensure better use of the funds. Practical training of skilled labor and subprofessionals can have immense long-term benefits.

The unavailability of counterpart financing and contribution in kind causes significant delays in aid programs. This touches on the real objectives of some of the aid programs as perceived by the donor. In many cases aid has been provided without regard to the benefits to, or the aspirations of, the recipient. The construction of uneconomic, small-scale smelters, the development of underground deposits in place of more competitive surface deposits, and exploration programs geared to specific minerals (often those needed by the bilateral donor) rather than a broader program more useful to host governments are all examples of less than honest aid programs.

8. Ibid., p. 7.

By and large, insufficient care is given to adapting the aid program, particularly the technology, to local conditions. To illustrate, in many of the developed countries the large-scale geological map has often provided the takeoff for detailed exploration. For the poorer nations, however, such maps are a luxury they cannot afford and accelerators have to be sought which, though perhaps not technically as satisfactory, can develop sufficient data to attract the needed capital fairly quickly. Similarly, making airborne geophysical measurements over very large areas is entirely reasonable in a developed country with plentiful capital, but to do so over tropical rainforest burdens the government with the impossible and expensive task of follow-up work on the ground, without which the airborne data cannot be interpreted and would go to waste. Groups often promote major regional geophysical surveys without mention of the time-consuming and costly follow-up work required.

Under most of the aid programs the cost of expertise is very high, sometimes up to three times what the expert earns at home. Hence, since most programs are financed by loan, even though on soft terms, the developing country often does not get a bargain. In fact, exploration costs in the developing countries are often considerably higher than in the developed ones. Many programs also seem more geared to providing the expert with data for a doctoral thesis than to mineral development.

This raises the question whether some of the aid agencies are as deficient as the multinationals in social consciousness. As emphasized above, many of the former's aid programs are ill conceived and designed for phases so preliminary that the end product cannot support economic development decisions. The multinationals are much more investment oriented. The aid agencies, bilateral and multilateral, are often too rigid in their approach and their procedures too bureaucratic to service the needs of the developing country.

Vast improvements in aid to the developing countries for mineral sector development can be realized by coordinating the activities of the various parties, the bilateral and multilateral agencies, the multinationals, the national agencies, and local mining industry. This requires preparation of a sector development strategy, a conscious determination by the host government to implement this strategy, and good administration. Many developing countries unfortunately do not have the expertise or resources to prepare, implement, or administer such strategy. One of the other parties therefore has to take the lead in a professional, unbiased manner.

Mineral sector development, especially the promotion of exploration by the host government, requires funds from sources other than the traditional multinationals. Most developing countries can ill afford to supply these funds from their own coffers—which leaves the multilateral and bilateral aid agencies as possible sources. The use of these sources, however, can have many pitfalls; developing countries should be cognizant of them and incorporate appropriate safeguards. Nevertheless, in our opinion, a major increase in multilateral and bilateral aid is needed to promote mineral exploration and development in the developing countries.

It is also of paramount importance not to overlook the already significant opportunities for cooperation among the developing countries, not only in training and research and development, where joint facilities may be established, but in all areas, including processing, where economies of scale and similarity of problems or community of interests may make them logical long-term partners. Other opportunities for such cooperation will be cited in the next chapter. Here, too, aid agencies and the UN regional commissions can play a useful role as catalysts.

Finally, both bilateral and multilateral programs have a role to play, and each has its different advantages. As noted in the proceedings of the St. John's Workshop, bilateral programs often give more control over projects to the recipient country and are thus especially useful in aiding institutions. On the other hand, they are more subject to the political views of the donor's country; tied to the donor's products, equipment, or personnel; and too little concerned with the follow-up stage. Multilateral programs are bound to be relatively apolitical and thus perhaps best suited to large mineral exploration projects, but a common criticism is that they are often less precise and well-planned than bilateral projects and suffer from the differences in background of the team members. Obviously, "there can be no single blueprint for aid to developing countries."[9]

9. Ibid., p. 4.

6 | Objectives and Policies
of Mineral Sector Development

IN THIS CHAPTER we set forth the institutional and policy steps we believe should be taken for establishing and administering a mining sector. The rather ambitious and many-faceted plan we describe raises two questions. One concerns the ability of any emerging country to deal with its mining sector on such a sophisticated level; this may, by extension, lead to questioning the relevance of the whole plan. The other concerns the appropriateness of describing a system as if it can be divorced from the political and ideological framework with which it will ultimately interact.

We would like to point out first that establishing a mining sector is a difficult undertaking whose requirements cannot be scaled down arbitrarily to fit the limited resources of a developing country if the operations are to be competitive in the long run—for mineral development is a long-term investment whose benefits to the country stretch far into the future. Second, our blueprint is in the nature of guidelines which have been shown to lead to efficiency. Efficiency ought not to be the prerogative of developed nations; it must inform the actions of any government involved seriously in mineral development no matter what the specific political context.

We are painfully aware of our failure to describe the particulars of mining development in centrally planned countries and the way their experience might be applicable to new nations. But in our discussion below, while being didactic on what steps should be taken, we do also deal with alternative ways of implementing these steps, depending on a country's political and structural preferences. We do so, however, within the bounds of the mining sector. While we do address ourselves to the requirements for establishing and operating a successful mining industry under central planning and state ownership or control, we do not consider the case where the entire economy is centrally planned and integrated into other centrally planned economies through a network of commercial and political agreements. Under such conditions, the determinants (even definition) of savings, investment, risk, prices, and trade are significantly different. The overwhelming reason for excluding the centrally planned economies from the analysis in this chapter, however, is that the information base is not nearly as complete as that obtaining for the market economies. To proceed on a sketchy basis might lead to wrong conclusions about the nature and performance of the mining industry in centrally planned countries and therefore to an unjustly distorted profile.

One further clarification is needed: many of the areas for action outlined below have been highlighted individually by others before, perhaps more effectively. What we hope to achieve by bringing them together here is an outline of the total role that public and private policy must assume in developing a viable mining sector. We wish to emphasize that, in addition to thoughtful action at each step, a concert of steps is required.

The Objectives

Mineral development in any country, whether developed or developing, constitutes only one element of total national development and must therefore be structured to fit into the total economic development plan. The broad objectives of mineral development can be categorized as follows: to ensure optimal use of available mineral resources; to earn or save foreign exchange; to create employment (direct or indirect), often in remote or depressed areas; to promote backward and forward linkages (service and supply industries and processing of raw material) in order to maximize value added within the country, to the extent that it is economically sound; to ensure an adequate supply of raw material inputs for industry; and to stimulate regional development, often in remote areas.

Figure 16 is a diagrammatic presentation of the mineral policy objectives of Canada by that country's Assistant Deputy Minister for Energy, Mines, and Resources. We are including it here not as a model—the sectoral objectives appropriate to individual countries depend on national economic, social, and political goals which transcend those of one sector alone—but to illustrate that there are many basic objectives shared by all producing countries, developed or developing, in terms of sovereignty, economic growth, and quality of life.

FIGURE 16 | CANADIAN MINERAL POLICY OBJECTIVES

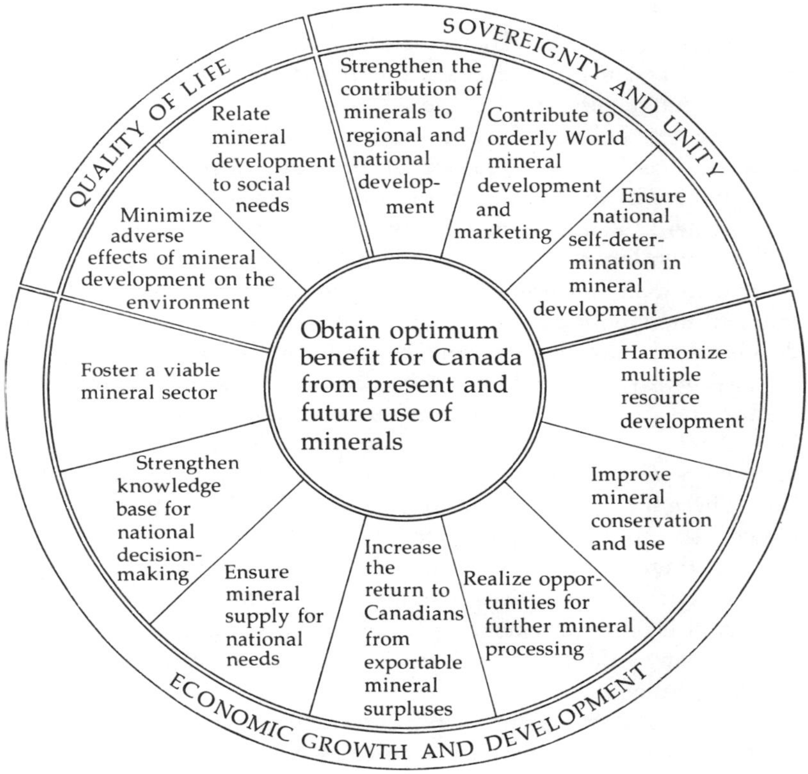

A circular diagram titled with segments around a central hub. Central hub reads: "Obtain optimum benefit for Canada from present and future use of minerals"

Outer ring labels: SOVEREIGNTY AND UNITY, QUALITY OF LIFE, ECONOMIC GROWTH AND DEVELOPMENT

Segments:
- Relate mineral development to social needs
- Strengthen the contribution of minerals to regional and national development
- Contribute to orderly World mineral development and marketing
- Ensure national self-determination in mineral development
- Minimize adverse effects of mineral development on the environment
- Foster a viable mineral sector
- Harmonize multiple resource development
- Strengthen knowledge base for national decision-making
- Improve mineral conservation and use
- Ensure mineral supply for national needs
- Increase the return to Canadians from exportable mineral surpluses
- Realize opportunities for further mineral processing

Source: Jean-Paul Drolet, "The Demand for Canada's Mineral Resources," paper presented at the International Symposium on Canada's Nonrenewable Resources, Toronto, March 25, 1974.

The Elements of a National Mineral Policy

To attain the goals illustrated in figure 16, a nation must have a mineral policy. Yet in the majority of developing countries no such policy has been formulated; decisions are made on an ad hoc basis and development of the mineral sector is often sporadic and ill-directed, at times even forfeited by the absence of a clearly defined policy.

As a first step in the formulation of a national mineral policy, the country must decide whether to develop its mineral sector on the basis of a private, public, or mixed system. The selection of one of these options, or a combination, should take into account not only political and social considerations but also the exploration, operating, and marketing characteristics of the sector. In practice, political judgments may prevent policymakers from considering anything but political factors, regardless of the long-term consequences. This can present an unfortunate obstacle to effective development of the mining sector unless there is scrupulously good management. While national sovereignty over natural resources is the governing principle, the nation can choose to exploit its resources in many different ways between the two absolutes of government monopoly and all-private development. In the case of state development, effectiveness will depend wholly on the ability and effectiveness with which the state can plan, provide technical and managerial expertise, commit financial resources, and secure markets. Development under the private sector depends for its success upon more detailed considerations, given its more fragmented situation. These include considerations of the following nature, many of which also apply to the state monopoly situation.

First, there should be a clear definition of the terms and conditions of operating practices, employment, training, ecology, safety, fiscal and legal requirements, and land tenure, under which a mining company—domestic or foreign, public or private—will be expected to function.

To help assure maximum returns to the country from a given mineral resource, the relative economics of processing the mineral domestically and exporting the raw material should be carefully evaluated.

Expansion of domestic ownership and control of mineral resource industries is the prerogative of a country, but it should take place on a clearly defined and well-publicized basis in order to maximize the country's share of the benefits derived from its mineral resources. The rate of such expansion will depend on the need for, and extent of reliance on, foreign technology, management know-how, capital, and markets.

Mineral policy should provide for mineral conservation measures, increasing orebody recovery and minimizing waste. The fiscal regime can have an important influence on the efficiency of the sector and the extent of resource waste.

Provision should be made in the formulation of mineral policy for procurement, maintenance, and dissemination of geological and mineral resource data. Such information is expensive; it should be carefully collected and used to prevent the duplication of exploration activity.

Mineral policy should encourage land reclamation and the elimination or control of air and water pollution. Environmental control in mining is of increasing public concern; it is generally accepted that the cost of that control is a component of operating costs, and therefore can be passed on to the consumer. While this may not be the case yet, over the long term, countries imposing reasonable ecological requirements are not expected to be at a disadvantage when competing for investment capital and markets.

Mining can often, on the one hand, serve as a basis for regional development, and provision may be made for it in mineral policy (through tax allowances as investment incentives, for instance), particularly in countries with wide regional disparities. On the other hand, mineral deposits by their very nature become exhausted, and the facilities and communities which came into existence because of them may cease to have a purpose. This has often led to community pressures to keep submarginal mines in operation, at great cost to the country, with inefficient use of labor, and a decline in the overall efficiency of the industry. Mineral policy should provide for programs to ease severe dislocations and to facilitate adjustment to change in case of mine closures.

Being frequently situated in remote areas, mineral projects often have significant new infrastructure needs such as housing and community facilities, roads, water power, railway, and ports. Mineral policy should provide guidelines for determining whether responsibility for the infrastructure lies with government, the private sector, or both. The government may wish to supply it in order to maintain control over public utilities, freight, and social services, and to increase its share of project benefits through rent on facilities. Often the responsibility is shared by the investor and the government. Project evaluation should take account of the cost of associated infrastructure and of the catalytic effect of such infrastructure on regional development apart from mineral development.

Mineral exploitation should be accompanied by adequate provision for training and employment of indigenous personnel.

Mineral policy should ensure that mining provides the host nation with an equitable share of the revenue from such activities. Furthermore, the nonrenewable nature of mineral resources makes it essential that government revenues from mineral resources exploitation be channeled into continuing productive investment in industry, agriculture, and supporting infrastructure. In many cases, the foreign exchange earnings from mineral exports go into the purchase of consumer goods; mineral tax revenues are used to support the government's current budget; and alternative productive capacity or revenue-earning facilities are not installed to take over from the depleted reserves.

Steps to Implement a National Mineral Policy

In contrast to the past, when multinational companies took the lead in setting standards for mineral policy, particularly in the developing countries, the host government is now considered to have primary responsibility for carrying out national mineral policy. Government action includes determining and executing policy through the preparation and promulgation of legislation and establishment of institutions and administrative framework to carry out mineral sector development. Mineral resources are of such significance for the national economy of many countries that they require specific legal status. Legislation for them should include a mining code and a special taxation regime compatible with existing investment codes and social laws. Exceptions should be clearly legislated.

Any plan of action for effective mineral sector development requires a factual basis. An inventory of the mineral resources is fundamental; hence, knowledge of the geology and mineral occurrences is a prerequisite. One of the first tasks, therefore, is to prepare a geological map of the entire country. Systematic geological surveys should be carried out and detailed mapping undertaken. The preparation of basic documentation of geologic and related data should be the responsibility of the state. Documentation of nongeological mining sector data is also required to keep abreast of activities within the country for supervision, planning, and control, and also of worldwide technological trends and devolpments. Laboratories for testing and analysis of rock and mineral samples are an early requirement. Research and development facilities are generally a subsequent and more advanced need.

In the field, in the laboratory, in the administration, and in operations, mineral resource development requires highly specialized personnel. The growth of the industry calls for a continuing flow of geologists; mining, metallurgical, mechanical, and other engineers; and financial and other technical men keyed to the industry. Any deficiency of trained personnel will compound the difficulties of the industry. Foreign experts may be hired to train local personnel, teach in local universities, and undertake actual field work. Mining, metallurgical, and geological education may be provided in the country, preferably by a shortened university term followed by a period in the field to provide a blend of theory and practice. Scholars may be sent abroad for post-graduate and specialized studies. A technological institute may be established at far less cost than a university or college to produce in a much shorter time a larger number of semiprofessionals for positions of secondary responsibility. Education in specialized fields may be provided with the assistance of multilateral and bilateral agencies.

The government, therefore, needs to set up six or seven administrative nodes. First, a policy, planning, and administrative agency is required. This usually means a Ministry of Mines, although it may be combined with Energy or with Transport or Economic Development. Second, an institute for geological survey is needed, often set up as an autonomous agency but under the direction of the Ministry of Mines. Third, educational facilities are a vital requirement. Separate departments need to be established and staffed in the local universities. Fourth, a research and development institute may be required to undertake research and provide technological assistance to the sector. Fifth, in countries where there is a strong desire to develop mining under the administration of the state, government-owned enterprise is the logical arrangement. Sixth, it is often necessary to provide channels for financing the sector. This may entail setting up a separate mining bank, or opening a "new window" at the development bank. Seventh, the government may also wish to centralize the marketing functions to strengthen its role as controller and coordinator.

Let us now examine each of these administrative structures in greater detail.

The Ministry of Mining

The Ministry of Mines or Mining is often a large, bureaucratic, and ineffective institution. It may suffer from overstaffing, low salaries leading to an inability to attract qualified personnel, inadequate budget, incorrect procedures, lack of planning and inability to formulate policies or monitor relevant legislation, and ineffective decisionmaking.[1]

Whether mineral development is through a private, public, or mixed system, an effective Ministry of Mines is needed. Planning

---

1. The description applies to other ministries as well. Normally a change is possible only on a national scale.

and coordinating current operations and future development should be among its primary responsibilities. Yet these are the functions most commonly lacking, usually because of poor staffing. To plan correctly, a highly qualified multidiscipline staff is required. The staff should be capable of: assessing mineral potential; identifying, preparing, and evaluating projects; establishing priorities; formulating long-term plans, including all technical, financial, and managerial aspects; and implementing and supervising such plans. People with such qualifications are scarce worldwide, and the few in the developing countries can command much higher remuneration in the private sector or in senior government administrative positions (often outside the mineral sector), particularly in view of the low salaries offered by the ministries. Staffing of the planning units which do exist is generally inadequate. Although some of the staff may have sufficient academic qualifications, it is rare to find many with sufficient practical experience. Lack of experience frequently makes it difficult for the staff to relate to the reality of the industry, and the assignment of sector priorities may appear a bewildering confusion. The linkages between projects are often ignored, as is the dependence of mining and processing operations on infrastructure. All too often political considerations override what should be strictly technical considerations in the assignment of priorities.

Planning for mineral sector development must be coordinated with the development of other sectors in accordance with set priorities. This requires a team approach. A group of mining engineers alone will not suffice; engineers in mining and metallurgy, financial analysts, and economists are needed; to complete the team, transport, power, water, and ecology experts are also needed. Though mounting a full, integrated team can be justified for a large country or one with an important mineral sector, for a small country or one with a small sector, this is obviously more difficult. Regional cooperation or heavy reliance on technical assistance is often required.

Apart from the planning function, effective documentation of data is often absent. Of course, many of the developing countries cannot afford the expensive electronic data-processing facilities used by some of the ministries in industrialized countries; but simple and workable methods can be established—and with relatively low-cost clerical help. Up-to-date and accurate data can provide a very large payoff in terms of improved planning, better decision-making, and control. Regrettably, the establishment of a documentation center is often viewed as a way of establishing a library rather than a data base; where a data base is established, an effective retrieval system may be lacking. Care must be taken to ensure that documentation does not become an end in itself; it is justified only to the extent that it is useful in establishing policies and monitoring the sector.

Supervising compliance with the mining legislation is an important and, sometimes, the only function of a mining ministry but, sadly, one which is often neglected. Exercising this function properly entails issuing exploration and exploitation licenses, policing safety and health regulations, ensuring observances of laws relating to the use of surface facilities, collection of royalties, issuing export licenses, and carrying out all other requirements of the mining code and related legislation.

The organization of a Ministry of Mines must be designed to fit the functions assigned to the ministry and the structure of the sector as a whole. It is not advisable to generalize beyond noting that a smaller staff is often preferable to a larger one (the problems of countrywide unemployment need other solutions) and decentralization of decisionmaking and authority is preferable to centralization, although a strong coordinating mechanism is a must. In several instances one is confronted with a situation where the sector and the ministry are administered on the premise of mistrust —a situation which can lead to excessive centralization and intolerable work conditions. Good people will not stay long under these circumstances. Drawing up or reviewing the organizational structure of the ministry requires careful consideration.

The Geological Survey

Beyond doubt, it is the responsibility of the government to supply basic geological data and maps, and to carry out the infrastructure geology without which detailed exploration surveys will be retarded. Since mineral deposits are a consequence of their geologic environment, a geological survey of an area can give a good understanding of the broad characteristics of its mineral resources. Good knowledge of the geologic environment of the country provides an appropriate framework for planning.

Most countries with a mineral sector of any significance have an established agency for geological surveying, commonly referred to as the Geological Survey. The Geological Survey should carry out a continuing program of background survey work and, in addition, collate the geological data obtained from surveys by private parties or other public agencies. Evaluation of mineral resources starts in the field and proceeds to the laboratory, requiring facilities to undertake tests and analyses. Such laboratories must be staffed by competent personnel and have modern equipment. Apart from engaging in basic geologic surveys and mapping (geological, topographical, and metallogenic maps), the Geological Survey should also act as a repository for all geological information available within the nation. It may also have a department for conducting mineral exploration on behalf of the government, or under contract for third parties, public or private. This, however, is a responsibility better delegated to another agency, if possible; if not, it must not be allowed to interfere with the basic function of a Geological Survey, namely, mapping.

Generally, the problems of staffing a Geological Survey are less formidable than those encountered by the Ministry of Mines. There are more suitably qualified geologists; the jobs tend to provide greater satisfaction; and the alternatives—except in an area undergoing an exploration boom—are not as many or as lucrative in relation to the number of available professionals. Nevertheless, agencies still suffer from the clean hands attitude discussed in the previous chapter, making it difficult to recruit good field geologists.

A Mining Bank

Large-scale mining projects have such large capital requirements that financing must come from international sources. Medium and small-scale mining operations, however, encounter difficulties when trying to tap these sources and often can be financed only from within the country. While the commercial banks will provide financing for working capital, they are not usually prepared to extend credit for capital investment. In some countries this gap may be filled by the development bank, if one exists, or alternatively, by a mining bank set up for this purpose.

Too often, the mining bank becomes a political pawn which loses sight of its objectives. Confusion arises over whether the bank is a source of finance for sector development or a channel for government subsidies to the small-scale mining operations. To assume the latter is wrong. A mining bank should be a financially viable entity with a well-qualified staff, autonomous both financially and managerially. Recipients of loans should be creditworthy companies with technically and financially viable operations and projects. If, on company and project grounds, a subsidy element is called for, the government should seriously review the economic justification for supporting what may amount to a nonviable proposition. If the government nevertheless wishes to extend assistance on political and social grounds, this should be done by means other than the lending operations of the mining bank.

By its very nature, medium- and small-scale mining may need a significant technical assistance input to justify financial support. Hence, the mining bank will have to be organized and staffed to assist in project preparation and evaluation, to conduct in-depth project and company appraisals, to introduce new managerial and financial control systems, to supervise project implementation, and to provide the small mine with continuing technical assistance.[2]

A mining bank is not an absolute necessity. If an efficient development bank already exists, opening up a "mining window" within this bank can serve the mining industry just as effectively and probably at much less cost. Commercial banks, too, may be prepared to channel capital funds into the small-scale mining sector, although they will not provide the necessary technical assistance. Care must be taken not to inundate a country with too many specialized banks.

The State-owned Operating Company

If the state wishes to form a state monopoly to exploit its mineral resources, or to participate in the exploitation with the private sector, it can set up a wholly government-owned but autonomous company. In free enterprise nations, this entity would be most effective if established as a stock company operating under the same rules and regulations as a private company. The company pays taxes as any other company, transfers earnings to the government only as dividends, is free from political interference in its day-to-day operations, recruits staff on a professional basis, and is headed by people who, though they may be political appointees, bring high professional competence to the job. The company should be accountable to its board (made up of representatives of the government) for its profitability, investment program, and production performance, as any private entity would. A rigorous cost-accounting and budgetary system should be implemented. Salaries should be competitive with the private sector (if it exists) and job motivation fostered.

---

2. The particular characteristics and problems of the small-scale mining sector are given more attention in appendix K.

A state company can function in several ways: it can operate as an individual producer; it can operate in partnership with a private company (joint venture), taking a majority or minority position with an active or passive role in management; it can function as a holding company with the operating units set up as wholly or partially owned subsidiaries; or it can purchase equity interest in the mining companies on the capital markets (this alternative is available only in the industrialized or more advanced developing countries).

Obviously, as nations move toward national control of natural resource development, state companies will become more prevalent. This raises the crucial issue of forming and staffing the companies correctly. In cases where the companies are formed by nationalizing the multinationals, every effort should be made to keep on the essential staff and minimize attrition. If a large number of expatriates are among the staff of the nationalized company, their phaseout should not be premature, but planned over a sufficiently long period to allow the training of nationals. Another means is to contract a firm to manage the operations under a management contract on the basis of a phaseout arrangement providing for the training of nationals.

Political pressure often prohibits the use of expatriates or foreign management teams which works to the detriment of the new company. Going it alone becomes a costly exercise in terms of incorrect project design; incorrect process selection; two-, three-, four-, and even five-year delays in project implementation; substantial cost overruns; and even project failures—all this because of the refusal to accept foreign technical and managerial assistance when it is truly required. Some countries have suffered considerable economic harm in consequence. Even when foreign experts are brought in, they are often confined to advisory positions and are unable to influence the operations, with the result that they are ineffective through no fault of their own. Foreign experts must have the full support of the management and, if necessary, be assigned to line functions. For some tasks it may be necessary to engage a team of experts to establish functional units dealing with, for example, cost accounting and budgeting, project preparation and planning, or specific technical problems. Foreign experts can also be engaged on a retainer basis as idea men and problem solvers. Of course, many problems can be avoided through joint venture operations where the partner, often with minority interest, is assigned full management responsibility. Again, a phaseout operation should be encouraged in the long-term interest.

A state-owned company must have managerial and financial autonomy.[3] Employment policies must be competitive with the private sector; otherwise the entity may prove merely a costly training ground for the private sector.

Marketing

The role of the state in the marketing of minerals will vary according to the economic system of the country. Even in the private enterprise system, however, the state generally plays a role in marketing the mineral products, particularly from the small-scale producers, who are widely dispersed and too small to conduct more than elementary beneficiation of the ore. The state can play an important part by providing regional or mobile concentrating plants, setting up a network of collection points and the necessary infrastructure to get the product to the marketplace. While medium and large-scale producers are generally adept at marketing their own products, governments are increasingly demanding a role in the marketing functions, even to the extent of setting up a state marketing monopoly through which all mineral sales transactions are handled. The rationale for this trend is the state's desire to exercise fuller control over its export earnings and over foreign exchange flows. But the ramifications of this ought to be taken into account. It should be remembered, for example, that the marketing agents who have traditionally performed this role have usually also been important sources of short- and medium-term finance for the small- and medium-scale mines. To replace these with a state monopoly can mean drying up this source of finance, which may retard the growth of the sector unless substitute sources are found. In addition, the viability of many large-scale projects depends upon the captive markets or market infrastructure provided by the project sponsors; financing of many large projects is often tied to special marketing arrangements, reciprocal agreements, repayment in kind, and firm marketing contracts. The taking over of marketing by the state is not a viable proposition in every case. Short of government takeover of this function, control can be exercised by laying down the ground rules (in terms of the level of domestic processing required) including the basis for establishing prices (London Metal Exchange quotation, and *Metals Bulletin*

3. The government of course retains the final say since it appoints the top managers.

or *Metals Week* quotations, for instance), and by exercising the right of prior approval of all sales contracts.[4]

Setting up a state marketing agency, whether it is to market part or all of the production, requires special care and caution. The marketing of minerals is a highly specialized field where inexperience and mistakes can be very costly. Simple mistakes can bring penalties many times higher than the charges of the international marketing agents. The cost of merely setting up a fully integrated marketing agency with foreign offices can be immense. A less costly and often more practical approach is to subcontract some of the marketing responsibilities or employ commission agents in the principal markets. The marketing arrangements for each mineral should be reviewed independently, since arrangements suitable for marketing one mineral are not necessarily those most suitable for another. Before taking any steps toward setting up a state marketing agency, therefore, an in-depth study is required. Marketing proposals should be analyzed on technical, financial, managerial, and economic grounds, much as a project is evaluated. In most cases foreign experts will be needed to assist in such a study and in the establishment and early operation of the agency.

In setting up a marketing agency, several pitfalls must be avoided. Transition from a free marketing system to one under state control should be gradual and planned. This may mean taking over the marketing of one mineral at a time. During the transition period, the private companies already in the country may maintain the marketing responsibility under contract to the agency to ensure continuity. The agency should be an autonomous and separate entity, not a division of the Ministry of Mines or a department of the mining bank. Marketing is a business, not a civil service function; the job philosophy is quite different. If borrowers from the mining bank have to rely on the bank for the sale of their product, this will lead to mistrust and a breakdown of relations

---

4. For every example of successful government control over or participation in marketing, there is a dramatic illustration of well-intended actions resulting in a step backward. A good example is the beach sand industry, which Australia dominates, accounting for a major part of world supply of ilmenite, rutile, zircon, and so on. Minimum prices were established in the boom year of 1973—for zircon, for example, at A\$200 a ton. Subsequently, the market value dropped to A\$130 a ton, yet the Australian producers were not allowed to sell at this price. Not being able to get the zircon they needed, consumers in Europe and Japan turned to cheaper substitutes of magnesite. While the new government has rescinded some of the legislation and reduced the minimum price to world market level, it remains to be seen if the substitution proves permanent.

between the producer and the bank. A compromise approach may be to assign the marketing responsibility to the sales department of the state mining company, if one exists, particularly if the private sector produces only one or two minerals also produced by the state company.

Research and Development

Research and development institutes serving the mining sector throughout the world are generally accessible to outside parties, domestic or foreign, public or private. Therefore, developing countries should not be too hasty in setting up an R&D institute of their own. When they do, the institute should be set up with a specific objective in mind and its facilities should be geared to the characteristics of the mineralogy of the country. Considerable savings can be realized through regional cooperation in R&D.

It must be borne in mind that the major asset of an R&D institute is its personnel. The expertise required for quality research is scarce worldwide and particularly in the developing countries; without it, equipment is of little value. Several R&D facilities are underused for this very reason; after they have been set up with extensive and expensive technical assistance, these institutions reduce their contribution as the experts withdraw. Establishing R&D in a country means acquiring the expertise and training, not building extensive facilities. One of the crucial requirements is the ability to identify problems and ascertain the type of research needed. When proper guidance is available, the physical testing can be readily subcontracted. This should not be interpreted as an effort to dissuade developing countries from establishing R&D facilities but as an attempt to stress the need to establish R&D only after serious planning and for specific objectives.

The Mining Code

After the government has determined its mining policy, the policy has to be translated into a legal framework. This is commonly expressed in a mining code. If a decision has been made to allow private capital to invest in mining activity, the code must provide the legal framework defining the relations between the investor and the government. It should cover the preconditions for investment, land tenure, rights and obligations of the operator, as well as investment and tax provisions. Without a mining law, no mining right can be established; without a right who would venture to risk his capital? A bad mining law can be as bad as no mining law at all, if not worse. For instance, it may grant rights without the corresponding obligations concerning exploration work and, at the same time, prevent others from doing the work. Conversely, it might be so restrictive and impose such heavy exploration obligations without commensurate rewards as to frighten off sound enterprising investment.

Mining legislation will create a feeling of confidence in the investor if the needs and requirements of the government and the rights and obligations of the operator are set out in clear and definite terms. Confidence is not built when laws and regulations cause needless delays to operators who have tied up large investments. Procedures must be laid out clearly. It is not enough to formulate and promulgate a mining code; careful preparation of the regulations for the mining code are necessary to eliminate ambiguity and prevent bitter controversy. It is helpful if the investor can deal with only one agency, the Ministry of Mines. In one country, obtaining mining exploitation rights requires obtaining approvals and agreements from no less than nine ministries and government agencies. This situation is so frustrating to the investor that he will divert his attentions to other countries if he is foreign, or to other sectors if he is a national.

It must be emphasized that there is no model code suitable for all countries. In each case the code has to be constructed in relation to the country's economic and political system. Also, the code has to be flexible and dynamic enough to adjust to changes in the economic and political situation. Yet it must remain reasonably stable if it is to instill confidence in the investor. While changes do become necessary from time to time and are legislated through supplementary laws, this procedure should not be carried to the extreme; periodically, it may be prudent to incorporate all into a revised mining code. The components of a modern mining code are outlined in appendix M.

Mining Taxation[5]

The fiscal regime applied to the mining sector is of major importance for the realization of many other policy objectives. A

5. The problems are too complex to deal with adequately here. For additional detail, see United Nations, *Taxation and Incentives* (ESA/RT/AC.7/9) (New York, 1973); and John S. Carman, "Fiscalité des Entreprises Minières," trans. Pierre Legoux, *Annales des Mines* (December 1971).

basic premise of all mineral policy is that the returns from mining activities should benefit the country under various forms: local expenses, salaries, reinvestment, taxation, and so on. With a wholly public-owned sector, the contribution to the economy depends on the efficiency of operations and the terms at which the required financial and technical assistance are available. With private participation the question is more complex. On the one hand, investors must be allowed a normal return on their capital—too heavy taxation will discourage investment and may jeopardize existing mines. On the other hand, governments are entitled to revenue from the exploitation of their nonrenewable resources.

A fiscal regime governing the mineral sector will contain many of the following nine elements. The first element comprises *administrative fees*, which are charges for services rendered by the government, such as granting exploration or mining rights, conducting mineral assays, providing property valuations, and registering documents. The fees are generally small and arbitrary, but should be calculated with a view to covering the costs of the service.

The second element is *surface taxes*—alternatively referred to as land rental, exploration, or exploitational tax—which are charges for the exclusive right to explore or exploit a specific area. The primary purpose of the tax is to ensure continuous and effective development work on the property in question. Even though the purpose of the tax is not to produce revenue, the rate charged is often too low. Though a high tax rate is resented by investors, it discourages the locking up of large areas for speculation and makes them available for serious exploration. An alternative to high tax rates may be a relatively low tax base and a minimum level of exploration expenditure a year for each unit area. If the minimum level is not reached, the difference between that and actual expenditure is levied as an additional tax. Neither alternative is without pitfalls: the high tax rate may encourage selective mining whereby the concessionaire high grades the deposit;[6] the second alternative can lead to padding or superfluous expenditures. Increasing the tax with the age of the concession will provide incentive to conduct intensive exploration and to relinquish areas considered less promising. Any area with delinquency in the payment of surface tax should automatically be deemed abandoned, thus lessening the administrative burden on the government. Since the surface tax is not a revenue-raising device but only an inducement to explore and

---

6. High grading refers to mining the richer parts of the orebody without regard to possible future exploitation of the lower-grade parts, which may be rendered uneconomic. The minerals may therefore be lost to the nation.

produce minerals, its usefulness ends with the start-up of production. At this stage, it may be offset by a royalty or, preferably, eliminated.

Third is *royalties*, the payments made to the government or the owner, discoverer, or developer of the deposit for the privilege of exploiting a mineral deposit. Generally, royalties are set as a percentage of the gross, market, or minehead value of the mineral extracted. They may be fixed as a flat rate or a graduated rate, depending upon the value and grade of minerals. The rates may be specified in the tax codes or negotiated project by project. Royalties are simple to administer but have several drawbacks. They represent a charge on production and, as such, are treated as a pretax charge on the mining operations. Any such charge running on top of the costs of production increases the fixed costs faced by the mine and hence reduces the maximum production costs the mine can support, thereby making it more vulnerable to world market changes; or it may increase the minimum treatable grade of ore, thus shrinking total reserves. All these dangers are real unless the royalty remains well within the taxable capacity of the operation.

Fourth, *export taxes*, like royalties, are simple to administer but have the same disadvantage: they are merely different forms of pretax charges and may directly weaken the country's competitive position. In some cases it may be necessary to limit exports in order to meet domestic demand preferentially, because further processing is considered in the best interests of the nation, or for strategic reasons. This can be better accomplished, however, by the licensing of exports than by export taxes.

The fifth element comprises *artificial exchange rates*, whereby the foreign exchange earnings of the mining enterprises are converted into local currency by the central bank at a pegged rate artificially lower than the free market or official rate. These are in effect export taxes but have even more far-reaching effects. For example, they can make domestic inputs (including labor) more expensive than imports and hence have a negative impact on the consumption of local goods, thereby favoring capital-intensive over labor-intensive methods.

Sixth, *import taxes*, in most countries, are very low or nil in the case of imported mining equipment and supplies. Since modern equipment for mineral resources development in the developing countries is almost always lacking, it ought to be in the national interest to encourage the import of specialized equipment, machinery, and spare parts for the mining industry. Though import fees should be low for this purpose, excessively low import duties can discourage local manufacturing of equipment and again favor capital-intensive over labor-intensive methods.

Seventh is *income taxes,* based on the profitability of an operation, avoid many of the difficulties encountered in the use of royalties and export taxes. But the absence of clearly definable world market prices and standardized accounting and valuation procedures present measurement problems. That exploitation of a mineral deposit leads to depletion of a nonrenewable source has been used to justify a depletion allowance as a tax deductible item. This supposedly allows the operator to retain a portion of income in order to "replace" the nonrenewable resource, or to provide funds to search for additional reserves. With increased government ownership of mineral resources, this rationale is becoming less and less acceptable. In mining, accelerated depreciation provides for double counting since exploration expenditures are often charged to operating expenditures in the year in which the costs are incurred. Accelerated depreciation is often permitted to lighten the tax burden in the early years of operation when technical risks are highest. Mining development, preproduction expenses, and even exploration are frequently capitalized and amortized over several years; in some cases, the operating company may have the option of writing off the expenditures as incurred. Many developed countries allow only income taxes to be taken as tax credits by the multinational firm, an important factor to be considered in designing a tax code. Superprofit taxes may become increasingly used as a way of avoiding an undue burden on a mining company in times of low mineral prices while assuring a more equal sharing between host country and mining company when mineral prices are buoyant.

Eighth, *tax concessions* are among the most widely used incentives to attract investment and promote mineral sector development. The question of tax payments weighs heavily in investment decisions since an investor's decision is very much influenced by his after-tax earnings. Initial tax holidays are commonly used to provide the mine with an opportunity to recover a large part of the capital expenditures before taxes are imposed, or for relief during the first few years of operation when low cash flows with high debt-servicing obligations and starting problems are faced. This encourages the stripping of high-quality ores and high extraction rates. Moreover, since these incentives are seldom accompanied by special tax credits in the investors' countries, they may result merely in a transfer of tax revenue from the developing nations to the developed nations.

Payments in the form of subsidies may be introduced to maintain production, particularly of vital and strategic minerals, which otherwise would have to cease because of the increasing production cost or fixed government prices for the mineral. The objective may be to supply local raw materials to industries using minerals, to continue production of valuable minerals, or to enable indigenous minerals to compete in external markets. One other important consideration is the support of key centers of population dependent upon the mineral project. Subsidies may also be used to promote exploration.[7]

Finally, *repatriation* of capital and earnings is of prime concern to a foreign investor. It is natural and reasonable for foreign capital to return home, and it is only fair that it be released in a straightforward and timely manner. The legal framework should provide for repatriation of capital plus interest and profits. Many projects have experienced considerable delays in reaching a solution to this problem. The reinvestment of earnings (or recouped capital), which may contribute significantly to the development of the sector, is worth consideration in formulating a tax policy. Tax deductions on reinvested earnings can help to promote such reinvestment.

Revenue Sharing

Some governments tend to concentrate on revenue sharing considerations to the detriment of other important issues when developing a mineral policy. While this does increase the government's share of revenues from existing investment, further investment may be discouraged and revenue to the host country be reduced over the long term. Such shortsightedness is evident throughout the world. For decades, mining development took place in the United States, Canada, and Australia by preference because of more stable politi-

---

7. Several developed countries give tax credit for certain taxes paid to developing countries. This enables the latter to raise tax rates to levels close to those prevailing in the developed countries without loading extra burdens on the investor. Other tax measures in the developed countries tend to work at cross purposes with the policies in the developing countries. For example, the fact that the United States allows a depletion allowance of 15 to 18 percent on mining activities for U.S. companies operating abroad encourages operation as a U.S. subsidiary rather than a foreign subsidiary. Furthermore, the tax laws of the developed countries often make no allowance for incentives offered by developing countries to encourage reinvestment of earnings. The incentive may thereby be nullified. There is a need for developed countries to review their tax policies in terms of their impact on operations in the developing countries.

cal and fiscal climates. The recent legislative action in Canada highlights the importance of an equitable taxation system. With the introduction of high taxes, exploration efforts in the country are
reported to have declined by almost 75 percent. A serious retarda-
tion in the growth of Canada's mineral sector appears inevitable.

TABLE 15 | ESTIMATES OF THE EFFECTS OF NEW TAXATION ON
AN ACTUAL COPPER MINE IN BRITISH COLUMBIA
(millions of Canadian dollars)

Item	Copper price assumption (dollars a pound)		
	74 cents	90 cents	$1.25
Loss in mine life (years)	−6.0	−7.7	−2.0
Loss in total wealth generated by mine	−163.0	−224.0	−30.0
Loss in wages	−47.0	−54.0	−9.0
Loss in equipment supplier revenues	−54.0	−62.0	−9.0
Loss in company cash flow	−0.5	−21.0	−50.0
Loss in federal government revenue	−0.2	−8.0	−20.0
Loss (−) or gain (+) in British Columbia government revenue	−6.0	−17.0	+62.0

Source: J. B. Evans, "How Bill Thirty-one Will Affect an Actual Copper Mine,"
The Northern Miner (June 6, 1974).

When preparing a fiscal regime for the mineral sector, it is wrong
to consider the short-term split of revenues only; the long-term picture is all important. Following the revolutionary tax changes a few
years back in British Columbia,[8] J. B. Evans, head of the Department of Mineral Engineering, University of British Columbia, estimated for an actual mine, the effect of the new taxes on federal
government revenue, mine life, salaries, equipment-supplier revenues, company cash flows, and British Columbia government gain.
Although these changes are reported to have been relaxed, and in
some aspects reversed, in 1976, Professor Evans's calculations are
still of interest because they throw light on the direction and magnitude of the impact that such changes can have and because they
may have influenced the change in policy. The estimates, which
are presented in table 15 and illustrated in figure 17, indicate that

8. A net royalty equal to 5 percent of the net value, that is, the world
selling price less 25 cents per pound of copper produced, and a super royalty
equal to 50 percent of the difference between the world selling price and 66
cents per pound of copper produced.

FIGURE 17 | THE EFFECT OF TAXATION ON MINING
IN BRITISH COLUMBIA, CANADA

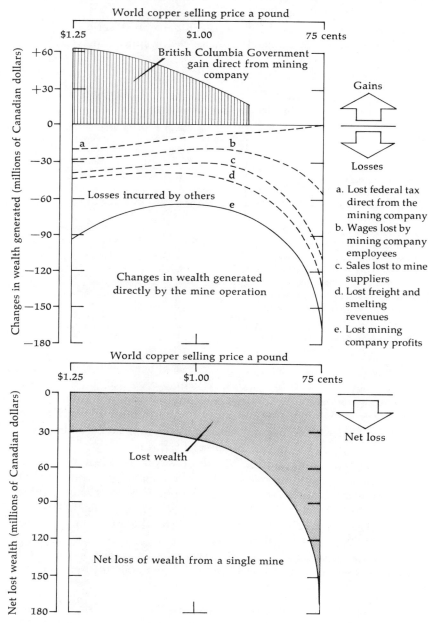

Source: J. B. Evans, "How Bill Thirty-one Will Affect an Actual Copper Mine,"
The Northern Miner (June 6, 1974).

the legislation would have had very serious implications for the operation.

These estimates do not cover all the consequences; an important consequence would have been the reduction in investment for new projects. In fact, the mere threat of the legislation was enough to cause a major curtailment in investment programs.

We add here, for the benefit of the specialist, a possible tax system which takes into account many of the problems associated with the mineral industry and eliminates many of the disadvantages of current tax systems. The government could provide that taxes would be applied to profits only after the mine had earned a discounted yield equivalent to the minimum return the management required a project to show before it decided to invest. This could be done simply by allowing all expenditure to be charged for tax purposes in the year in which it was incurred and carrying forward any outstanding loss to the following year, with a percentage increase equivalent to the discounted cash flow return the mine is allowed to earn free of tax. By this means, the discounted cash flow on the original sum invested will have been obtained when the unrecouped expenditure is reduced to zero. Subsequent profits would be taxable at a standard rate. This system does not form an obstacle to investment; there is no waste of revenues to the state if profits are higher than expected; and the tax rate could be fixed at what the investors would bear—which is probably significantly higher than the rate for ordinary income tax, and may be either fixed or progressive. This type of tax structure enables the government to control the flow of investment to the mining industry by adjusting two variables: the discounted cash flow return allowed tax free, and the subsequent tax rate. Perhaps the most important feature of the system is that the interests of the two parties are considered openly, as compared to other systems which contain large elements of smoke screen. The system does, however, have the major disadvantage that while the revenues accruing to the state may be greater over the long term, they are received at a later stage in the development of the mine. Consequently, the tax rate must be higher to reach the same present value.

Other Legislation

Other forms of legislation besides the mining and tax codes impinge in the mining sector. For example, in a country where private capital, local or foreign, is used to develop the sector, an enlightened investment code and guarantees are required. These may include the following: freedom of establishing commercial activities and free movement of people, capital, and goods; respect for the right of property, official protection of private investment, and fair compensation on expropriation, convertible into the recipients' national currency; freedom of employment, hiring, and firing; free choice of suppliers and contractors (subject to local preferences); cooperation from public agencies; tariff or quota protection; stability concerning the juridical, economic, financial, fiscal, labor, and health laws in force; provisions and procedures for settlement of disputes; and guarantees for the provision of infrastructure.

On the other hand, several undertakings or commitments have to be sought from the private investors. These may include: implementation of the project within an agreed time frame; pricing procedures, local and foreign; giving domestic consumers right of first refusal; giving domestic supplier preferences at comparable prices and qualities; employing nationals preferentially or providing training; reinvestment of part of earnings; transfer of stock to local investors; provision of necessary social and educational facilities for employees; and compliance with all legislation.

Dealing with Multinationals

Even with a well-defined mineral policy and legislative system, a country relying upon private foreign capital for development of its mineral sector should pay particular attention to its policies and procedures as they apply to the foreign enterprises. The precise relationship between the multinational corporation and the host country must therefore be clearly defined and a mechanism established for coordinating and monitoring this relationship. These functions are often widely scattered among various ministries, few of which are even remotely equipped to deal with the whole range of problems that may arise or are in a position to play a central role in developing a consistent set of policies. One solution is to set up a coordinating body which can gradually develop a nucleus of people who are capable of understanding the operations of the multinational corporations and of conducting negotiations with them. Such people are very scarce in the developing countries. In countries where some form of participation in the decisionmaking of the multinationals is aimed at, this can be done through joint ventures, majority or minority ownership. This has the advantage of working from the inside so that cumbersome procedures are avoided. Both sides need to know who they are dealing with—

there should be no ambiguity and the lines of communication should be drawn clearly.

A major problem area is that of negotiation between the multinationals and host governments. Most developing countries lack the expertise to conduct these negotiations in a manner to ensure that their interests are protected in seeking agreement. Results may vary from giving away excessive concessions (in order to buy the participation of the corporation) to a hard line which frightens away potential investors. Both extremes are equally unsatisfactory. Implementation of a good project has in many cases been delayed years and years, at great cost to both the host country and the multinational. The negotiators on both sides must consider themselves as entering a partnership which has to be mutually satisfactory. Countries should not hesitate to engage experts to assist in such negotiations.

Technical Assistance: the Where, What, and How

In the majority of developing countries there is unquestionable need for substantial technical assistance. Assistance may be needed in assessing the country's mineral potential; defining the role that the mineral sector should play in the country's economic development; preparing and assisting in formulation of policy for mineral sector development; preparing and advising on promulgation of legislation governing the mineral sector; reviewing the administrative set-up for the sector and establishing an action plan for improving it; reorganizing and strengthening the institutions servicing the sector; training and educating nationals in all aspects of sector administration and operation; increasing exploration activity; negotiating with the multinationals and other foreign private investors; and identifying, promoting, and implementing projects in both the public and private sectors.

Even those developing countries with reasonably well-developed mineral sectors can use large technical assistance inputs. Many, however, refuse to recognize or accept this fact and persuade themselves that they have sufficient internal capability. Technical assistance is particularly resisted in the area of formulating policy and legislation, since it involves political decisions. Often a team or commission of semiqualified people is set up to review existing policies and legislation and prepare new legislation, which may then be kicked around as a political football before becoming effective. A better approach would be to seek full technical assist-

ance at the outset; develop policy and legislation on strictly technical grounds; test them within the political framework; and, only
then, if the issues they raise are considered politically sensitive,
make political adjustments.

Individuals and groups capable of providing good technical
advice on policy and legislative matters are scarce, although a great
many claim such qualifications. This expertise can be found in
bilateral and multilateral aid agencies, individual consultants, consulting firms, state agencies in the developed countries, universities,
and the mining industry itself. Few single individuals are capable
of providing a full complement of advice to governments, and a
team approach is to be recommended. One may hear a lawyer,
economist, mineral economist, or engineer claim to be an expert
in mineral policy or legislation, with broad capabilities. Some may
truly be so, but a country is often better off paying more and
getting a team of specialists. Establishing a mineral policy requires
expertise in such subjects as development strategy and legislation,
geology, exploration, mineral economics, macroeconomics, public
organization and administration, mining and mineral processing,
mineral marketing, law, and taxation regimes. Any country con-
templating a major policy and legislative reform should therefore
seek proposals for assistance. These proposals bear scrutinizing
carefully before selection is made. Ironically, many countries do not
have the expertise even to prepare documents inviting proposals
or to evaluate those received. An expert is needed even for this step.
The aid agencies could play an important role by providing personnel for this first step.

Another area requiring a team approach is assistance to the
governments in evaluating the proposals of, and negotiating concession contracts with, the multinationals. An individual advisor
can perform a useful but not complete function. These services
are better provided by several public and private sector consulting
groups.

More specific expertise is required for strengthening the administrative ability of the government, which might include complete
reorganization of the public sector. Many countries have an administrative framework but lack qualified staff and procedures. Duplication of effort and responsibilities is common, and coordination
and cooperation between agencies is generally lacking. Individual
experts can assist in rectifying the problems, provided the administration steers them to the heart of it. Often, however, the administration is too weak to monitor the activities of the sector or implement the experts' recommendations. In such a case, the team, while
reporting to the very highest levels of the administration, might

take over some implementation functions and train nationals to carry out these tasks at a later date. Too often, a good technical assistance program is wasted because a proper course of action is not carried through.

Project identification and preparation, including investment planning, is an essential function often inadequately carried out in developing countries by either the government, the state-owned companies, or the private sector. Because of it, one often comes across situations where projects are justified solely on technical grounds; financial and economic considerations may be ignored or not understood; and the need to arrange for the requisite infrastructure is overlooked. Consultants and operating companies may prove the best source for assistance in this vital area.

A final word of caution: While it is understood that the most reliable expertise resides with reputable firms and agencies, countries seeking assistance would be well advised to question the qualifications of each individual expert assigned to them. For, in practice, it is the individual who provides the assistance, not the agency.[9]

9. One African official is reported to have observed, "Just two months ago I had some experts from . . . and they could jolly well have been my first year students. I had to take them in the field to show them what they were supposed to be advising on." See A. R. Berger (ed.), *Geoscientists and the Third World: A Collective Critique of Existing Aid Programs*, Geological Survey of Canada, Paper 34–57, 1975.

7 | Performance, Prospects, and Problems of the Industry

IN THE PRECEDING SIX CHAPTERS we have examined the raw material base, structure, and operation of the world mining industry and focused on the problems of mineral sector development in the developing countries. In tracing the various stages of mineral development we have tried to define policy objectives, identify operational problems, outline choices of approach, note the most common misconceptions, and warn against the most costly mistakes. In this final chapter we summarize our assessment of the overall performance of the industry, its future direction, and the major problems along the way.

The Performance of the Industry

There are no objective or universally applicable criteria for judging the performance of the world mining industry. The needs and interests of consuming nations and the developing exporting nations vary widely. Developed countries are primarily interested in security of supply at reasonable prices, though price is secondary to security; reasonable prices might be defined as the lowest possible levels that guarantee secure sources and a steady supply. Developing countries wish to promote mineral development and at the same time to extract a significant rent. Their needs and interests include ensuring the reinvestment of the proceeds from mineral exploitation in other productive activities, gaining greater control over the planning and operation of the industry, increasing value added in the country, and promoting greater employment. All these needs are accentuated by their level of underdevelopment.

These basic differences notwithstanding, the dichotomies between groups of nations should not be overemphasized, since nations are not neatly categorizable into consumers and producers along lines of economic development. As shown in chapter 3, a number of developed countries figure prominently among the world's large producers and exporters of nonfuel minerals; they have common interests with developing countries that are mineral producers and they are susceptible to some of the same mistakes. Furthermore, in a dynamic world, the factors that shape self-interest can change rapidly. For example, although the process of becoming a large consumer of minerals through development is undoubtedly slow, populous countries like India, Brazil, Nigeria, and Pakistan, already possessing or planning to establish a large manufacturing sector, can find their raw material requirements swell swiftly. What affects the size of mineral demand is the absolute size of the industrial sector, not the country's degree of industrialization.

Are there, then, economic interests which all nations share or which transcend national self-interest? In the case of the mining sector, the obvious common interests are adequate supplies at equitable yields and a distribution favoring the developing countries without interfering with global efficiency. If the professed goal of international economic and development cooperation is progress for all, the mining industry must be expected to play a role in fulfilling the aspirations of the developing countries. Proposing this as one of the standards of the industry's performance means taking seriously the importance of a global commitment to narrowing the gap between the rich and the poor countries.

The record of the world mining industry in responding to the needs of the developing countries is dismal. The industry's total effort has been directed to obtaining sufficient supplies for the consuming nations, who are predominantly the developed countries; that is a task in which the industry has been highly effective and innovative. Only recently has the industry even shown awareness of the needs of the developing countries, and very few consuming nations and firms have reacted earnestly to meet the challenge; the record remains largely uncorrected.

The industry has performed reasonably well in terms of efficiency. It has provided consumers with an expanding variety and steady source of mineral raw materials, many of which are exploited as efficiently as man is able, though with some glaring omissions, such as failure to bring the best deposits on stream first. Political climate has had a major impact on the industry's decisions on where to mine and has tended to discriminate against the developing countries. This is particularly apparent in the disproportionate allocation of exploration expenditures to developed regions.

There is also reason to question the industry's efficiency with respect to use. The proportions in which mineral resources are exploited and used today do not reflect their relative abundance, largely because of imperfections in the orientation of research and in the pricing mechanism. Far from being directed systematically towards abundant materials, research in end use is sporadic, ad hoc, and very uneven among minerals and over time. Often, major breakthroughs have been achieved during and in response to emergencies (wars) or as a by-product of advances in other fields (aerospace). Mineral prices have traditionally been determined on the basis of capital, operating, and distribution costs, modified by bargaining power, with no allowance made for the inherent value of the mineral in the ground. A more appropriate yardstick (if adopted by all mineral producers) might be the price just below that of the closest substitute or the cost of secondary (recycled) material. The difference between this price and that based on costs can be taken to represent the intrinsic value of the mineral in the ground which ideally should accrue to the host country. The imperfection of the pricing mechanism has undoubtedly led to inefficient use, aside from maldistribution of benefits.

A related question is how much government interference has hindered or helped the industry. It is hard to draw general conclusions from past experience, since government action has tended to be irregular in degree and quality. At times it has been completely irrational and has aborted efficient mineral development; in numerous cases it has been so tentative as to be virtually ineffective. With regard to worldwide resource use and production efficiency, of course, nonuniform tax burdens and tariffs and other government barriers to trade and processing lead to inefficiency compared to the ideal economic model. But an ideal model exists only in a vacuum; the usefulness of such a measure is nullified by the reality of political and economic divisions and inequalities.

Despite the shortcomings listed above, our conclusion is that on strictly technical grounds the industry has not performed too badly in the past.

Meeting Future Requirements

The world mining industry faces a dynamic future. Continued population growth and universal demand to improve physical standards of living guarantee that. While the intensity of use of nonfuel minerals (the volume of consumption per unit of GNP) has been declining over the long term in the industrially advanced countries and is bound to bring about a deceleration in the growth rate of world demand, this need not be fully manifested in the next ten years, constitute an openended trend or imply that the task of meeting future requirements will become progressively easy—far from it.

In the next five to ten years, world demand for nonfuel minerals is likely to grow at rates not materially different from those of the sixties (4 to 5 percent a year). The factors combining to sustain growth rates over this period, despite the steady decline in intensity of use in a major consumer like the United States, include: differences in the structure of demand, in accumulated stocks, or reservoirs (physical structures or goods with long life cycles); the redistribution of income under way through adjusted oil prices, particularly the capital intensiveness of many of the projects undertaken or financed by OPEC countries with a surplus of resources; and pent-up demand everywhere resulting from the combination of recession and inflation.

The force of declining use by the large producers will very likely be felt more strongly in the late 1980s and the 1990s. Available projections for the year 2000 point to considerably slower growth rates in the last quarter of the century than in the third quarter. Because of the progressive expansion of the consumption base, however, the amount of additional yearly requirements is hardly likely to decline in absolute terms and, given the fixed stock of resources (at least of superior grades), meeting these requirements will pose a constant challenge.

With regard to the very long term, it suffices to note that the deceleration in the growth rate of demand need not last indefinitely nor give way to stable growth rates of unlimited duration. Not only the hoped-for industrialization of the developing countries but also programs to eradicate pockets of relative poverty, to redistribute income, or to reallocate and improve the volume and quality of mass consumption in the rich countries can revitalize, even revolutionize, demand for minerals. Therefore, it is not farfetched to suggest that the S-shaped curve of the relation between mineral consumption and economic growth over time—historically verified and theoretically anticipated—may be followed by another and another similar curve.

In short, world demand for minerals is likely to continue to expand rapidly in the next ten years, at decelerating rates thereafter, but with spurts or even sustained periods of rapid growth again.

What about the product mix of future consumption? It would be sheer folly to speculate on it at a time when the world is facing major readjustments in relative prices, when the impetus for technological change is getting stronger, and when policies of self-sufficiency, even at the cost of changing the product mix, have obvious appeal. Available projections do not point to any significant change in the mix in the foreseeable future: the metals growing fastest in the past (aluminum and nickel) still top the list in terms of projected growth rates, with tin at the bottom, and copper and iron in the middle. Most of these projections were made before the energy crisis, however, and do not take into account, for example, the implications of new forms of energy generation or of energy-saving adjustments in consumption patterns for specific minerals.

It is even more difficult to predict the future supply of minerals product by product, though some estimates exist on short- to medium-term expansion plans worldwide, the most comprehensive being those published annually by the *Engineering and Mining Journal*. Even these are subject to wide margins of error,[1] and can at best be used to provide orders of magnitude on new capacity, investment requirements, and location of new investment.

The *Engineering and Mining Journal* list of projects forecast to come on stream between 1975 and 1980, published in January 1975 (modified here by the authors on the basis of their personal knowledge of specific projects), indicates that among the major minerals, aluminum, copper, iron, and nickel are all forecast to have very substantial increases in supply over the next five years. Even after refinements resulting in significant downward adjustments in the figures, the projected increase in capacity between 1975 and 1980 comes to 40 to 50 percent, or 6 to 8 percent annually. Except in the case of aluminum, this is significantly higher than the growth rate forecast for demand and would tend to indicate surpluses, at least in the medium term.[2] Several projects will inevitably be postponed because of lack of finance, hesitancy in the face of political instability, and limitations on the absorptive

1. For example, there is a considerable amount of double counting since different stages of production located in separate places are treated as separate projects. Also, it is almost certain that the *Engineering and Mining Journal* survey significantly underestimates new investments in the centrally planned countries.

2. In an analysis of the outlook for twenty-seven commodities, Takeuchi and Varon concluded: "The anticipation of more surpluses than shortages, while comforting to the consuming nations, suggests that our concerns are skewed in the wrong direction." Kenji Takeuchi and Bension Varon, "Commodity Shortage and Changes in World Trade," *Annals of the American Academy of Political and Social Science*, vol. 420 (July 1975), p. 56.

capacity of the industry. In any case, supply is not likely to fall below demand in the medium term although short-term imbalances cannot be ruled out.

For the longer term, there is little information available which permits predicting with confidence shortages or surpluses of major consequence. Nevertheless, as pointed out in chapter 2, presently known reserves for most minerals appear adequate to the year 2000, with only moderate increases in the real price needed to precipitate new mine development. The most notable exceptions appear to be silver, tin, and zinc. However, data on ore reserves are even less reliable than those on investment in new projects, and to attempt to draw more than indicative conclusions from them is hazardous.

Future discoveries of major importance are sure to occur, particularly if we consider the relatively large areas which remain virtually unexplored and the progress being made with new exploration techniques and the increasing awareness of many nations of the need to promote exploration in their territories. The Earth Resources Technology Satellite (ERTS) program is already having some far-reaching effects on the exploration for minerals. It has identified major fault zones, previously undetected, and provided a new direction to exploration in several areas. To date, the potential exploration benefits from the ERTS program have barely been tapped. New and more sophisticated exploration techniques are leading to further significant discoveries in areas previously heavily explored. A major breakthrough is needed, however, to assist in finding orebodies at depth. Up to now most orebodies discovered have been located at or relatively close to the earth's surface. The development of new exploration techniques for tropical areas could also provide substantial mineral discoveries, as shown by the discovery of major iron ore and bauxite deposits in the Amazon region.

Although we can expect new discoveries to be adequate for the long-term demand for minerals, the matter of timing is far from clear. Can we expect a sufficient acceleration in exploration effort to meet the exponential growth in demand? To what extent will mineral prices have to increase (in real terms) to attract the necessary funds? With the increased trend toward national control, many of the traditional sources of exploration capital have dried up. With increasing worldwide acceptance of national sovereignty over natural resources, will these sources open up again? If so, will they be sufficient to meet the worldwide exploration needs? To what extent will new sources of exploration capital be required? From where will the new funds come? We are dealing here with worldwide problems not easily solved within national contexts; while national self-interest may be a legitimate starting point, national self-sufficiency would be a dubious goal, in no way ensuring a balanced worldwide satisfaction of requirements.

Problems and Challenges

The principal problem and challenge facing the industry in the short run is most definitely the business cycle and the excessive volatility of prices which makes planning difficult, followed by the industry's tendency to overreact to business cycles, the rapidly weakening fiscal stability of some of the large mineral-producing countries, and rapidly rising capital costs and increased costs of finance, coupled with the decreasing availability of finance for mining.

In the long run, the industry faces and has to respond to: changes in the rules of the game, increased nationalism, and inevitable changes in ownership; the limited capacity of the developing countries to absorb their own mineral development, coupled with problems of transfer of technology caused by the inflexibility of the developed countries and the blindness of many developing countries to their own limitations; and the need to swing back to a more realistic balance between national control and joint ventures. Energy and pollution should not prove to be major problems for the industry overall.

The increases in energy prices were at first expected to have an important bearing on the future location of mining and mineral-processing facilities. It is not now so certain that, given time for the situation to stabilize, the higher energy costs will lead to radical changes. Of course, transport costs have already increased significantly, making the processing of minerals closer to the mine more attractive. Deposits and process technologies requiring less energy have also become more attractive. With the higher energy prices, greater attention will no doubt be given to economizing on the use of energy, for example through greater use of waste-heat boilers, modification of plant design, minimizing of heat losses, and better harnessing of the heat generated from exothermic reactions. Turning to geothermal steam as a source of energy will bring more attention to recovering minerals from the steam and geothermal brines. It is far too early at this stage to determine whether or not the energy crisis will have a significant influence on the competitiveness of different minerals, promoting or retarding substitution of one mineral for another.

Following the implementation of the first rigorous environmental protection legislations in the industrialized countries, a tendency developed to relocate mineral-processing facilities, that is, to export pollution—a trend welcomed by the developing countries since it meant greater value added within their territories. While increased environmental awareness initially had a disruptive influence in terms of mineral production (for example, by forcing the closure of smelters and modifications of strip mining design), it is not expected to affect radically the future distribution of production capacity. Research into the means by which environmental requirements are met has resulted in the development of new processes and new by-product uses with some economic return, thereby lessening what had earlier been feared as a major investment with no return. For instance, the recovery of sulfur dioxides from the gases of smelters has led to the production of significant quantities of sulfuric acid which are used in many cases to leach the minerals from the waste dumps or areas of lower-grade ores, thereby increasing recovery of the orebody. In addition, the developing countries are now following the developed ones in imposing antipollution controls, which may slow the trend to relocate smelting and refining capacity. On the other hand, these countries' demands that the mineral mined in their territories be processed at least to the metal ingot stage will persist. Although what may be called an initial overreaction in favor of environmental protection is being brought back more into balance (responding to the need to remain competitive), several projects will continue to be hindered by environmental considerations, some perhaps rightly, but quite a number unjustifiably.

The Special Problem of Capital Requirements

The lack of capital can be a major barrier to mineral development. It is now apparent that a capital shortage of significant proportions exists in the industry. The rash of expropriations, the uncertainties of future energy supplies and costs and of future environmental legislation, as well as the recent radical changes in mineral industry taxation, even in countries thought to be stable, have all added to the already high risk factors of the industry, and these uncertainties have affected the industry's ability to raise debt or equity financing. The increase in project size and the effect of rapid inflation on capital costs has made it increasingly difficult to finance projects from internal cash flow and has forced companies to turn more and more to external sources of finance. MacGregor and Vickers show that for the twelve leading producers of base metals, ferroalloys, and industrial minerals in North America, deteriorating financial conditions between 1966 and 1972 have led to a drop in return on sales from nearly 14 percent to about 8 percent; an increase in the average debt-to-equity ratio from 9:91 to 26:74; and a decrease in the coverage of fixed capital requirements from operations from 84 percent to 62 percent. Over a similar period, the debt-to-equity ratio for U.S. nonferrous mineral producers as a group increased from 29:71 to 50:50.[3]

As pointed out at the beginning of this chapter, the demand for nonfuel minerals is projected to increase significantly between 1975 and 1985; the world productive capacity in existence—the result of cumulative investment over almost three-quarters of a century— must be increased by as much as 50 percent in ten years or so. For most minerals sufficient projects appear to have been identified to meet this demand into the early 1980s (if all projects are carried out). What is not clear, however, is the availability of sufficient capital to finance these projects. According to the figures in the *Engineering and Mining Journal* survey of January 1975, the capital requirements for projects up to 1980–81 are in the order of $55,000 million, or extrapolating this through to 1985, $90,000 million, equivalent to $8 to $9 million a year. In 1974, MacGregor and Vickers, by using past ratios of assets to sales, estimated investment requirements for the period 1972 to 1985 at $50,000 to $100,000 million, or an average of $4 to $7 million a year. Industry spokesmen have recently mentioned figures in the range of $100,000 to $120,000 million (in 1975 prices) for the period 1975 to 1985, or $14,000 to $15,000 million a year by the mid-1980s. We favor the higher estimates, fully recognizing the financial limitations that may force the lower estimates to come true; this would cause serious supply shortages unless a major worldwide effort at conservation were to lower significantly the rate of demand—an event we see as possible but not probable.

On the basis of historical ratios and various assumptions about future worldwide taxation policies and environment requirements, MacGregor and Vickers estimated that $35,000 to $70,000 million would be available for capital investment from internal cash generation by the mining industry itself. This would leave $30,000 to $60,000 million to be sought from outside sources. Where will this financing come from? A look at the past indicates that while

3. See Wallace MacGregor and Edward L. Vickers, "Capital and the U.S. Resources Crunch," *Engineering and Mining Journal* (September 1974).

substantial amounts have been provided by the banking system in the developed countries and significantly smaller amounts by the insurance companies, bilateral and multilateral institutions, and export-credit agencies, these contributions, in aggregate, still fall far short of the future needs. This leaves public issues of bonds and equity, a source with very definite limitations. It also raises the question of the debt-carrying capacity of the industry as a whole and of individual companies in particular. To raise all this additional capital as debt would distort the capital structure of the industry, tearing it away from its historically conservative stance to a position probably unacceptable to bankers used to considering the risks of the industry. Furthermore, it appears unlikely that sufficient amounts of new equity can be raised to alleviate this problem. The industry faces a financial crunch—a situation which, in a few years, through the resultant supply shortages, may force significant and longlasting increases in mineral prices.

The developing countries, which require much more than half the capital of the nonsocialist world, will experience most of the financial shortages because the financiers associate higher political and fiscal risks with them than with the industrialized countries. Though it is quite possible that significant amounts of oil revenues will be channeled into mining projects in the developing countries, unless much of it is in the form of equity, it will not alleviate the problem and may merely replace capital available from other sources. With the current spate of nationalism, the multinationals hesitate to pour significant amounts of equity into the developing countries and are asking the nationals to increase their equity participation. This appears to be one of the most crucial problems in the future financing of the nonfuel mineral sector. Where is the equity base for development in the developing regions to come from? A change in the policies of the aid agencies may be warranted. On the other hand, to help secure supplies, we may see more and more consumers willing to provide small amounts of equity finance, a trend already apparent in recent years.

The Role of Policy

The problems of the nonfuel mineral sector are only some of the many facing the world community in these troubled times. What sort of priority do they deserve and why? Obviously, they fall below the problems of food, nutrition, family planning, and the prevention of armed conflict. But they must come next. Industrialization and social advancement as measured by the standard of living relate to material wealth, which is based on minerals. Non-fuel minerals, together with energy, are the foundation of the ever widening assortment of goods and services. Without minerals societies would still be physically in the Stone Age.

What is the role that public and private policy must assume to safeguard the interests of nations and the industry? The first requirement is that all public policies affecting the mining sector directly or indirectly be clearly defined. Unambiguous and stable investment and tax codes are a must. Also needed is a clear definition and delineation of the public and the private sectors, a realistic assessment of the ability of each country to go it alone, and an appraisal of the need for outside assistance, financial, technical, and commercial. Policy must start with identifying objectives so that all parties with a role to play can move in the same direction. It must be accompanied by the creation of adequate mechanisms and agencies to monitor and administer the sector. Finally, governments must respect their agreements except when national interest has been grossly, illegally, or unfairly violated. Bullying companies is bad practice; curtailing excess is a sound policy objective.

Companies, on their part, must learn to recognize and respect the needs and aspirations of the countries in which they operate. Be they national or foreign, they must show increased social awareness, increased willingness to participate in joint ventures, and increased readiness to train nationals as well as to promote local processing, and hence domestic value-added, where economic.

There Is No Looking Back

The mining industry is facing fundamental changes. The root cause of these changes and the need to adjust to them have been stated as follows in a *Mining Journal* editorial, and we can hardly improve on it:

> The old world order, in which the industrially developed countries of the West had considerable political and economic mastery over much of the rest of the globe, has passed into history. So, too, has their power to secure largely unfettered access to raw materials overseas. These facts are recognized publicly by the international mining industry, both through utterances of its leaders and in the many changes in mining's corporate structure over the past two decades.

Nevertheless, there are some in the industry who have not yet come to terms with the changing world for mining. There still lingers in some quarters a nostalgia for times past when mining overseas was, from today's viewpoint, far less onerous and frustrating. To look back in this mood is natural and might be harmless. On the other hand, such indulgence may subconsciously lead to policy decisions which are touched by deep-rooted dismay and the rejection of an evolution that is almost certainly irreversible.

At a personal level, it has to be recognised that attitudes moulded over many years may sometimes become too rigid for any real change of basic outlook to be possible. For others, willingness to modify long-cherished concepts will always be half-hearted in private, although not in public. If elements of the international mining industry can be viewed as having an Achilles Heel in this respect, they are no more fallible than many governments which have often been myopic about the fundamental changes in the world's social, political and economic structure.

Certainly, it must be unwise, in the longer term, for the mining industry to react to economic nationalism in the developing world merely by taking rearguard or otherwise purely defensive actions. That this has so often seemed to have happened is understandable, however. It has usually appeared to be the only response possible in the extremely complex situation now facing the mining industry and its operations in the Third World. Quite apart from the tensions involved in working out conditions under which mining corporations and the new mineral owners in the developing countries can co-exist, there have been the serious distractions of changing government policies towards mining in the more developed of the resource-rich nations. Again, there is the confusing factor that the Third World countries themselves are not wholly sure of where they are going and how best they should obtain greater benefits from the extraction of their mineral resources. . . . Even if the tide of economic nationalism has begun to ebb a little in some parts of the world, the social, political and economic conditions under which metals and minerals were won from overseas in the not too distant past will certainly never return.[4]

The mining industry has always been long-term future oriented —more so than other industries—because of the high cost of

4. *Mining Journal* (November 22, 1974).

exploration, the high capital intensiveness of exploitation, and the exhaustible character and location-bound nature of mineral resources. But from this point on planning for the future has to go beyond meeting the micro and purely economic objectives of the firm and be responsive to larger concerns which are at once macro (contribution to national economies), social (resource creation, environmental protection), political (harmonizing international relations), and even moral (safeguarding the interests of the poor countries). The industry must reform. It now operates in a climate of suspicion and hostility on the part of the public and policy-makers, the result of past abuses and transgressions. But if the industry is to meet the expanded tasks, chastisement must give way to intelligent guidelines and fair-minded supervision.

The time for international resource planning, covering both exploitation and use, is here. Increased international cooperation and commodity agreements taking careful account of the needs and aspirations of both producers and consumers is a must if major and unpredictable disruptions to the world economy and trade are to be avoided. The problem of international cooperation becomes evident when the question of the exploitation of the seabed's mineral resources is considered. Not in the short term but possibly in the medium term, and almost certainly in the longer term, the oceans will become a significant factor in mineral supply, as discussed in chapter 2. Past attempts to reach international agreement on the terms for exploiting this potential have been unsuccessful. No doubt the question of exploitation of ocean resources is extremely complex, with important ramifications for both consumers and producers; but future commodity agreements may prove just as complex. A greater commitment to expanding the benefits to the developing countries from the development of their mineral resources will be important to a continued smooth flow of minerals to the marketplace and will improve the climate for international cooperation.

Minerals have been as much a development agent of civilization as agricultural products and communication, and a steady supply of them is essential to its continuation. Though the primary challenge to the mining industry will continue to be, as in the past, the provision of adequate supplies, in the coming decades the industry itself, rather than its product, will have to become a conscious agent for worldwide economic development. This is admittedly an enormous task.

All the complex difficulties the industry faces in its normal course of operations are now compounded by the unrelenting pressure for additional supplies. Population growth and improvement in individual income translate into one basic imperative: more! While steadily increasing production, the industry must also find ways to safeguard the environment in which its activities are located and to conduct them harmoniously in a more demanding political and social setting. Governments increasingly seek a role in the making of decisions or, at the very least, demand compliance with sectoral goals and guidelines. The world has become feverishly aware of the importance of natural resources for the survival of civilization and anxious to know how well their providers are safeguarding the future. A fundamental requirement of the mining industry, therefore, is to respond to the challenge by planning, investing—in knowledge and capacity—and operating in such a way as to inspire confidence in man's ability to manage natural resources on a global basis and over time.

The mining industry is truly international in character, by definition and necessity. Mineral development requires the combination of physical, financial, and technical resources from varied sources, and its products travel across national boundaries. The industry thrives best in a climate of cooperation among disciplines, countries, investment sources, the public and private sectors, management and labor, and the various elements of the research and information networks. The potential for cooperation will be enhanced by the industry's efforts to distribute its investment and earnings equitably over countries. This will require a continuous resolve on the part of the industry to commit its vast know-how and in-house resources to international development, particularly that of the developing countries.

It is widely argued that the mining industry should shift its base of operations to the developing countries because the developed countries are depleting their existing mineral resources. This has to be pursued systematically, as a matter of policy, both because, over the long run, intelligent resource planning and management must truly cover the globe, and because the strain on civilization, over the short and medium term, of a world divided into economic classes—of a standoff between the have and have-not nations—is insupportable.

Appendixes

A | Mineral Exploration Costs, Expenditures, and Risks: Selected Examples

BECAUSE OF THE CONFIDENTIALITY of mineral exploration, data on costs and risks are incomplete and available for only a few countries. Data are perhaps more complete for Canada than for any other nation. The Canadian experience, while not typical of exploration in the rest of the world, is outlined below as an example and illustrated in a series of charts. The Canadian data are followed by some estimates for the United States and the implications of this experience for the developing countries.

Canadian Experience

Exploration expenditure in Canada has increased substantially in the postwar years:[1] from an average of Can$12 million a year in the late 1940s to Can$80 to 90 million a year in the late 1960s to early 1970s, in constant 1971 Canadian dollars (figure A.1). Over the same period, the value of the mineral discoveries also increased, but to a much lesser extent (figure A.2), and exploration costs per ton of metal doubled (figure A.3). Between 1945 and 1970, the number of ore discoveries a year declined (figure A.4); hence, the average exploration expenditure per discovery increased significantly, namely, from Can$2 million in the periods 1946–50 and 1951–55, to about Can$6 million in the periods 1956–60 and 1961–65, Can$15 million in 1966–70 (figure A.5) and an estimated Can$25 to 30 million in 1971–72. (The figures for the recent periods may be artificially high, since companies often do not announce discoveries for

1. See D.A. Cranstone and H. L. Martin, "Are Ore Discovery Costs Increasing?" *Canadian Mining Journal* (April 1973); and P. Going, "An Industrial Analysis of Exploration Activity," *Canadian Mining Journal* (April 1973).

FIGURES A.1–A.6 | CANADIAN MINERAL
EXPLORATION EXPERIENCE

FIGURE A.1 | AGGREGATE EXPLORATION
EXPENDITURES A FIVE-YEAR PERIOD

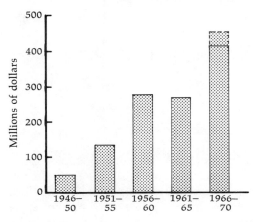

FIGURE A.2 | AGGREGATE VALUE OF DISCOVERIES
A FIVE-YEAR PERIOD

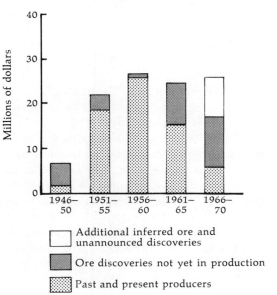

FIGURE A.3 | VALUE OF METAL DISCOVERIES A
MILLION DOLLARS OF PROSPECTING
OR EXPLORATION EXPENDITURES

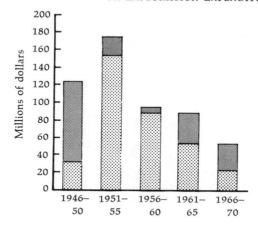

FIGURE A.4 | NUMBER OF DISCOVERIES A
FIVE-YEAR PERIOD

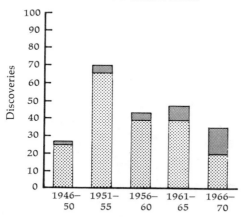

Ore discoveries not yet in production

Past and present producers

FIGURE A.5 | AVERAGE EXPLORATION
EXPENDITURE PER DISCOVERY

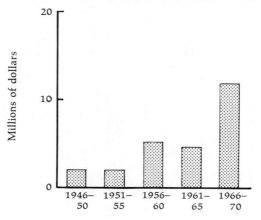

FIGURE A.6 | AVERAGE VALUE OF A DISCOVERY

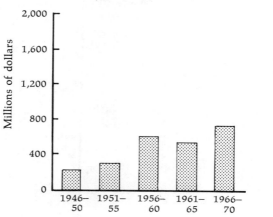

Note: Dollars are constant 1971 Canadian dollars throughout.

Source: Mineral Resources Branch, Canadian Department
of Energy, Mines, and Resources.

several years.) However, this notable increase in discovery costs per deposit was compensated considerably by the greater value of the average discovery, which increased from an estimated Can$245 million in 1946–50 to at least Can$750 million in 1966–70 (figure A.6).

The experience of Cominco, Ltd., a major mining company formerly known as the Consolidated Mining and Smelting Co. of Canada, provides some insight into the relation of cost to risk in exploration in Canada. In the 1937–69 period, Cominco spent more than Can$300 million on exploration. Over 1,000 properties were examined (all in Canada), of which 78 warranted major programs, with capital investments ranging from Can$100,000 to Can$75 million. Eventually, only 7 of the 1,000 properties became profitable mines.

United States Experience

The past fifteen years have seen a significant increase in the costs of exploration in the United States.[2] At least three times as many people are being used in the search for metallic minerals in the western part of the United States today as in 1955. In addition, exploration technology has become considerably more sophisticated and expensive; the cost of putting a prospecting team in the field has increased to an estimated $100,000 a year for each geologist. These two factors—manpower and technology—have combined to increase the total expenditures of the mining industry, stated in terms of 1970 dollars, by about 2.5 to 3.0 times between 1955 and 1969. (See figure A.7.)

The number of discoveries more than doubled between the 1955–59 and 1965–69 periods but the average gross value of each discovery in the 1965–69 period was only about 60 percent of the average ten years earlier. The estimated gross value of all discoveries in the western United States increased by a factor of only about 1.5 (figure A.8). Therefore, even though increased exploration activity has brought about an increase in the number of deposits discovered, the cost of finding $1,000 worth of product was about twice as great in the latter period. This corresponds closely with the Canadian experience.

Although forty-seven significant deposits were discovered from 1955 through 1969, only sixteen of these are currently under ex-

2. See "U.S. Exploration Is Very High Risk, Development More Costly," *World Mining* (November 1971).

FIGURE A.7 | EXPLORATION EXPENDITURES IN THE WESTERN
UNITED STATES

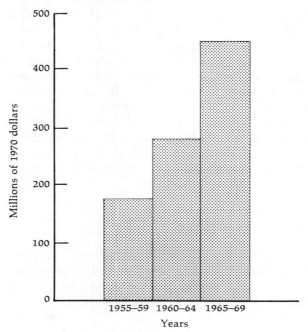

Source: "U.S. Exploration is Very High Risk: Development More Costly," *World Mining* (November 1971).

ploitation. Exploration expenditures in the western United States over the period 1955–69 averaged $18 million per significant discovery, but $60 million per mine brought into production.

Implications for Exploration Expenditures in the Developing Countries

Very little quantitative information is available on exploration expenditures in the developing countries and much of what is available is unreliable. To put the Canadian and the United States experience in the context of exploration costs in the developing countries, it is important to note the following:

The results obtained in these two countries depend to a very

FIGURE A.8 | GROSS VALUE OF ORE DEPOSITS VALUED AT $100 MILLION OR MORE DISCOVERED IN THE WESTERN UNITED STATES

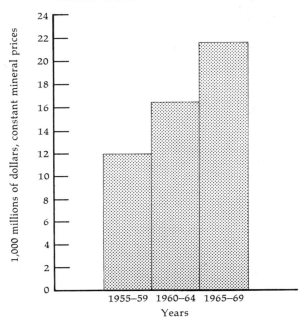

Source: "U.S. Exploration is Very High Risk: Development More Costly," *World Mining* (November 1971).

large extent on the geological maps and surveys already substantially completed. Such information is generally not available in the developing countries, which would make costs significantly higher.

On the other hand, Canada and the United States have been thoroughly explored, and new mines are becoming more difficult to find, while costs are increasing. This is reflected in the age of the mines currently in operation: 50 to 60 percent of Canada's current production comes from mines discovered before 1910, 25 percent from 1910 to 1920, and 11 percent from 1920 to 1930; of the 150 to 200 mines started or restarted since 1955, more than 50 percent were discovered before 1950 and 20 percent before 1920.

Exploration costs and risks in the developing countries will, of course, vary considerably from country to country but can be expected to be considerably lower than in Canada and the United States, especially in countries with known potential such as Bolivia,

Peru, Chile, Brazil, and Zambia. Overall, taking into account the large areas unexplored in the developing regions, exploration costs and risks there can be expected to be considerably below those in Canada and the United States.

B | Expansion of Mineral Capacity

THE FOLLOWING TABLE summarizes the investment costs of announced projects for the mining of bauxite-alumina-aluminum, copper, iron ore, lead and zinc, nickel, and other metallic and nonmetallic minerals on the basis of 1973 data in most cases. Since then, inflation and escalation have raised costs considerably—in some cases, to almost double the original estimate. In copper projects, for example, the increase in 1974 alone was about 15 percent on the average and as high as 25 percent in some countries. Furthermore, postponements or cancellations are common. Taking copper again as an example, in 1974 net additions (expansions minus closures) of some 500,000 tons were projected for 1976 by one reputable source. In 1975 the estimate was reduced by half of the original projection, and now it appears that even the revised estimates will not be achieved.

TABLE B.1 | MINERAL PROJECTS UNDER CONSTRUCTION OR IN ADVANCED STAGES OF PLANNING

Project	Total number of projects	Projects for which no cost estimates were provided	Total reported investment	Size of investments (millions of dollars)					
				0–9	10–49	50–99	100–150	150–199	200+
Bauxite, aluminum, and aluminum industry									
Number of projects	62	32	30	3	10	4	2	6	5
Percentage of reported projects	100	52	48	5	17	6	4	10	8
Total reported investments[a]	3,564			19	319	274	241	1,027	1,690
Percentage of total reported investment	100			0	9	8	7	29	47
Copper mining, beneficiating, smelting, and refining									
Number of projects	84	42	42	3	12	11	8	1	7
Percentage of reported projects	100	50	50	4	14	13	10	1	8
Total reported investments[a]	5,629			19	297	796	850	180	3,487
Percentage of total reported investment	100			0	5	14	15	15	62
Iron mining, beneficiating, and pelletizing									
Number of projects	41	19	22	1	3	6	0	1	11
Percentage of reported projects	100	47	53	2	7	15	0	2	27
Total reported investments[a]	4,676			8	107	419	0	190	3,952
Percentage of total reported investment	100			0	2	9	0	4	84
Lead and zinc mining, beneficiating, smelting, and refining									
Number of projects	50	22	28	8	15	5	0	0	0
Percentage of reported projects	100	44	56	16	30	10	0	0	0

Total reported investments[a]			680	37	329	314	0	0	0
Percentage of total reported investment	100		100	5	48	46	0	0	0
Nickel mining, beneficiating, smelting, and refining									
Number of projects	31	14	17	1	6	3	2	3	2
Percentage of reported projects	100	46	54	3	18	9	6	9	6
Total reported investments[a]			1,621	6	161	207	237	490	520
Percentage of total reported investment	100		100	0	10	13	15	30	32
Other metallic minerals, mining, beneficiating, smelting, and refining[b]									
Number of projects	70	38	32	17	7	5	2	0	1
Percentage of reported projects	100	55	45	24	10	7	3	0	2
Total reported investments[a]			1,041	74	96	306	265	0	300
Percentage of total reported investment	100		100	7	9	30	25	0	29
Total metallic minerals									
Number of projects	338	167	171	33	53	34	14	11	26
Percentage of reported projects	100	49	51	10	16	10	4	3	7
Total reported investments[a]			17,211	163	1,309	2,316	1,593	1,887	9,949
Percentage of total reported investment	100		100	1	8	13	9	11	58
Nonmetallic minerals, mining, beneficiating, and processing[c]									
Number of projects	56	30	26	10	12	2	0	0	2
Percentage of reported projects	100	54	46	18	21	4	0	0	4
Total reported investments[a]			938	55	348	135	0	0	400
Percentage of total reported investment	100		100	6	37	14	0	0	43

Note: The majority of these projects is scheduled to start up in 1975, 1976, or 1977, although a few are scheduled to start up as late as 1980.

a. In millions of dollars.

b. Includes antimony, bismuth, magnesium, platinum, silver, titanium, tungsten, and uranium.

c. Includes phosphate, potash, asbestos, fluorspar, salt, sulfur, soda ash, strontium, and diamonds.

Source: Engineering and Mining Journal, 1974 International Directory of Mining and Mineral Processing Operations.

C | United Nations Assistance in Mineral Resources Development

OPERATIONAL ACTIVITIES in the mineral sector have been conducted mainly by the United Nations Resources and Transport Division, now called the Centre for Natural Resources, Energy, and Transport, on behalf of the United Nations Development Programme (UNDP). Over 100 full-scale mineral resource development projects have been undertaken with cooperation and joint financing by the recipient governments. These programs, which started in the early 1960s, generally combine the search for ore deposits with the establishment or strengthening of national mineral resources departments. Nonoperational activities include dissemination of information on technological developments through seminars, research studies, and working groups on a worldwide basis, the results of which appear as United Nations publications. While the overall program focuses primarily on land-based mineral resources, near-shore and offshore surveys are also undertaken in certain countries with mineral potential in that environment.

The major thrust of the program has been operational activities which have embraced virtually all aspects of mineral resources development—geological survey and mineral resources department organization; geological mapping; photogeology; mineralogy and petrology; mineral exploration using all modern methods such as geochemical prospecting, exploration geophysics (airborne, ground, and offshore), diamond and other types of drilling, analytical chemistry and assaying, economic feasibility studies, mining, mineral processing and metallurgical extraction, and mining legislation. The following paragraphs set out briefly the sectors covered and give some indication of the magnitude of the program as of January 31, 1972.[1]

---

1. For additional details, see United Nations, *Comprehensive Plan of Action for the Co-ordination of Programmes Within the United Nations in the*

Organization and Strengthening of Government Departments Dealing with Geology and Mineral Resources Development

In essence, virtually all projects executed assist in the organization and strengthening of government institutions, and training of national personnel at all levels is an important part of that effort. A number of projects, however, have as their primary objective the establishment or strengthening of institutions, while concurrently carrying out the geological, mineral exploration, or other field surveys required by the development program of the recipient country. They, too, encourage mineral resources development, the Geological Survey Institute project in Iran being a case in point.

Total funding in this sector amounts to $5.1 million in UNDP financing and $5.0 million in recipient government contributions. Projects have been or are being executed in Benin, Ethiopia, Guinea, Mauritania, Iran, and Jordan. A number of others are anticipated, notably in Burma.

Mineral Exploration Programs Using Modern Methods

The largest single operational sector involves exploration using modern methods, since the direct search for ore deposits (along with simultaneous training of national personnel in modern methods) has been the prime motivation for the bulk of the projects assisted by the UNDP. Institute strengthening is inherent in all these programs through training, equipment financing, and other provisions. Some sixty-five projects have been or are being executed in fifty-five countries, thirty of them in Africa. The extent of the funding totals about $55.0 million of UNDP resources and $45 million contributed by recipient governments. The operations have involved all appropriate methods of ground, airborne, and offshore surveying.

This sector also contains a number of combined mineral and groundwater projects—in Madagascar, Somalia, Togo, Upper Volta, and Cyprus—which involve UNDP inputs totaling $7.3 million, with some $5.7 million of counterpart contributions.

Field of Natural Resources Development, Report of the Secretary General, Addendum on Mineral Resources (E/C.7/47/add. 2) (New York, February 10, 1975).

Programs in Mining and Mineral Processing

Mineral processing activities have figured in several of the mineral exploration projects listed above. The reason for this is obvious; mineral deposits identified in these programs cannot be evaluated without establishing that the ore can in fact be beneficiated economically. It is not unusual for mineral deposits of otherwise satisfactory tonnage and grade to be considered unworkable because of mineral processing difficulties. Processing must therefore be taken into account in establishing economic feasibility.

There are, however, a number of projects in which mining and mineral processing investigations form the major part of operations, that is, projects not necessarily tied to exploration activities but rather designed to meet the needs of an existing mining industry. Projects of this kind have been executed in Burma and Bolivia.

Establishment of University Schools in Applied Geology

The emphasis placed by certain developing countries on applied rather than purely scientific university training has resulted in several projects providing such training. They were executed jointly with national universities, usually in close cooperation with national geological or mining organizations which will be employing a number of the specialists turned out. Training has centered on mineral exploration techniques, taught at the postgraduate level or after a grounding in basic sciences through undergraduate courses; it combines academic course work with concentrated practical field training in the physical, geological, and metallogenetic environment of the students' home country. While the field training programs may not have the location of mineral deposits as a primary objective (instead focusing on applied research and development of exploration methods in different environments), positive exploration results are by no means neglected in these programs, as has been demonstrated by the "Institute of Applied Geology" project in the Philippines.

Other Technical Assistance Activities

In addition to the larger-scale projects dealt with above, considerable assistance on a more modest scale has been given to developing countries in the form of individual experts assigned to advise governments or to meet specific needs, but usually not charged with assuming operational responsibility, as in the case of full-scale projects. To indicate the nature and extent of these services, it may be noted that 353 man-years of expert services were provided during 1966–74; for general exploration and economic geology (135); mining and mineral processing (82); geological and mining institute organization (35); mineral economics (22); drilling (23); mining legislation (14); chemists, mineralogists, and other laboratory work (28); geophysics (10); and geochemistry (4).

D | Past Activities of the World Bank in the Mining Sector

THE WORLD BANK has been actively engaged in the financing of mineral resource development for many years.[1] From 1957, when it made its first loan in this sector, through FY75, the IBRD and IDA financed eighteen projects for a total of $610 million, and IFC participated in nine projects with total investment of $119 million. The total cost of mineral projects financed by the Bank through June 30, 1973, was in the order of $2,500 million, and the Bank contribution (approximately $570 million) came to about 23 percent of total project costs. While its own direct contribution to mineral sector investment in developing countries has been only 1 to 1.5 percent, the Bank participated in projects accounting for 6 to 8 percent of total mineral sector expenditures in these countries.

Roughly 45 percent of the commitments through FY73 were made in Africa (Botswana, Congo, Gabon, Guinea, and Mauritania); 37 percent in Latin America (Brazil, Chile, Dominican Republic, and Mexico); 9 percent in India; and the remainder in Greece, Israel, and the Philippines. The largest recipients were Brazil and Mauritania, with $148 million and $66 million, respectively. In two countries, Botswana and the Dominican Republic, projects financed by the Bank accounted for more than 80 percent of total mineral sector investments and made a major contribution to national product and export earnings.

The twenty-two projects financed by the Bank between FY57 and FY73 display differing characteristics. By and large, financing has been limited to the exploitation stage, although some technical

---

1. Here and throughout the World Bank is understood to comprise the International Bank for Reconstruction and Development (IBRD) established in 1945, the International Development Association (IDA) established in 1960, and the International Finance Corporation (IFC) created in 1956.

assistance lending has also been extended for the final stages of exploration and for the preparation of feasibility studies. The loans themselves have been made not only for the mining and beneficiation facilities but also to build townships, road and rail transport facilities, port-loading facilities, and electric power generation. Eleven loans financed production facilities, four loans financed infrastructure facilities, and the remainder covered both production and infrastructure. IBRD loans involved the production of iron ore, nickel, manganese ore, potash, bauxite, aluminum, and coal; IFC investments were for the mining and production of copper, nickel, aluminum, and iron ore. All IFC finance was for private enterprises, in accordance with the corporation's charter; IBRD loans went about equally to the private and the government sectors.

While the main thrust of its effort has been directed toward the financing of production and infrastructure facilities, the Bank has also been active in assisting governments in reviewing the mineral sectors of their economies. This has been done through special sector or subsector surveys undertaken at its own initiative or at the request of member governments. As of June 1973, twenty-five such surveys had been undertaken or were planned; these ranged from an assessment of the mineral potential of Bolivia and Upper Volta to a brief review of the investment needs for geological surveys of a group of African countries. In some cases the objective of these surveys has been to collate the geological knowledge of mineral resources within the country to determine its mineral potential and to identify promising projects. In other cases, such surveys have assisted governments in assessing the effectiveness of administrative arrangements, policies, and legislation in the sector. Many of these surveys, however, have been exploratory in nature so far.

The importance of the mining industry to the economies of many of its member countries has led the Bank to engage regularly in studies of the long-term prospects and problems of individual minerals, especially those of current or potential export interest to the developing countries, both for internal use and for the benefit of its constituents.

E | Profitability of the Mineral Sector

THE DATA are not sufficient for a full analysis of the earnings experience of the mineral sector as a whole. In this appendix, some isolated available statistics are presented in order to provide some background.

In Canada, for example, more than 3,500 mines are currently registered, of which 1,000 are quoted on the Canadian Stock Exchange. Of these stocks, quoted since 1956, only fifty to sixty have paid dividends for any one year; that is, less than 1 percent of all incorporated mining companies pay dividends. A review of the mines making a profit indicated that return on investment has been generally low, ranging from 2.2 percent for gold mines to 9.7 percent for nonmetallic mines.[1]

A survey of mines conducted by the *Financial Post* showed that between 1894 and 1967, 283 Canadan mines paid dividends totaling Can$5,000 million. The largest, INCO, paid more than $1,000 million and INCO with seven others (Cominco, Noranda, Hudson Bay Mining, Hollinger, Falconbridge, McIntyre-Porcupine, and Lake Shore) accounted for two-thirds of total payout. Seven mines paid dividends for over fifty years and account for two-thirds of the total payout, whereas 106 of the 283 paid dividends for one year only.

In 1969, the U.S. Bureau of Mines contracted with Charles River Associates, Inc., for a study on "The Contribution of the Nonfuel Minerals Industry to International Monetary Flows." This study indicated that average annual earnings on U.S. foreign investment fluctuated between 10 and 15 percent of net investment for the period 1954 to 1967. Broken down by region the investment re-

---

1. F. C. Kruger, "Mining: A Business for Professionals Only," *Mining Engineering* (September 1969), p. 85.

turned less than 10 percent in Canada but up to 25 percent in Latin America. (See figure E.1.) Furthermore, income returned to the parent companies, although averaging 60 percent of earnings from the Canadian investments, was close to 100 percent of earnings on the Latin American investment. This is clearly indicative of the additional return required by the companies to compensate for the higher political risks.

Fortune Magazine's tables on the top 1,000 U.S. corporations and top 200 non-U.S. corporations for 1970 and 1973 provide a brief overview of how the larger and more successful of the mining companies fare compared to the large companies in other sectors. Of the top 1,000 U.S. corporations only about thirty are mining companies (twenty in the top 500 and ten in the second 500). When we look at industry medians we find that mining companies clearly display the highest return in terms of profit on sales, the ratio varying between 10 and 15 percent. The return for individual companies varied up to 35 percent, with a few at less than one percent.

On the other hand, as mining is a capital intensive industry, returns in terms of profits on assets, or profits on equity, compare much less favorably. In recent years, profits on total assets, while remaining slightly above the average for all industries, have been well below those of many industries. Furthermore, the very conservative debt to equity ratios maintained by most of the mining companies has meant that mining is barely able to maintain a return (profit on equity) above the average for all industries. Some of the individual companies display a return on equity of up to 20 percent, but rarely up to the 30 and 40 percent common in companies of other industries; in most cases, returns lie between 10 and 15 percent, and for a notable number they lie below 5 percent.

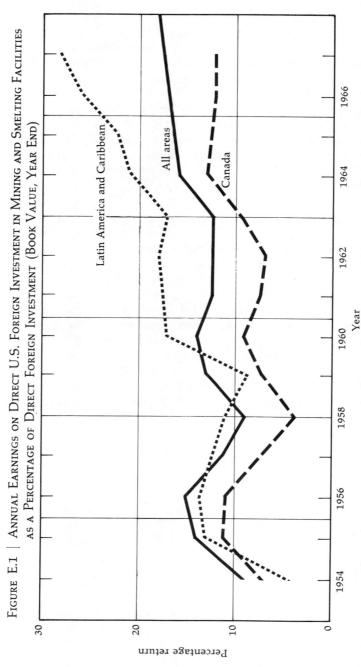

FIGURE E.1 | ANNUAL EARNINGS ON DIRECT U.S. FOREIGN INVESTMENT IN MINING AND SMELTING FACILITIES AS A PERCENTAGE OF DIRECT FOREIGN INVESTMENT (BOOK VALUE, YEAR END)

Note: Earnings defined as the sum of the U.S. share in net earnings (or losses) of foreign corporations and branch profits after foreign taxes and before U.S. taxes.

Source: U.S. Department of Commerce, Office of Business Economics, *Survey of Current Business* (October 1968), p. 26; and *Balance of Payments Statistics Supplement,* pp. 190, 193, 212, and 215.

F | Classification and Reliability of Reserves and Resources

WITHIN THE INDUSTRY, mineral resources are classified into reserves —proven, indicated, and inferred—and resources. Several variations of this classification exist, such as: measured, indicated, inferred; or proven, probable, possible. A mineral resource is not classified as a reserve or, more specifically, an orebody until there is sufficient indication that its size and grade are sufficient for it to be economically exploitable. The common distinction among the subgroups is explained below.

Proven reserves: These are reserves that have been blocked out or delineated in three dimensions, with sufficient sampling intensity and accuracy to allow the exploration crew to estimate size and grade of the deposit with a reasonable degree of certainty. *Reasonable degree of certainty* is a commercial term which varies between operator, mineral, and type of orebody. Hence, a level of knowledge sufficient to classify reserves as proven in one deposit may not be sufficient for another deposit.

Indicated reserves: These are reserves that have been partially delineated and computations of quantity and grade made by extrapolation from assay and sampling results. Before being classified as proven, they require additional sampling and perhaps the collection of bulk samples to verify sampling and measurement methodology.

Inferred reserves: These are reserves inferred from limited geological and sampling information. They may be inferred by extrapolating from proven or indicated reserves solely on the basis of knowledge of continuous rock structures. The degree of certainty with which the quantity and grade of the reserves can be computed is very low.

In its most recent appraisal of U.S. and world resources,[1] the

---

1. U.S. Department of the Interior, *United States Mineral Resources,* Geological Survey Paper no. 820 (Washington, D.C., 1973).

U.S. Geological Survey has adopted a new classification which divides resources into three categories—conditional, hypothetical, and speculative. *Conditional resources* are defined as specific *identified* mineral deposits whose contained minerals are not profitably recoverable with existing technology and economic conditions. *Hypothetical resources* are undiscovered mineral deposits, whether of recoverable or subeconomic grade, that are geologically predictable as existing in known districts. *Speculative resources* are undiscovered mineral deposits, whether of recoverable or subeconomic grade, that may exist in unknown districts or in unconventional form.

Unlike earlier definitions, the classification outlined above places less emphasis on levels of economic recoverability and more emphasis on evaluating the undiscovered, because of the conviction that the long-range potential lies in resources that have not yet been discovered. The relation of the four principal categories under this classification is illustrated schematically in figure F.1.

Published reserves have no uniform classification and are not uniformly reliable. Some entities announce only those reserves that are proven, others those that are proven and indicated, and still others announce all three categories proven, indicated, and inferred. In some cases announcements are highly speculative (a recent announcement in Australia, for instance, referred initially to enormous, very high-grade uranium deposits, but the assessment was later discounted and modified to medium size, slightly above average grade). In other cases the announcements are extremely conservative. The latter is often the case for operating companies, which often announce only proven reserves, yet restrict their exploration activity to proving up sufficient reserves for adequate mine planning. Some governments require a minimum rate of exploitation based upon the size of the reserves; hence, companies purposely understate reserves. Other factors of equal importance when reviewing published reserves are the mineral price and technology assumptions used in the computation of reserves. Whether a mineral occurrence is regarded merely as an occurrence or a reserve will depend upon the economic feasibility of exploiting the reserves. In some cases, what is merely an interesting mineral occurrence (but under existing prices and technology is noneconomic) is announced as a reserve.

All these factors point to the extreme caution that must be used when using published reserves to draw regional and global conclusions. It is relevant to note that a 1971 survey of eighty-one mineral commodities by the U.S. Bureau of Mines indicated that roughly four-fifths of the data on reserves (even on U.S. reserves)

FIGURE F.1 | CLASSIFICATION OF MINERAL RESOURCES

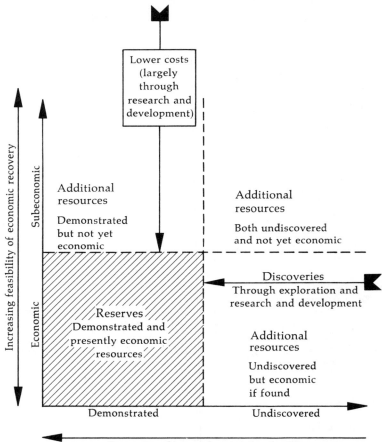

Source: Jean-Paul Drolet, "The Demand for Canada's Mineral Resources," paper presented at the International Symposium on Canada's Nonrenewable Resources, Toronto, March 25, 1974.

are poor, having a confidence level of 65 percent. (See table F.1.)[2]

2. This account barely scratches the surface. For a comprehensive review and analysis, see Resources for the Future, John J. Schanz, principal investigator, *Resource Terminology: An Examination of Concepts and Terms and*

TABLE F.1 | APPARENT RELIABILITY OF DATA ON
EIGHTY-ONE MINERAL COMMODITIES

Item	Data classification			
	Good[a]	Fair[b]	Poor[c]	
	(number of commodities)		(number of commodities)	(percentage)
United States				
Supply				
Production	54	2	25	31
Stocks	34	6	41	51
Imports	54	0	27	33
Exports	37	4	40	49
Reserves	13	2	66	81
Demand				
Consumption by end use	28	3	50	62
Total consumption	54	3	33	41
Rest of the World				
Supply				
Production	6	48	27	33
Reserves	4	10	67	83
Demand				
Total consumption	2	29	50	62

a. Amount estimated, less than 15 percent; confidence level greater than 85 percent.
b. Amount estimated, less than 35 percent; confidence level greater than 65 percent.
c. Amount estimated, more than 35 percent; confidence level less than 65 percent.
Source: U.S. Congress, Hearings before the Joint Committee on Defense Production, *Potential Shortages of Ores, Metals, and Minerals, Fuels and Energy Resources, etc.* 92nd Cong., 1st sess., August 2, 1971, p. 61.

Recommendations for Improvement (Palo Alto, California: Electric Power Research Institute, August 1975). The study reproduces and reviews several classifications, including the joint U.S. Geological Survey–Bureau of Mines classification recently adopted in a landmark agreement. A good exposition of the complexities of the subject can be found in Jan Zwartendyk, "Problems in Interpretation of Data on Mineral Resources, Production, and Consumption," *Natural Resources Forum* 1 (October 1976): 7–15.

G | Estimates of Reserves and Adequacy

THE RESERVE AND OUTPUT ESTIMATES in the following tables are from the U.S. Bureau of Mines, *Mineral Facts and Problems*, Bulletin 650, 1970; *Commodity Data Summaries*, 1971; *Minerals Yearbook* (various issues); and *Metal Statistics*, 1971. Volume estimates were converted into value terms solely for the purpose of estimating regional distribution and to permit aggregation. As noted in the text, the true value of a deposit cannot be determined until all the ore is mined.

The demand assumptions used in measuring adequacy (reserve life) are from Leonard L. Fischman and Hans H. Landsberg, "Adequacy of Nonfuel Minerals and Forest Resources," in Ronald G. Ridker, ed., *Population, Resources and the Environment* (Washington, D.C.: U.S. Government Printing Office, 1972). The Fischman and Landsberg estimates for projected growth in world consumption compare with the following 1970 growth estimates from the U.S. Bureau of Mines (all differences reflect differences in the estimates for the United States):

Mineral	U.S. Bureau of Mines[a] 1968–2000	Fischman and Landsberg 1968–2020
	(percentage a year)	
Bauxite	6.4	6.4
Chromium	2.6	2.7
Cobalt	1.5	1.9
Copper	4.6	4.6
Iron	1.8	2.3
Lead	2.0	2.3
Manganese	2.9	2.9
Molybdenum	4.5	4.7
Nickel	3.2	3.2
Silver	2.7	2.7
Tin	1.1	1.2
Tungsten	2.5	3.5
Zinc	2.9	3.0

a. Average of high and low estimates.

TABLE G.1 | DISTRIBUTION OF WORLD MINERAL RESERVES BY VALUE AT COMMON STATE OF TRANSFER IN THE WORLD MARKET

| | World reserves | | | Value of reserves by region | | | | | |
| | | | | Developed countries | | Developing countries | | Centrally planned economies | |
Mineral	Quantity	Unit value (dollars)	Gross value US$1,000 million	US$1,000 million	Percent of world	US$1,000 million	Percent of world	US$1,000 million	Percent of world
Iron ore	100,000 million short tons of recoverable iron	15[a]	1,500	525	35	450	30	525	35
Phosphate rock	21,800 million short tons of P content	50[a]	1,090	340	31	570	53	180	16
Aluminum	1,200 million short tons of Al content	500[a]	600	210	35	330	55	60	10
Potash	1,310 million short tons of K_2O content	25[a]	325	154	47	21	7	150	46
Copper	320 million short tons of Cu content	1,000[a]	320	109	34	160	50	51	16
Asbestos	Not accurately delineated	100[a]	250–350	—[b]	—[b]	—[b]	—[b]	—[b]	—[b]
Magnesium	2,600 million short tons of Mg content	75[a]	195	15	8	4	2	176	50
Nickel	147,000 million pounds of Ni content	1.25[c]	184	69	38	88	48	27	14
Titanium	147 million short tons of Ti content	900[a]	132	79	60	31	23	22	17
Diatomite	2,000 million short tons	58[a]	116	—[d]	—[d]	—[d]	—[d]	—[d]	—[d]
Chromium	775 million short tons of Cr content	100[a]	77	53	75	18	23	1	5

Mineral	Units	Price						
Columbium	20,500 million pounds of contained Co	2.6[e]	53	6	12	29	54	18	34
Manganese	728 million short tons of Mn content	55[a]	40	19	47	12	31	9	22
Zinc	124 million short tons of Zn content	300[a]	37	24	66	6	16	7	18
Sulfur[e]	2,100 million long tons of contained S	30[a]	62	13	21	37	60	12	19
Lead	95 million short tons of Pb content	270[a]	26	18	68	5	21	3	11
Tin	4.3 million long tons of contained Sn	3,750[f]	16	1	4	12	80	3	16
Silver	5,500 million troy ounces of Ag content	2.2[g]	12	4	35	4	29	4	36
Feldspar	1,000 million long tons	10[f]	10	—[d]	—[d]	—[d]	—[d]	—[d]	—[d]
Fluorspar	39 million short tons of fluorine content	100[f]	4	—[h]	—[h]	—[h]	—[h]	—[h]	—[h]
Tungsten	2,800 million pounds of WO$_3$	0.45[e]	1.4	negligible	5	negligible	5	1	90
Total minerals				1,639	35	1,787	38	1,249	27
Total minerals (excluding iron ore)				1,114	35	1,337	42	724	23
Total metallic minerals (excluding iron ore)				607	36	710	42	382	22
Total metallic minerals (excluding iron ore, copper, and aluminum)				288	37	220	28	271	35

Note: Value of reserves is based upon estimated long-term price of the mineral, at the commonly used points of transfer in the international market. A more representative price would be international market price of ore or concentrates. However, data are inadequate to compute all values in these terms.

a. Per short ton.
b. No details available, but major reserves in South Africa.
c. Per pound.
d. No details available, but United States alone has sufficient reserves to supply total world needs for more than thirty years.
e. Includes petroleum and natural gas as sources.
f. Per long ton.
g. Per ounce.

TABLE G.2 | WORLD RESERVES OF SELECTED MINERALS

Mineral	Major reserves	Major producers[a]	Value of world output, 1968[b]
	(percent of world total)		(millions of dollars)
Minerals with ample reserves			
Reserve life 150 years plus			
Columbium	Latin America (45) Soviet Union (35) Africa (10) Canada (10)	Brazil (6) Canada (26) Nigeria (12)	29
Phosphorus	Morocco (42) United States (31), Soviet Union (12)	United States (42) Soviet Union (24) Morocco (13)	835
Potash	Centrally planned economies (45) Canada (38) Germany, Fed. Rep. of (7)	Centrally planned economies (19) Canada (17) Western Europe (27) United States (15)	370
Reserve life 120 to 150 years			
Magnesium	China, People's Rep. of (53) North Korea (31) New Zealand (6)	United States (45) Soviet Union (22) Norway (16)	115
Reserve life 100 to 110 years			
Chromium	South Africa (74) South Rhodesia (22)	Centrally planned economies (40) South Africa (23) Philippines (9)	190
Reserve life 90 to 100 years			
Feldspar	not available— widespread	United States (30) Europe (35) Soviet Union (12)	55
Iron	Soviet Union (32) South America (19) Canada (12) Australia (10)	Soviet Union (26) Western Europe (17) United States (11) Australia (8) Canada (6)	6,190
Vanadium	Soviet Union (59) South Africa (20) Australia (15)	United States (49) South Africa (25) Finland (13)	60

Table G.2 | *Continued.*

Mineral	Major reserves	Major producers[a]	Value of world output, 1968[b]
	(percent of world total)		*(millions of dollars)*
	Reserves presenting no serious problem		
Reserve life 50 to 60 years			
Cobalt	Zaïre (31) New Caledonia (18) Zambia (16)	Zaïre (59) Zambia (9) Canada (8) Morocco (4)	110
Nickel	Cuba (24) New Caledonia (22) Canada (14) Soviet Union (14)	Canada (40) Soviet Union (22) New Caledonia (19)	1,100
Reserve life 40 to 50 years			
Asbestos	not available— widespread	Canada (50) Soviet Union (30) South Africa (8)	323
Manganese	South Africa (38) Soviet Union (25) Gabon (12)	Soviet Union (38) South Africa (12) Brazil (12) India (9)	475
Molybdenum	United States (58) Soviet Union (18) Chile (16)	United States (70) Canada (21)	not available
Reserve life 30 to 40 years			
Antimony	China, People's Rep. of (50) South Africa (6) Soviet Union (6)	South Africa (25) China, People's Rep. of (20) Bolivia (18) Soviet Union (10)	66
Bauxite	Guinea (34) Australia (34) Surinam (11) Jamaica (5) Soviet Union (3)	Jamaica (20) Australia (15) Surinam (11) Soviet Union (10) Guyana (7)	340
Sulfur	Near East and South Asia (45) Eastern Europe (16) United States (12)	United States (39) Centrally planned economies (21) Canada (20)	710
Titanium	Norway (20) United States (17) Canada (17) Soviet Union (17)	United States (60) Japan (30)	60

TABLE G.2 | *Continued.*

Mineral	Major reserves	Major producers[a]	Value of world output, 1968[b]
		(percent of world total)	(millions of dollars)

Reserves that are tight or critical

Reserve life 20 to 25 years

Barite	United States (40) China, People's Rep. of (13) Other centrally planned economies (15) Germany, Fed., Rep. of	United States (23) Western Europe (33) Centrally planned economies (6)	35
Bismuth	Japan (45) Latin America (21) United States (13) Centrally planned economies (10)	Latin America (48) India (18) Canada (8)	28
Copper	United States (28) Chile (19) Soviet Union (13) Zambia (10) Peru (8)	United States (23) Soviet Union (15) Zambia (13) Chile (12) Canada (8)	7,740
Tungsten	China, People's Rep. of (74) United States (7) Korea, Rep. of (4)	China, People's Rep. of (24) Soviet Union (20) United States (13) North Korea (7) Korea, Rep. of (6)	105

Reserve life 15 to 20 years

Lead	United States (37) Canada (13) Australia (12)	United States (14) Australia (14) Soviet Union (14) Canada (9)	775
Tin	Thailand (32) Malaysia (14) Indonesia (12) Bolivia (10)	Malaysia (32) Bolivia (13) Soviet Union (12) Thailand (9)	750
Zinc	United States (27) Canada (20) Western Europe (11) Eastern Europe (11)	Canada (22) Soviet Union (12) Australia (10) United States (9) Peru (6)	1,450

TABLE G.2 | *Continued.*

Mineral	Major reserves	Major producers[a]	Value of world output, 1968[b]
			(millions of dollars)
	(percent of world total)		

Reserves that are tight or critical (continued)

Reserve life under 15 years

Mineral	Major reserves	Major producers[a]	Value of world output, 1968[b]
Fluorspar	not available—reserves mainly in Mexico and western Europe	Mexico (27) Western Europe (27) Centrally planned economies (20) Thailand (7) United States (6)	81
Mercury	Centrally planned economies (35) Spain (31) Italy (22)	Western Europe (50) Soviet Union (17) United States (11) China, People's Rep. of (9)	125
Silver	Centrally planned economies (36) United States (24) Mexico (13) Canada (12)	Mexico (15) Canada (15) United States (14) Soviet Union (13) Peru (12)	595

a. In the late 1960s.
b. At the commonly accepted point of transfer in world markets.

Several revised estimates of some components of the demand and supply picture have appeared recently. In most cases, especially on the demand side, the revisions have been minor. While major new resource discoveries have been reported (especially in the Amazon region of Brazil, Oceania, Siberia, and south central Africa), these have not yet been reflected in the official statistics. Some sources give nickel and bauxite figures significantly higher than those in the following tables. Most mineral prices are higher than in 1970, despite the recession; some (like phosphate rock) having attained what appear to be new plateaus. On this score alone, many of the reserve estimates can be considered conservative.

TABLE G.3 | COMMERCIALLY RECOVERABLE RESOURCES OF
SELECTED ORES UNDER SELECTED PRICE ASSUMPTIONS

					Reserves		
Mineral	Price[a]	Index[b]	World[c]	Index[b]	Developed countries	Developing countries	Centrally planned economies
Bauxite	0.27	100	3,280	100	38.1	56.6	5.3
	0.31	115	3,420	104	37.8	56.2	6.2
	0.34	126	3,705	113	37.5	55.0	7.5
	0.37	137	4,695	143	35.9	52.7	11.4
Copper	0.50	100	296	100	37.3	47.2	15.5
	0.60	120	332	112	38.5	47.3	14.2
	0.80	160	402	136	36.8	50.1	13.1
	1.00	200	516	174	38.8	49.5	11.5
Iron ore	15.65	100	97	100	35.6	29.1	35.3
	18.65	119	129	133	34.8	32.2	33.0
	21.65	138	206	212	40.1	28.7	31.2
	n.a.[d]	n.a.	n.a.	n.a.	n.a.	n.a.	n.a.
Tin[e]	1.64	100	4,180	100	3.7	79.2	17.1
	2.00	122	5,492	131	4.7	72.3	23.0
	2.50	152	7,465	179	6.1	68.3	25.6
	3.00	183	9,133	218	6.5	66.5	27.0

a. Prices in dollars a pound, constant 1969 dollars.
b. First price assumption equals 100.
c. Volume (metal content) in millions of short tons, except tin.
d. n.a. means not available.
e. Volume in thousands of long tons.

H | Estimates of Production, Consumption, and Trade

THE DATA presented in the following tables were compiled from statistics in various issues of Metallgesellschaft A.G., *Metal Statistics*; United Nations, *Statistical Yearbook*; United Kingdom Overseas Geological Survey, Mine Resources Division, *Statistical Summary of the Mineral Industry*; United Nations, *Yearbook of International Trade Statistics*; and World Bank, *Commodity Price Trends*. The estimates cover nine major minerals: bauxite and aluminum, copper, iron ore, lead, manganese ore, nickel, phosphate rock, tin, and zinc.

Tables H.1 and H.2 give mine production and estimates of consumption and net trade in terms of minehead value (value of the ore and concentrate). Tables H.3 through H.5 give mining plus processing output and estimates of consumption and net trade in terms of the value of the final product.

Table H.6 presents estimates of the degree of processing conducted in individual regions, defined as the ratio of the value of mineral produced over the value of mineral mined if processed through to its final stage, namely, metal ingot. The ratio was computed as:

$$\text{Degree of processing} = \frac{A - B}{C - B} \times 100,$$

where A = value produced (mining and processing value); B = mine value of production; and C = value produced, had all ore mined been processed to refined metal or product, except that iron ore upgraded to be suitable for blast furnace feed (sinterized or pelletized), ferromanganese, and superphosphate fertilizer were taken as representing the processed product.

The minerals produced, consumed, and traded are not uniform in grade and quality. In addition, for a number of minerals there is no international market price as such, and no prices approximating mine value. Therefore, rough estimates had to be used in a number of cases.

TABLE H.1 | MINING OUTPUT AND ESTIMATED MINEHEAD VALUE OF CONSUMPTION AND NET TRADE, BY REGION, NINE MAJOR MINERALS COMBINED, 1950, 1960, AND 1970[a]

Region	Production			Consumption			Net exports (imports)		
	1950	1960	1970	1950	1960	1970	1950	1960	1970
				($1,000 millions of dollars)					
Developed market economies	3.1	4.4	7.3	4.6	7.0	11.6	(1.5)	(2.6)	(4.3)
Developing market economies	1.8	3.5	5.3	0.2	0.5	0.8	1.6	3.0	4.5
Centrally planned economies	0.8	2.5	4.4	0.9	2.6	4.6	(0.1)	(0.1)	(0.2)
Total	5.7	10.4	17.0	5.7	10.1	15.56		0.3	
Developed market economies				(percent)					
United States and Canada	39	27	25	47	29	26	(17)	(5)	(1)
Western Europe	11	10	7	30	34	27	(65)	(71)	(73)
Japan	1	2	1	1	5	12	(17)	(71)	(89)
Australia and South Africa	3	4	8	2	2	3	32	47	60
Total developed	54	43	41	80	70	68	(33)	(39)	(39)
Developing market economies	32	33	33	4	5	6	87	86	83
Centrally planned economies	14	24	26	16	25	26	9	6	2
Total	100	100	100	100	100	100			

a. See explanation at the beginning of the appendix.

229

TABLE H.2 | MINING OUTPUT AND ESTIMATED MINEHEAD VALUE OF CONSUMPTION AND NET TRADE, BY REGION AND BY MINERAL, 1950, 1960, AND 1970[a]

(millions of dollars)

Item	Production			Consumption			Net exports (imports)		
	1950	1960	1970	1950	1960	1970	1950	1960	1970
Bauxite and alumina									
United States and Canada	10	15	16	42	129	302	(34)	(114)	(286)
Western Europe	9	26	41	10	62	199	(1)	(36)	(158)
Japan	0	4	0	1	8	43	(1)	(4)	(43)
Australia and South Africa	0	1	158	0	0	45	0	1	113
Total developed market economies	19	46	215	53	199	589	(34)	(153)	(374)
Developing market economies	34	168	443	0	25	98	34	143	345
Centrally planned economies	10	39	68	10	38	66	0	1	2
Total	63	253	726	63	262	753	0	9	(27)
Distribution (percentage)[b]									
Developed	30.2	18.2	29.6	83.9	76.0	78.2	(5.4)	(76.8)	(63.4)
Developing	54.0	66.4	61.0	0	9.5	13.0	100.0	85.1	77.8
Centrally planned economies	15.8	15.4	9.4	16.1	14.5	8.8	0	0	2.9
Total	100.0	100.0	100.0	100.0	100.0	100.0			
Growth rates (percentage)									
Developed		9.2[c]	16.8[d]		14.6[e]	11.5[d]			

Developing		17.1	10.0		0	14.9			
Centrally planned economies		14.9	6.0		14.8	6.1			
Total		15.0	11.2		15.5	11.3			
Copper									
United States and Canada	1,018	1,318	2,075	1,119	1,020	1,772	(101)	298	303
Western Europe	109	124	201	748	1,548	2,089	(639)	(1,424)	(1,888)
Japan	38	85	114	12	233	698	26	(148)	(584)
Australia and South Africa	47	153	315	38	83	133	9	70	182
Total developed market economies	1,212	1,680	2,705	1,917	2,884	4,692	(705)	(1,204)	(1,987)
Developing market economies	975	1,778	2,239	108	169	224	867	1,609	2,015
Centrally planned economies	228	598	1,136	283	702	1,229	(55)	(104)	(93)
Total	2,415	4,056	6,080	2,308	3,755	6,145	107	302	65
Distribution (percentage)[b]									
Developed	50.2	41.6	44.5	83.0	76.9	76.4	36.7	41.7	42.3
Developing	40.4	43.8	36.8	4.7	4.5	3.6	89.0	90.4	89.9
Centrally planned economies	9.4	14.6	18.7	12.3	18.7	20.0	24.1	17.5	7.5
Total	100.0	100.0	100.0	100.0	100.0	100.0	4.5	7.5	1.0

a. See explanation at the beginning of the appendix.
b. Net exports as a percentage of production, net imports as a percentage of consumption.
c. Growth rate 1950–60.
d. Growth rate 1960–70.

TABLE H.2 | Continued.

Item	Production			Consumption			Net exports (imports)		
	1950	1960	1970	1950	1960	1970	1950	1960	1970
Copper (continued)									
Growth rates (percentage)									
Developed		3.3[c]	5.0[d]		4.2[c]	4.8[d]			
Developing		6.2	2.6		4.6	3.0			
Centrally planned economies		10.1	6.6		9.5	5.4			
Total		5.3	4.1		5.0	5.1			
Iron ore									
United States and Canada	671	767	1,014	714	989	1,027	(43)	(222)	(13)
Western Europe	367	675	689	384	865	1,339	(17)	(190)	(650)
Japan	7	21	13	16	118	858	(9)	(845)	(702)
Australia and South Africa	27	65	494	27	59	104	0	6	390
Total developed market economies	1,072	1,528	2,210	1,141	2,031	3,328	(69)	(503)	(1,118)
Developing market economies	127	657	1,339	59	150	221	68	507	1,118
Centrally planned economies	338	1,152	2,106	338	1,156	2,106	1	4	0
Total	1,537	3,337	5,655	1,538	3,337	5,655	0	0	0
Distribution (percentage)[b]									
Developed	69.7	45.8	39.1	74.2	61.0	58.9	(6.0)	(24.8)	(33.5)
Developing	8.3	19.7	23.7	3.8	4.5	3.9	54.0	77.4	83.4

Centrally planned economies	22.0	34.5	37.2	22.0	34.5	37.2	0	0.3	0
Total	100.0	100.0	100.0	100.0	100.0	100.0	0	0	0
Growth rates (percentage)									
Developed	3.6[c]	3.7[d]		5.9[c]	5.1[d]				
Developing	17.8	7.2		9.8	4.0				
Centrally planned economies	13.0	6.2		13.0	6.3				
Total	8.1	5.4		8.1	5.4				
Lead									
United States and Canada	107	81	172	168	135	174	(61)	(54)	(2)
Western Europe	51	73	91	130	217	267	(79)	(144)	(176)
Japan	2	8	13	5	20	41	(3)	(12)	(28)
Australia and South Africa	44	62	104	11	13	18	33	49	86
Total developed market economies	204	224	380	314	385	500	(111)	(161)	(120)
Developing market economies	97	129	125	18	18	54	79	111	71
Centrally planned economies	32	116	172	37	113	196	(5)	3	(24)
Total	333	469	677	369	516	750	(36)	(47)	(73)
Distribution (percentage)[b]									
Developed	61.2	47.7	56.1	85.0	74.5	66.7	(35.4)	(42.0)	(24.0)

a. See explanation at the beginning of the appendix.
b. Net exports as a percentage of production, net imports as a percentage of consumption.
c. Growth rate 1950–60.
d. Growth rate 1960–70.

Table H.2 | Continued.

Item	Production 1950	Production 1960	Production 1970	Consumption 1950	Consumption 1960	Consumption 1970	Net exports (imports) 1950	Net exports (imports) 1960	Net exports (imports) 1970
			Lead (continued)						
Developing	29.2	27.5	18.5	4.9	3.5	7.2	81.2	86.0	56.8
Centrally planned economies	9.6	24.8	25.4	10.1	22.0	26.1	(15.5)	2.4	(12.2)
Total	100.0	100.0	100.0	100.0	100.0	100.0			
Growth rates (percentage)									
Developed		0.9[e]	4.8[d]		2.1[e]	3.0[d]			
Developing		3.2	0		0	12.0			
Centrally planned economies		13.9	4.2		11.7	5.6			
Total		3.5	4.0		3.4	4.1			
			Manganese						
United States and Canada	4	3	3	62	71	104	(58)	(68)	(101)
Western Europe	1	2	2	30	66	102	(29)	(64)	(100)
Japan	3	7	5	5	13	100	(2)	(6)	(95)
Australia and South Africa	20	28	94	3	4	0	(17)	(24)	94
Total developed market economies	28	40	104	100	154	306	(72)	(114)	(202)
Developing market economies	72	124	168	2	7	7	70	107	161

234

Centrally planned economies	84	181	211	83	173	179	1	8	32
Total	184	345	483	185	344	492	1	1	(9)
Distribution (percentage)[b]									
Developed	15.1	11.7	21.5	53.9	44.8	62.2	(72.0)	(74.1)	(66.0)
Developing	39.2	36.0	34.8	1.1	4.8	1.4	97.4	86.9	95.8
Centrally planned economies	45.7	52.3	43.7	45.0	50.4	36.4	1.5	4.0	15.1
Total	100.0	100.0	100.0	100.0	100.0	100.0			
Growth rates (percentage)									
Developed		4.1[c]	9.2[d]		4.6[c]	6.4[d]			
Developing		5.6	3.2		23.5	0			
Centrally planned economies		8.0	1.5		7.7	0.3			
Total		6.5	3.3		6.5	3.7			
Nickel									
United States and Canada	163	297	420	135	148	225	28	149	195
Western Europe	1	3	7	48	136	252	(47)	(133)	(245)
Japan	0	0	0	1	25	142	(1)	(25)	(142)
Australia and South Africa	7	81	259	1	3	14	6	78	245
Total developed market economies	171	381	686	185	312	633	(14)	69	(53)

a. See explanation at the beginning of the appendix.
b. Net exports as a percentage of production, net imports as a percentage of consumption.
c. Growth rate 1950–60.
d. Growth rate 1960–70.

TABLE H.2 | Continued.

Item	Production			Consumption			Net exports (imports)		
	1950	1960	1970	1950	1960	1970	1950	1960	1970
Nickel (continued)									
Developing market economies	0	22	106	0	2	12	0	20	94
Centrally planned economies	43	89	168	43	107	187	(14)	(18)	(19)
Total	214	492	960	228	421	832	(14)	71	128
Distribution (percentage)[b]									
Developed	80.0	77.5	71.5	81.2	74.2	76.1	(7.4)	17.9	(11.5)
Developing	0	4.5	11.0	0	0.5	1.4	75.0	89.0	89.1
Centrally planned economies	20.0	18.0	17.5	18.8	25.3	22.5	(1.4)	(16.5)	(10.7)
Total	100.0	100.0	100.0	100.0	100.0	100.0	(6.4)	14.3	(0.6)
Growth rates (percentage)									
Developed		8.4[c]	6.2[d]		5.4[c]	7.2[d]			
Developing		0	16.4		19.1	17.8			
Centrally planned economies		7.6	6.7		9.5	6.0			
Total		8.7	6.9		6.4	7.0			
Phosphorus									
United States and Canada	106	167	327	93	129	250	13	38	77
Western Europe	1	0	1	68	117	180	(67)	(117)	(179)
Japan	0	0	0	11	23	29	(11)	(23)	(29)

Tin

Australia and South Africa	0	2	12	23	30	27	(23)	(28)	(15)
Total developed market economies	107	169	340	195	299	486	(88)	(128)	(146)
Developing market economies	91	161	250	4	30	93	87	131	157
Centrally planned economies	27	77	214	27	79	225	1	(2)	(11)
Total	225	407	804	226	408	804	0	0	0
Distribution (percentage)[b]									
Developed	47.5	41.6	42.3	86.3	73.2	66.2	(44.8)	(43.2)	(30.0)
Developing	40.4	39.6	31.1	1.7	7.4	6.0	96.0	81.0	62.8
Centrally planned economies	12.1	18.8	26.6	12.0	19.4	27.8	0	2.7	(5.1)
Total	100.0	100.0	100.0	100.0	100.0	100.0			
Growth rates (percentage)									
Developed		4.7[c]	7.1[d]		4.4[c]	5.5[d]			
Developing		5.9	4.6		22.5	12.0			
Centrally planned economies		10.9	11.0		11.5	11.3			
Total		6.1	7.1		6.1	7.0			
United States and Canada	0	0	0	175	128	133	175	(128)	(133)
Western Europe	6	5	6	125	155	156	119	(150)	(150)

a. See explanation at the beginning of the appendix.
b. Net exports as a percentage of production, net imports as a percentage of consumption.
c. Growth rate 1950–60.
d. Growth rate 1960–70.

TABLE H.2 | Continued.

Item	Production			Consumption			Net exports (imports)		
	1950	1960	1970	1950	1960	1970	1950	1960	1970
			Tin (continued)						
Japan	1	2	2	11	33	58	(10)	(31)	(56)
Australia and South Africa	6	8	25	9	14	14	(3)	(6)	11
Total developed market economies	13	15	33	320	330	361	(307)	(315)	(328)
Developing market economies	362	299	392	29	33	39	333	266	353
Centrally planned economies	28	117	115	39	93	140	(11)	(24)	(25)
Total	403	431	540	388	456	540	15	(25)	
Distribution (percentage)[b]									
Developed	3.2	3.5	5.6	82.5	72.4	67.4	(95.8)	(95.5)	(92.0)
Developing	89.7	69.4	72.9	7.5	7.2	7.9	91.9	88.6	88.7
Centrally planned economies	7.1	27.1	21.4	10.0	20.4	24.7	(27.1)	(20.0)	(17.4)
Total	100.0	100.0	100.0	100.0	100.0	100.0	3.7	(5.9)	(4.5)
Growth rates (percentage)									
Developed		1.6[c]	8.1[d]		negligible[e]	1.0[d]			
Developing		negligible	2.8		1.5	2.0			
Centrally planned economies		15.2	0		9.2	4.1			
Total		0.6	2.4		1.6	1.7			

Zinc

United States and Canada	180	160	340	203	177	248	(23)	(16)	(108)
Western Europe	58	91	153	142	229	321	(84)	(138)	(168)
Japan	10	29	59	11	40	131	(1)	(11)	(72)
Australia and South Africa	36	56	112	14	25	35	22	30	77
Total developed market economies	284	336	664	370	471	735	(86)	(135)	(171)
Developing market economies	95	160	216	14	42	77	81	118	139
Centrally planned economies	53	152	242	52	134	220	1	18	22
Total	432	648	1,122	436	647	1,032	(4)	1	(10)
Distribution (percentage)[b]									
Developed	65.9	51.8	59.2	84.6	72.8	71.2	(23.5)	(28.7)	(23.2)
Developing	21.9	24.7	19.2	3.3	6.5	7.5	85.0	74.4	64.6
Centrally planned economies	12.2	23.5	21.6	12.1	20.7	21.3	7.7	11.8	9.1
Total	100.0	100.0	100.0	100.0	100.0	100.0	(1.3)	0	2.6
Growth rates (percentage)									
Developed		1.7[c]	7.0[d]		2.5[c]	4.6[d]			
Developing		5.4	2.9		11.4	6.5			
Centrally planned economies		11.2	4.7		9.9	5.0			
Total		4.2	5.7		4.0	4.8			

a. See explanation at the beginning of the appendix.
b. Net exports as a percentage of production, net imports as a percentage of consumption.
c. Growth rate 1950–60.
d. Growth rate 1960–70.

TABLE H.3 | MINING AND PROCESSING OUTPUT AND ESTIMATED FINAL PRODUCT VALUE OF CONSUMPTION AND NET TRADE, BY REGION, NINE MAJOR MINERALS COMBINED, 1950, 1960, AND 1970[a]

Region	Value of mining and processing output			Consumption			Net exports (imports)		
	1950	1960	1970	1950	1960	1970	1950	1960	1970
	(thousand millions of U.S. dollars)								
Developed market economies	6.3	10.1	16.9	8.1	12.9	21.4	(1.81)	(2.81)	(4.5)
Developing market economies	2.4	4.5	7.0	0.4	0.8	1.9	2.0	3.6	5.11
Centrally planned economies	1.6	4.7	8.3	1.7	4.9	8.4	(0.11)	(0.1)	(0.1)
Total	10.3	19.3	32.2	10.2	18.6	31.7	0.07	0.72	0.5
Developed market economies	(percentage)								
United States and Canada	41.8	31.4	28.5	46.9	29.5	27.9	(11.0)	6.2	1.9
Western Europe	14.9	14.6	13.1	28.7	32.5	26.6	(47.9)	(55.1)	(50.5)
Japan	1.4	2.6	4.7	1.5	4.9	10.9	(4.8)	(46.9)	(57.4)
Australia and South Africa	3.1	3.6	5.7	2.4	2.4	3.0	22.9	32.9	47.1
Total developed	61.2	52.2	52.0	79.5	69.3	68.4	(22.9)	24.7	(21.0)
Developing market economies (percentage)	23.1	23.2	22.2	3.7	4.6	5.4	84.0	80.4	
Centrally planned economies (percentage)	15.7	24.6	25.8	16.8	26.1	26.2	(7.0)	(5.8)	(1.1)
Total	100.0	100.0	100.0	100.0	100.0	100.0			

a. See explanation at the beginning of appendix.

TABLE H.4 | Mining and Processing Output and Estimated Final Product Value of Consumption and Net Trade, by Region, and by Mineral, 1950, 1960, and 1970[a]
(millions of dollars)

	Production			Consumption			Net exports (imports)		
	1950	1960	1970	1950	1960	1970	1950	1960	1970
	Aluminum, alumina, and bauxite								
United States and Canada	546	1,299	2,148	528	1,084	2,000	18	215	148
Western Europe	141	459	929	132	709	1,484	9	(250)	(555)
Japan	12	67	369	5	78	531	7	(11)	(162)
Australia and South Africa	0	6	260	11	42	118	(11)	(36)	142
Total developed market economies	699	1,831	3,706	676	1,913	4,133	23	(82)	(427)
Developing market economies	36	265	757	57	158	462	(21)	107	295
Centrally planned economies	120	494	933	120	453	736	0	41	197
Total	855	2,590	5,396	853	2,524	5,331	2	66	65
Distribution (percentage)[b]									
Developed	81.8	70.7	68.7	79.2	75.8	77.5	3.3	(4.3)	(10.3)
Developing	4.2	10.2	14.0	6.7	6.3	8.7	(36.8)	40.3	39.0
Centrally planned economies	14.0	19.1	17.3	14.1	17.9	13.8	0	8.3	21.1
Total	100.0	100.0	100.0	100.0	100.0	100.0			

a. See explanation at the beginning of appendix.
b. Net exports as a percentage of production, net imports as a percentage of consumption.

TABLE H.4 | *Continued.*

Copper

	Production			Consumption			Net exports (imports)		
	1950	1960	1970	1950	1960	1970	1950	1960	1970
Growth rates (percentage)									
Developed		10.1[e]	7.3[d]		11.0[e]	8.0[d]			
Developing		22.0	11.0		11.0	11.0			
Centrally planned economies		15.1	9.7		14.2	5.0			
Total		11.8	8.0		10.2	7.7			
United States and Canada	1,487	1,958	2,884	1,598	1,457	2,374	(111)	501	510
Western Europe	215	278	434	1,068	2,211	2,628	(853)	1,933	(2,914)
Japan	53	162	348	17	332	977	36	(170)	(629)
Australia and South Africa	66	197	413	54	119	146	12	78	267
Total developed market economies	1,821	2,595	4,079	2,737	4,119	6,125	(916)	(1,524)	(2,046)
Developing market economies	1,292	2,347	2,973	154	241	392	1,138	2,106	2,581
Centrally planned economies	334	871	1,648	404	1,003	1,949	(70)	(132)	(301)
Total	3,447	5,813	8,700	3,295	5,363	8,466	152	450	267
Distribution (percentage)[b]									
Developed	52.8	44.6	46.9	83.1	76.8	72.3	(33.5)	(36.3)	(33.4)
Developing	37.5	40.4	34.2	4.7	4.5	4.6	88.1	89.7	86.8
Centrally planned economies	9.7	15.0	18.9	12.2	18.7	23.1	17.4	13.1	(15.4)
Total	100.0	100.0	100.0	100.0	100.0	100.0	4.4	7.7	

Growth rates (percentage)

Developed	3.6^c	4.6^d	4.2^c	4.0^d
Developing	6.1	2.4	4.6	4.7
Centrally planned economies	4.0	6.7	9.5	6.8
Total	5.3	4.1	5.0	4.7

Iron ore

United States and Canada	934	1,132	1,409	977	1,355	1,422	(43)	(223)	(13)
Western Europe	508	994	1,204	525	1,184	1,854	(17)	(190)	(650)
Japan	12	65	343	21	162	1,118	(9)	(97)	(845)
Australia and South Africa	37	87	534	37	80	144	0	7	390
Total developed market economies	1,491	2,278	3,490	1,560	2,781	4,608	(69)	(503)	(1,118)
Developing market economies	149	712	1,424	80	205	306	(69)	507	1,119
Centrally planned economies	463	1,579	2,916	463	1,582	2,916	0	(3)	0
Total	2,103	4,569	7,830	2,103	4,568	7,830			

Distribution (percentage)^b

Developed	70.9	49.9	44.6	74.2	60.9	59.9	(4.4)	(18.1)	24.2
Developing	7.1	15.6	18.2	3.8	4.5	6.3	46.2	71.3	78.5
Centrally planned economies	22.0	34.5	37.2	22.0	34.6	34.7	0	0.3	0
Total	100.0	100.0	100.0	100.0	100.0	100.0			

Growth rates (percentage)

Developed	4.3^c	4.4^d	6.0^c	5.2^d
Developing	13.1	7.1	9.8	6.1
Centrally planned economies		6.3	13.0	6.3
Total	8.1	5.5	8.1	5.5

b. Net exports as a percentage of production, net imports as a percentage of consumption.
c. Growth rate 1950–60.
d. Growth rate 1960–70.

TABLE H.4 | Continued.

Lead

	Production			Consumption			Net exports (imports)		
	1950	1960	1970	1950	1960	1970	1950	1960	1970
United States and Canada	189	163	298	280	226	330	(91)	(63)	(32)
Western Europe	117	186	253	217	362	452	(100)	(176)	(199)
Japan	4	18	44	8	33	68	(4)	(15)	(24)
Australia and South Africa	70	89	140	19	22	24	51	67	116
Total developed market economies	380	456	735	524	643	874	(144)	(187)	(139)
Developing market economies	140	178	184	30	30	82	110	148	102
Centrally planned economies	54	191	294	62	188	291	(8)	3	3
Total	574	825	1,213	616	861	1,247	(42)	(36)	(34)
Distribution (percentage)[b]									
Developed	66.1	55.2	60.2	85.0	74.6	70.1	(27.4)	(29.1)	(15.2)
Developing	24.4	21.5	15.2	4.9	3.5	6.6	78.4	83.2	55.4
Centrally planned economies	9.5	23.3	24.2	10.1	21.9	23.3	(13.2)	1.6	1
Total	100.0	100.0	100.0	100.0	100.0	100.0	(6.8)	(4.2)	(2.7)
Growth rates (percentage)									
Developed		1.8[c]	4.7[d]		2.0[c]	3.1[d]			
Developing		2.4	0.5		0	11.0			
Centrally planned economies			4.3		11.7	4.6			
Total		3.6	3.9		3.4	3.7			

244

Manganese

United States and Canada	179	196	168	246	284	289	(67)	(88)	(121)
Western Europe	101	195	340	120	265	440	(19)	(70)	(100)
Japan	18	51	239	19	54	339	(1)	(3)	(100)
Australia and South Africa	28	51	174	11	16	53	(17)	(35)	121
Total developed market economies	326	493	921	396	619	1,121	(70)	(126)	(200)
Developing market economies	77	184	237	8	66	71	(69)	118	166
Centrally planned economies	332	701	807	331	693	772	1	8	35
Total	735	1,378	1,965	735	1,378	1,964			1
Distribution (percentage)[b]									
Developed	44.2	35.8	46.9	53.9	44.9	57.1	(17.8)	(20.2)	(17.8)
Developing	10.5	13.4	12.1	1.1	4.8	3.6	89.8	64.1	70.0
Centrally planned economies	45.3	50.8	41.0	45.0	50.3	39.3	0.4	1.0	4.3
Total	100.0	100.0	100.0	100.0	100.0	100.0			
Growth rates (percentage)									
Developed		4.3[c]	6.4[d]		4.6[c]	6.1[d]			
Developing		9.1	2.8		0	0.5			
Centrally planned economies		8.6	1.5		7.6	1.1			
Total		6.5	3.6		0	3.6			

b. Net exports as a percentage of production, net imports as a percentage of consumption.
c. Growth rate 1950–60.
d. Growth rate 1960–70.

TABLE H.4 | *Continued.*

Nickel

	Production			Consumption			Net exports (imports)		
	1950	*1960*	*1970*	*1950*	*1960*	*1970*	*1950*	*1960*	*1970*
United States and Canada	242	431	619	225	246	367	17	185	252
Western Europe	34	78	96	79	227	413	(45)	(149)	(317)
Japan	0	18	98	2	42	238	(2)	(24)	(140)
Australia and South Africa	8	93	296	1	6	19	7	87	277
Total developed market economies	284	620	1,109	307	521	1,037	(23)	99	72
Developing market economies	0	36	156	1	4	14	(1)	32	142
Centrally planned economies	71	148	291	72	178	312	(1)	(30)	(21)
Total	355	804	1,556	380	703	1,363	(25)	101	193
Distribution (percentage)[b]									
Developed	80.0	77.1	71.3	80.8	74.2	76.1	(7.4)	16.0	(12.0)
Developing	0	4.5	10.0	0.2	0.5	1.0	(71.4)	89.4	87.5
Centrally planned economies	20.0	18.4	18.7	19.0	25.3	22.9	1.3	(16.4)	(10.8)
Total	100.0	100.0	100.0	100.0	100.0	100.0	(6.4)	12.7	(1.6)
Growth rates (percentage)									
Developed		8.1[e]	6.0[d]		5.4[e]	6.9[d]			
Developing		20.2	15.5		14.5	12.2			
Centrally planned economies		7.6	7.3		9.4	6.0			
Total		8.5	6.8		6.4	6.8			

Phosphorus

United States and Canada	346	519	921	332	460	741	14	59	180
Western Europe	183	308	473	244	419	636	(61)	(111)	(163)
Japan	27	61	77	38	81	95	(11)	(20)	(18)
Australia and South Africa	57	78	111	81	106	150	(24)	(28)	(39)
Total developed market economies	613	966	1,582	695	1,066	1,622	(82)	(100)	(40)
Developing market economies	95	215	408	14	108	328	81	107	80
Centrally planned economies	98	275	811	98	283	843	1	(8)	(32)
Total	806	1,456	2,801	807	1,457	2,793	0	1	8
Distribution (percentage)[b]									
Developed	76.1	66.3	56.4	86.2	73.2	58.1	(11.7)	(9.3)	(2.5)
Developing	11.8	14.8	14.6	1.7	7.4	11.7	85.4	49.6	19.6
Centrally planned economies	12.1	18.9	29.0	12.1	19.4	30.2	0	(2.7)	(3.8)
Total	100.0	100.0	100.0	100.0	100.0	100.0			
Growth rates (percentage)									
Developed	4.6[c]	5.3[d]		4.9[e]	4.3[d]				
Developing	8.6	6.8		22.8	12.0				
Centrally planned economies	11.0	11.3		11.2	11.6				
Total	6.1	6.8		6.1	6.8				

b. Net exports as a percentage of production, net imports as a percentage of consumption.
c. Growth rate 1950–60.
d. Growth rate 1960–70.

TABLE H.4 | Continued.

	Production			Consumption			Net exports (imports)		
	1950	1960	1970	1950	1960	1970	1950	1960	1970
Tin									
United States and Canada	52	22	0	292	214	236	(240)	(192)	(236)
Western Europe	101	83	66	209	258	258	(108)	(175)	(192)
Japan	1	5	5	18	56	110	(17)	(51)	(105)
Australia and South Africa	9	12	36	16	24	27	(7)	(12)	9
Total developed market economies	163	122	107	535	552	631	(370.8)	(430)	(524)
Developing market economies	477	429	597	48	56	68	428.8	373	529
Centrally planned economies	47	195	190	65	155	232	(17.5)	40	(42)
Total	687	746	894	648	763	931	40.5	(17)	(37)
Distribution (percentage)[b]									
Developed	23.8	16.2	12.0	82.6	72.3	67.8	(69.4)	(78.1)	(83.0)
Developing	69.4	57.7	66.8	7.4	7.3	7.3	89.9	87.1	88.6
Centrally planned economies	6.8	26.1	21.2	10.0	20.4	24.9	(27.1)	20.1	(18.1)
Total	100.0	100.0	100.0	100.0	100.0	100.0	5.9	(2.3)	
Growth rates (percentage)									
Developed		0[e]	0[d]		0.3[c]	1.2[d]			
Developing		0	3.4		1.4	3.0			
Centrally planned economies		15.2	0		10.9	4.2			
Total		0.8	1.7		1.6	2.0			

Zinc

United States and Canada	321	304	555	338	294	409	(17)	10	146
Western Europe	139	215	343	237	382	529	(98)	(167)	(186)
Japan	17	55	153	18	66	221	(1)	(11)	(68)
Australia and South Africa	47	72	152	23	42	59	26	30	93
Total developed market economies	524	646	1,203	616	784	1,218	(92)	(138)	(15)
Developing market economies	108	191	268	24	70	129	84	121	139
Centrally planned economies	87	252	397	87	224	359	0	28	38
Total	719	1,089	1,868	727	1,078	1,706	(8)	10	162
Distribution (percentage)[b]									
Developed	72.9	59.4	64.4	84.8	72.8	71.4	(15.0)	(17.7)	(1.2)
Developing	15.0	17.5	14.3	3.3	6.4	7.6	78.0	63.6	51.2
Centrally planned economies	12.1	23.1	21.3	11.9	20.8	21.0	7	11.1	9.6
Total	100.0	100.0	100.0	100.0	100.0	100.0	(1.1)	(1.0)	8.7
Growth rates (percentage)									
Developed		2.1[c]	6.5[d]		2.4[c]	4.5[d]			
Developing		5.9	3.5		11.4	6.0			
Centrally planned economies		11.2	4.6		10.0	4.8			
Total		4.2	5.5		4.0	4.7			

b. Net exports as a percentage of production, net imports as a percentage of consumption.
c. Growth rate 1950–60.
d. Growth rate 1960–70.

TABLE H.5 | Estimated Net Import Requirements as a Percentage of Consumption, Nine Major Minerals, by Industrialized Region and by Commodity, 1950, 1960, and 1970[a]

Mineral	1950			1960			1970		
	United States	Western Europe[b]	Japan	United States	Western Europe[b]	Japan	United States	Western Europe[b]	Japan
Bauxite and alumina	74	14	100	86	35	100	93	51	100
Copper	23	85	c	8	92	63	4	89	83
Iron ore	6	4	58	33	22	83	35	40	98
Lead	51	61	56	65	66	60	46	67	67
Manganese ore	93	97	33	95	98	45	96	98	91
Nickel	99	99	100	88	98	100	89	97	100
Phosphorus	c	99	100	c	100	100	c	100	100
Tin	100	95	94	100	97	94	100	96	97
Zinc	38	59	10	50	60	28	62	62	60
Total for all nine minerals	32	65	17	31	72	72	27	73	89

a. See explanation at the beginning of the appendix.
b. Excludes intra-Western European trade.
c. Net exporter.

TABLE H.6 | DEGREE OF MINERAL PROCESSING CONDUCTED
IN DIFFERENT REGIONS, NINE MAJOR MINERALS
COMBINED, 1950, 1960, AND 1970[a]

Region	Percentage of mine production		
	1950	1960	1970
United States and Canada	146	179	179
Western Europe	250	250	295
Japan	235	381	1,046
Australia and South Africa	89	72	38
Developing market economies	30	28	29
Centrally planned economies	99	102	108
Total	100	100	100

a. See explanation at the beginning of the appendix.

I | The Share of the Developing Countries in World Mineral Exports

TABLE I.1 PRESENTS DATA on the value and share of exports of nine major minerals from the five most important exporting developing countries. Whereas one single developing country accounts for about 30 percent or more of world exports of bauxite, phosphate rock, and tin, all developing countries together account for less than one-fourth of world exports of lead and zinc, and less than two-fifths in the case of iron ore. It should be underlined that these data are for 1970–72 and that the configuration can change both in the short or medium term and in the long run. Changes in the short or medium term can be brought about by closure or expansion of existing facilities (expansions do not require as much time as the development of new mines) as well as by increased processing within the exporting countries, which tends to raise the revenue per unit and affect both the export share and rank of individual countries. The potential dynamism of shares over the long run in some cases stems from the wide distribution of unexploited or not fully exploited resources—for example, copper—and the even wider distribution of unexplored areas or insufficiently delineated or appraised resources. In short, it is misleading to view the distribution of mineral production and exports as static for physical reasons alone. While the location of mineral resources is fixed for eternity, man's knowledge of this location is very far from complete. We have come to associate copper with Chile, and vice versa, as a conditioned reflex. But the constraints on the location of production imposed by terrain and climate—in the case of coffee or cocoa, for example—make the market structure of certain agricultural commodities more rigid, and rigid for a longer period, than that of mineral commodities.

TABLE I.1 | PRINCIPAL EXPORTERS OF SELECTED MINERALS AMONG
DEVELOPING COUNTRIES
(Five largest exporters in descending order of value)

Commodity, SITC[a] number, rank, and country	Value of exports, average 1970–72 (millions of dollars)	Country share of	
		Total developing country exports (percentage)	World exports (percentage)
Bauxite (283.3)			
1. Jamaica	89.4	44.3	32.2
2. Surinam	46.0	22.8	16.6
3. Guyana	19.2	9.5	6.9
4. Dominican Republic	15.3	7.6	5.5
5. Sierra Leone	6.9	3.4	2.5
Other developing	25.0	12.4	8.9
Total developing	201.8	100.0	72.6
All others	76.1		27.4
World total	277.9		100.0
Copper (283.1/682.1)			
1. Zambia	765.0	31.5	17.0
2. Chile	731.0	30.1	16.3
3. Zaïre	449.0	18.5	10.0
4. Peru	208.3	8.6	4.6
5. Philippines	187.0	7.7	4.2
Other developing	90.3	3.6	2.0
Total developing	2,430.6	100.0	54.1
All others	2,064.4		45.9
World total	4,495.0		100.0
Iron ore (281)			
1. Brazil	226.0	22.7	8.5
2. Liberia	165.0	16.5	6.2
3. India	153.7	15.4	5.8
4. Venezuela	139.7	14.0	5.3
5. Mauritania	73.3	7.3	2.8
Other developing	240.2	24.1	9.1
Total developing	997.9	100.0	37.7
All others	1,650.9		62.3
World total	2,648.8		100.0
Manganese ore (283.7)			
1. Gabon	39.0	35.8	20.1
2. Brazil	31.9	29.3	16.5
3. India	15.2	14.0	7.9

a. Standard International Trade Classification.
Source: World Bank, Commodity Trade and Price Trends, August 1974.

TABLE I.1 | *Continued.*

Commodity, SITC[a] number, rank, and country	Value of exports, average 1970–72 (millions of dollars)	Country share of	
		Total developing country exports (percentage)	World exports (percentage)
4. Ghana	7.6	7.0	3.9
5. Zaïre	5.9	5.4	3.0
Other developing	9.2	8.5	4.7
Total developing	108.8	100.0	56.1
All others	85.2		43.9
World total	194.0		100.0
Lead (283.4/685.1)			
1. Peru	32.0	30.7	6.5
2. Mexico	21.3	20.5	4.3
3. Morocco	13.3	12.8	2.7
4. Namibia	13.2	12.7	2.7
5. Bolivia	7.3	7.0	1.5
Other developing	17.0	16.3	3.4
Total developing	104.1	100.0	21.1
All others	389.6		78.9
World total	493.7		100.0
Phosphate rock (271.3)			
1. Morocco	124.9	54.5	29.2
2. Gilbert, Ellis Is.	32.1	14.0	7.5
3. Tunisia	21.4	9.3	5.0
4. Togo	16.6	7.3	3.9
5. Senegal	13.9	6.1	3.3
Other developng	20.2	8.8	4.7
Total developing	229.1	100.0	53.6
All others	198.0		46.4
World total	427.1		100.0
Tin (283.6/687.1)			
1. Malaysia	318.3	49.9	42.6
2. Bolivia	102.3	16.0	13.7
3. Thailand	77.3	12.1	10.3
4. Indonesia	63.3	9.9	8.5
5. Nigeria	36.3	5.7	4.9
Other developing	40.6	6.4	5.4
Total developing	638.1	100.0	85.4
All others	109.3		14.6
World total	747.4		100.0

a. Standard International Trade Classification.
Source: World Bank, *Commodity Trade and Price Trends,* August 1974.

TABLE I.1 | *Continued.*

Commodity, SITC[a] number, rank, and country	Value of exports, average 1970–72 (millions of dollars)	Country share of	
		Total developing country exports (percentage)	World exports (percentage)
Zinc (238.5/686.1)			
1. Peru	54.7	32.2	7.1
2. Mexico	49.7	29.2	6.4
3. Zaïre	25.3	14.9	3.3
4. Bolivia	14.0	8.2	1.8
5. Zambia	13.0	7.7	1.7
Other developing	13.3	7.8	1.7
Total developing	170.0	100.0	22.0
All others	602.9		78.0
World total	772.9		100.0

a. Standard International Trade Classification.
Source: World Bank, *Commodity Trade and Price Trends,* August 1974.

J | The Experience of the Quebec Mining Exploration Company: A Case Study

THE MINERAL EXPLORATION and development experience of Société Quebecoise d'Exploration Minière (SOQUEM) is extremely instructive, as it demonstrates that success can apparently be achieved quite quickly, when the objectives, policies, functions, and operations of the company are essentially those of a private mining company, even though the government owns all the issued share capital.

The Quebec Mining Exploration Company was founded in November 1965 as a joint stock company. Its main objectives, as embodied in its charter, are three: (a) to carry out mining exploration by all methods; (b) to participate in the development of discoveries, including those made by others, with power to purchase and sell properties at various stages of development and to associate itself with others for such purposes; and (c) to participate in bringing mineral deposits into production either by selling them outright or by transferring them in return for a participation.[1]

Staffing

SOQUEM began operating on November 1, 1965, with three officer-directors and two geologists. The first five months of operation were spent hiring personnel and planning the exploration program for the next season, and by April 1966 the company was fully operative.

On the date of the first annual report, July 8, 1966, the president described the technical staff as nearly complete. Of twenty-

---

1. Subsections (b) and (c) defining the objective of the company seem to have been drafted so as to adopt a low posture, emphasizing the dominant role to be accorded to private firms at all stages beyond exploration.

four permanent employees, twelve were geologists or geological engineers, three were prospectors, and two were in charge of laboratories. The summer seasonal field staff numbered eighty-eight— university professors and students, engineers engaged in post-graduate studies, and prospectors.

Of the approximately eighty university students, about half had no previous experience. SOQUEM had to face the fact, as many mining and exploration companies are doing today, that technical personnel are scarce. From two training camps organized in the Eastern Townships it embarked on a program of training inexperienced students and prospectors and familiarizing them with all modern geochemical sampling and processing techniques, geophysical instrument handling, and interpretation. The training program, which started about May 1 and lasted from two to six weeks, supplied enough men to form fourteen field groups. During this period SOQUEM was aided by several mining companies, especially the Anglo-American Corporation of Canada, Ltd., which provided training crews and equipment.

On the date of the second annual report, July 17, 1967, the permanent staff had grown to thirty including nine geologists and engineers, and there were eleven temporary employees including nine geologists and engineers. More than one hundred seasonal employees were recruited from among university professors and students.

The third annual report does not give information on staff in the same format. However, the August 1969 publication "SOQUEM —General Information" gives the backgrounds of twenty non-clerical personnel. Besides the officers, these include five geologists, one geophysicist, one geophysical technician, three geochemists, one geochemical technician, two mining engineers of whom one is an oredressing specialist, two accountants, one lawyer as legal counsel, and a public relations man. Five of the staff, including the president and vice president, hold Ph.Ds. Turnover, to date, has been rather low.

Operations

On November 4, 1966, in an article entitled "SOQUEM Looks for Partners in Exploration Endeavours," the president of SOQUEM, after reviewing the company's first year activities, quoted the company's three objectives as stated in the charter and said: "Two of these three tasks call for participations and joint ventures." We may note that the two tasks referred to were development and bringing deposits into production, rather than exploration, so that the company's decision to invite private participation in exploration as well represented a genuine initiative, based on the desire to "spread . . . exploration budgets over a greater number of targets in order to increase the chances of discovery."

"Needless to say," the president went on, "the company has been flooded with all sorts of proposals from prospectors, amateur or professional, and mining syndicates or companies." (According to the Third Annual Report, by March 1968 the company had received 316 proposals and accepted 27.) "However, offers to join in far-reaching exploration programs have been scant and came mostly from French-controlled international concerns used to dealing with government-sponsored companies."

During the first eight years of its activities, SOQUEM has made four discoveries and acquired properties that are either revenue-producing at present or likely to be so in the future.

Financing

SOQUEM's charter provided the company with an authorized capital of Can.$15 million divided into 1.5 million shares of a par value of Can.$10 each to be purchased out of the consolidated revenue fund by the Minister of Finance at the rate of 150,000 shares (Can.$1.5 million) per year each year for ten years.

Between incorporation on July 15, 1965, and the balance sheet date of March 21, 1966, the minister subscribed Can.$625,000 for 62,500 shares. The company, which was just getting organized, spent Can.$111,000 on administrative expenses and Can.$37,000 on furniture and equipment and held just over Can.$490,000 in cash and short-term deposits at the end of the period.

During fiscal 1966–67, the minister subscribed the full Can.$1.5 million; again the company spent less than the amount subscribed (Can.$92,000 for mining rights, Can.$882,000 on exploration, and Can.$188,000 on administration) and ended the year with Can.$744,000 in cash and short-term deposits.

During fiscal 1967–68, the minister again subscribed Can.$1.5 million, and this and more were spent (Can.$1.25 million on mining rights and exploration, Can.$237,000 on administration, and about Can.$100,000 on furniture and equipment) so that at the end of the year the company's cash and short-term deposits were down to some Can.$440,000.

The same situation persisted during fiscal year 1968–69. Borrowing was no answer, as, under its charter, the company can contract loans without prior authorization by the lieutenant-governor in Council only if these new loans do not increase its total outstanding borrowings to more than $500,000. The company found it difficult for a while to put up the necessary share of joint venture money required to uphold its interest in projects at the advanced development and bringing into production phase. Exploration funds had to be used for this purpose, leaving less available for exploration and early development. Eventually, in 1971, the share capital and the annual share purchases tempo were both increased, which alleviated the situation to some extent.

The annual budget is now Can.$2.75 million and total share capitalization has been increased from Can.$15 million to Can.$45 million. The original budget figure of Can.$1.5 million had been established as follows: In 1960, 50 percent of all mining exploration in Canada was carried out by only thirteen companies, with an average expenditure of Can.$1,675,000 each. Inflation alone, however, required an additional Can.$300,000 a year. Furthermore, total exploration expenditures in Canada almost doubled from 1960 to 1966, International Nickel's share going from Can.$5 million to Can.$11 million. It is understandable that SOQUEM wished to keep pace.

Under the percent financing scheme, it is anticipated that SOQUEM will be able to self-finance the new yearly expenditure of Can.$2.75 million by 1985, twenty years after incorporation. Furthermore, the curve of earnings is such that SOQUEM could increase its exploration activities beyond Can.$2.75 million yearly under its own steam. In fact, SOQUEM could possibly beat the 1985 date. This would involve discovering or acquiring and putting in production one or two mines between now and 1985, which is feasible if the new discoveries or acquisitions present no crucial problems.

Implications for the Possible Exploration Funds in the Developing Countries

The success story of SOQUEM calls for a number of comments relevant to the establishment of similar organizations elsewhere. First, the company is truly autonomous, and the various provisions of the charter regarding the composition of the board and the code of ethics applicable to its members have assured the independent character of the company's decisions.

Next, none of the operations normally carried out by ministries or geological surveys has been undertaken by SOQUEM (except for one occasion, where a reconnaissance geological survey operation was performed out of urgent necessity).

Last, the difficulties experienced by SOQUEM in obtaining additional funds suggest that programs of this kind should be planned in such a way that additional funds are available from government or other sources, under the form of an accelerated purchase of shares accompanied by an increase in authorized share capital, when heavy advanced development expenditures jeopardize the normal exploration and early development program.

K | Small-scale Mining

A NUMBER OF MINERALS are produced predominantly on a small scale or have an important small-scale mining component, as indicated in table K.1.

The prevalence of small-scale mining is influenced by geological factors, although the end uses and value of the mineral play an important role. For instance, construction materials may be found in very large deposits, but economic considerations (especially the high cost of transport, for example, in the case of stone and gravel) dictate serving only limited, local markets and hence small-scale operations.

A rough idea of the geographic and commodity distribution of small-scale mining can be obtained from table K.2, which lists those developing countries with a small-scale sector in one or more minerals. Since intermittency of operations is characteristic of small-scale mining, a specific mineral commodity may be shown in the table if production occurred during only one or more years of the past decade. The information shown is known to be incomplete: In many instances, even the countries themselves do not attempt to collect, collate, and verify data in the face of the overwhelming difficulties these activities present.

Small-scale mining can vary from a one-man operation, involving handpicking of minerals from a waste dump, to a highly mechanized and efficient operation with good management. Such mining is generally characterized by labor intensive and inefficient work methods, inefficient exploitation of deposits, substandard work conditions, poor management, and undependable output. Nevertheless, small-scale mining can make an important contribution to the economy—if not of the country, of a province—by providing employment, very often in remote areas with no alternative sources of employment. Often, however, the small-scale mines are

TABLE K.1 | SMALL-SCALE MINING OF SPECIFIC MINERALS

Mineral	Usually small-scale	Important small-scale component
Barite	x	
Beryl	x	
Bismuth		x
Chromite		x
Copper		x
Diamond		x
Feldspar	x	
Fluorspar	x	
Gemstones, precious stones	x	
Gold		x
Graphite		x
Lead		x
Lithium	x	
Magnesite	x	
Mercury	x	
Mica	x	
Rare earth minerals	x	
Silver		x
Strontium minerals	x	
Talc, soapstone		
Tin		x
Tungsten	x	
Uranium		x
Vermiculite	x	
Construction & industrial materials		x

Source: United Nations, Small-Scale Mining in the Developing Countries, (ST/ECA/155) (New York, 1972).

viable only because of their lower wages. When the price of the mineral drops, the miner tightens his belt or ceases operation and diverts his attention to agriculture.

The major problems of small-scale mining are nine: Excessive fragmentation of the land prohibits the rational exploitation of the mineral resources. Primitive and inefficient mining methods often mean mining only higher-grade ores and poor recovery of the ore-body, leading to a substantial wastage of the nation's resources. Operations are generally too small to justify the provision of adequate infrastructure facilities, and often, because of their widely dispersed nature, the cost of inputs and marketing expenses is high. Collecting data and monitoring the sector are difficult; small operations require a large administrative staff and are expensive, so coordination of planning is virtually impossible. Work conditions and health standards are often appalling, and policing compliance

TABLE K.2 | SMALL-SCALE MINING IN SELECTED
DEVELOPING COUNTRIES, 1960–70

Country	Mineral subject to small-scale mining
Africa	
Algeria	Antimony, barite, bentomite, diatomite, mercury, zinc
Central African Republic	Diamonds, gold
Ethiopia	Gold, manganese, platinum
Gabon	Gold
Ghana	Diamonds, gold
Kenya	Beryl, copper, gemstones, gold, silver, vermiculite, wollastonite
Lesotho	Diamonds
Liberia	Diamonds, gold
Madagascar	Bismuth, colombite, gold, rare earth minerals, tantalite
Morocco	Antimony, barite, lead, manganese, tin, zinc
Nigeria	Asbestos, barite, colombite, gold, lead, tantalite, tin, zinc
Rhodesia	Antimony, beryl, chromite, copper, gemstones, gold, lithium, manganese, mica, silver, tantalite
Rwanda	Beryl, gold, tin, tungsten
Sierra Leone	Diamonds
Tunisia	Lead, mercury, zinc
Tanzania	Diamonds, gold, magnesite, mica, precious stones, tin, tungsten
Uganda	Beryl, bismuth, tungsten
Asia	
Burma	Antimony, manganese, tin, tungsten
India	Barite, borax, iron, manganese, mica, tin
Iran	Barite, copper, lead, zinc
Malaysia	Gold, iron, manganese, tin, tungsten, zinc
Turkey	Chromite, copper, lead, magnesite, mercury, zinc
Latin America	
Argentina	Antimony, asbestos, beryl, bismuth, columbite, lithium, mercury, tantalite, tungsten, vermiculite
Bolivia	Antimony, copper, gold, mercury, silver, sulphur, tin, tungsten, zinc
Brazil	Beryllium, chromite, columbium, gold, precious stones, tin, titanium
Chile	Barite, copper, gold, lead, manganese, mercury, sulfur
Colombia	Antimony, chromite, emeralds, iron ore, lead, mercury, precious stones, zinc
Cuba	Copper, manganese, pyrite
Dominican Republic	Gold
Guatemala	Antimony, lead, manganese, mica, tin, wolfram
Mexico	Fluorspar, mercury, sulfur, tin, uranium
Peru	Antimony, bismuth, copper, diatomite, lead, manganese, molybdenite, silver, tin, zinc
Venezuela	Asbestos, diamonds, gold

with the mining code is extremely difficult because of the large number and wide dispersal of the mines. Large deposits may be fragmented into several unrelated operations, preventing medium- or large-scale development and therefore resulting in significantly lower output, lower revenues, and lower foreign exchange earnings. Small-scale mining generally has very high technical and financial risks; funding the operations is hence difficult and expensive. The people operating much of the small-scale sector lack technical and managerial skills; any upgrading of the operations therefore must be accompanied by training. The grossly inadequate accounting procedures typical of small-scale mines render the application of an income tax nonviable and often make it necessary to depend on production royalties or export taxes as a vehicle for collecting government revenues.

Though it has many problems, the small-scale mining sector cannot be ignored. On the contrary, it requires special attention when formulating policies and drafting mineral and fiscal legislation, when staffing the ministries, and when preparing a mining sector development plan. Some of the special measures needed are mentioned in the following paragraphs.

A special agency is often required to collect the output from the small operating mines distributed over a wide area. This involves setting up a network of collection points, a related communication and transportation system, and institutional arrangements to market the product (a marketing agency).

Since limited scale often prohibits beneficiation of the ore by the miner, his product may be a hand-sorted raw ore. With few exceptions, this has to be upgraded to a concentrate or a refined product before it can be sold. The marketing agency may therefore have to install processing facilities to treat the ore. Two more useful approaches are: first, to establish regional concentrators to treat the ore from all the small operations within a specified area (this, of course, requires collection and transportation of the ore to a central plant); or, second, to set up mobile concentrators which can be readily moved from mine to mine. The ore can be custom treated for the miner who is then free to sell his upgraded product, or it can be purchased by the concentrator on its own account.

A further step in this direction is to install a smelter and refinery to treat the concentrates and ores from the small-scale producers. In several cases, the government has a monopoly in smelting operations, requiring that all minerals produced be sold to the domestic smelters. Again, the smelter can custom treat the ore or purchase it on its own account.

Because of the very high risk associated with small-scale mining operations, finance may not be available on favorable terms. The government may therefore have to take the lead by establishing special credit facilities for the sector. This can be done by setting up a special mining bank or by opening a "mining window" in the national development bank. Other arrangements may include the provision of government guarantees on commercial financing (local and foreign).

Technical assistance to train the miners in mining methods, management techniques, and planning functions is essential. This often requires a major effort. A special agency can be established to perform this function, or a new department could be formed in the Ministry of Mines. Generally, the preferred approach is to form a technical group in the financing agency, the area with which developing countries have the most difficulty. Qualified people are not available in the numbers required, and this leads to undertaking extensive training programs and the use of foreign consultants. The role of the financing agency in evaluating and supervising the projects cannot be neglected.

Many of the small mines are too small to justify the purchase of equipment for exploration drilling and mine development. Access to such equipment can be very beneficial, however, in terms of cutting costs and expediting development of the mine. Establishing an equipment pool from which the equipment can either be rented out or contracted out with an operator deserves consideration. This could be a government operation, a joint venture with the private sector, or a fully private enterprise.

Many countries with small-scale mining have a very large number of mines which are widely dispersed. Policing the mining code can require a very large staff and even additional regional offices of the Ministry of Mines. Although expensive, this may be indispensable to ensure the health and safety of the workers. Data collection from the small-scale operators is especially difficult and requires additional documentation facilities and staff.

Lack of exploration by the small miners may necessitate exploration assistance from the government in the form of subsidies, contract exploration, equipment lending, and so forth.

Policies and legislation must take into account the requirement of the small-scale mining sector for a much greater administrative input from the government than the large-scale sector.

L | A Modern Mining Code

OWNERSHIP OF OPERATION must be clearly spelled out in a mining code, together with the requirements for state participation and rules governing maximum foreign ownership, phase-out investment requirements, and corporate capital structure.[1] Areas that need definition, if not clarified under a separate investment code, include methods of accounting, valuing inventories, valuing assets, permissible dividend payouts, depreciation allowances, writeoffs for capital development or preinvestment, and so on. Of course, the applicable tax regime should be described under the mining code, if not covered under separate tax legislation. Beyond these fundamentals, a modern mining code should address itself to the following points:

First, a classification of minerals should be adopted for determining the different types of mining licenses, leases, and concessions. The categories adopted will depend very much on the individual country's basic economic and political philosophy and may be predicated upon relative values, mode of occurrence (placer, vein, or lode), end use, strategic importance, and methods of mining. Generally, because of their very different characteristics and end uses, building materials (stones, gravel, sand, clay, possibly also limestone, granite, marble) are separated as a category. Other categories such as strategic minerals, vital minerals, and all other minerals may be appropriate, the two former categories being placed under more rigid government control, or being assigned the responsibility of the central government rather than the state governments. For obvious reasons, nuclear minerals generally fall under special legislation. Coal and lignite, or petroleum, natural gas, and

---

1. This appendix draws heavily on United Nations, *Proceedings of the Seminar on Mining Legislation and Administration* (E/CN11/I and NR/L90) (Manila, 1969).

asphalt can also justifiably be placed under separate legislation. A special category may also be assigned to minerals on the continental shelf. In drafting mining legislation, each country should carefully establish categories that fit its policies and objectives.

The question of mineral ownership should be clearly defined. The accession system, where mineral ownership is linked to land ownership, is outdated and has generally been replaced by the domanial system, whereby mineral ownership is distinctly separated from surface ownership. Mineral ownership could be in private hands, but it is being increasingly treated as the prerogative of the state. This raises the question of separation of mineral ownership from mining rights in cases where mineral ownership rests in the state and the minerals are mined by private parties under license. This obviously provides the rationale for production royalties.

There is need for a clear definition of the procedures for the granting of prospecting and exploration rights. These may be separate or combined. The administrative burden (a real problem in developing countries) is reduced by combining the two into a single right. The alternatives are: first, grant to the discoverer; second, grant to the first occupier or first applicant; or third, grant at the government's discretion.

Grant to the discoverer. This is difficult to apply: who is the discoverer? By what legal criteria can he be recognized?

Grant to the first occupier (indicated by staking a claim) or first applicant (with or without staking a claim). This is generally the favored approach. It promotes interest in exploration and avoids conflict, although it does lead to fragmentation into blocks which are too small to be viable and may spoil the deposits through lack of expertise, machinery, and finance by high grading.[2] For there is no guarantee that the holder will be technically and financially competent and this may result in undue speculation. Such problems can be countered to some extent by establishing prequalification standards and minimum expertise and financial requirements, though this tends to favor the large enterprise. On the other hand, grant to first occupiers hinders large-scale surveys of large areas by modern prospecting techniques and does not give the government adequate means to direct the country's mineral development.

Grant at the government's discretion. This gives the state tighter control so that it can select from among applicants who are con-

2. High grading refers to mining the richer parts of the orebody without regard to possible future exploitation of the lower-grade parts, which may thus be rendered uneconomic. The minerals may therefore be lost to the nation.

sidered technically and financially fully competent. The selection should be based on clearly defined rules and procedures for seeking and evaluating proposals and applied by an expert team. If such a team is not available from within the state administration, it could be subcontracted.

As to prospecting and exploration, exclusive rights should be awarded. To discourage speculation, however, minimum work programs and reporting requirements should be established. It is also necessary to allow an adequate period of time for prospecting so that the preliminary survey can be as complete and accurate as possible. One or two years are bound to be insufficient, except when a very small area is involved; longer periods with renewals are advisable. The prospecting and exploration license may cover large areas, with specified relinquishments at specified periods. The license should clearly specify all rights and obligations of the holder and detail the causes for termination and forfeiture.

The holder of a prospecting license must be guaranteed automatic mining rights (exploitation title) with the discovery of an economic ore deposit, provided he has met all his obligations under the license. Without such assurances the licensee is unlikely to spend large sums of risk capital exploring for minerals. Furthermore, he must be assured of full possession of the granted rights as long as he meets the legal and agreed obligations. The rights and obligations of the holder must be clearly delineated, and a development and production schedule should be agreed upon to prevent speculation and tying up of good mineral deposits. The schedule must be realistic, making full allowance for the nature of the orebody. The duration of the mining right should be fixed. Twenty- or thirty-year periods, with right of option to renew, are normal and desirable. Inactivity is cause for forfeiture. The obligation of the mineral rights holder would include his periodic submission of production, financial, and statistical reports, as well as maps. To maintain the miners' trust, the government should keep a clear separation between information which is confidential and that which may be published.

The government may wish to reassess the technical and financial competence of the licensee, taking into account the nature of the deposit to be exploited, and specify steps to be taken (the need to take in partners, for instance, or to obtain technical and managerial assistance) to meet minimum requirements. The government's right to reevaluate the licensee should be agreed upon in the prospector's license.

Mining rights may also be granted by public auction, tender, or special contract. This is generally valid only if the government is disposing of mining properties under its control through expiration or forfeiture of a previous concession, or for particular minerals reserved for the state, or when detailed exploration conducted either by the state or on its behalf by a third party results in a discovery. Granting of mining rights by special contract is becoming more frequent and can be expected to become even more so in the future as the incidence of exploration done by and for the state increases. The main feature of such a contract is its bilateral and limited aspect, in contrast to the mining code whose objective is to establish general rulings for across-the-board application. However, to prevent conflict, the code must make provision for rules governing special contracts, and the terms of the contract must fit within the code framework. The code may require that a contract be annexed to each mining right, specifying the terms and conditions of exploitation, so that granting by special contract differs in approach only.

The code should clearly specify the degree of processing required for each mineral. Beneficiation is generally regarded as a part of the mining activity. In some countries, smelting and refining are considered as industrial activities regulated by the general legislation-governing industry. A few countries have provided for special licenses for smelting and refining in their mining codes, though these activities are increasingly becoming state functions.

Ecological and environmental requirements should be specified in the code, detailing for example the measurements needed, maximum level of pollutants, and reforestation. If separate laws have been promulgated to cover all industry, a cross-reference to this law will suffice. The obligations of the departing miner, after the closing down of facilities or the expiration of mining title, need defining; they include safety measures, rehabilitation of the surface, and removal of structures.

The code should spell out safety requirements and standards, for example, for protective clothing, equipment, work procedures, blasting procedures, special equipment designs, atmospheric and ventilation levels, lighting requirements, and minimum noise levels. Regulations governing the storage, transport, and use of explosives may also come under the mining code.

Guidelines concerning the conservation of resources are advisable. Legislation can cover the efficient exploitation of a mineral deposit by avoiding premature abandonment of parts of the deposit, fixing the cutoff grade at the lowest level compatible with the economic situation, and good recovery rates in the beneficiation of ores.

Employment policies must be incorporated in the law; they should include guidelines for phasing out expatriates, training nationals, hiring and termination practices, equality clauses, health and social facilities, and the general minimum terms of employment.

Marketing responsibilities and rights of the operator must be defined. Any requirements to sell through a state monopoly, to obtain prior approval of sales contracts, to report details of sales transactions, and to sell preferentially to domestic purchasers should be listed and the procedures spelled out.

The use rights to water, forests, and other natural resources should be defined, together with the procedures for obtaining such rights.

Rights to the use of public infrastructure—rail, roads, power, communications, housing, schools, and hospitals, for example—need defining. The obligation to make captive infrastrucure available for public use should similarly be defined.

Reference should also be made to the rights and conditions of exploiting minerals on the continental shelf, to overflight privileges for aerial photography, geophysical work, the availability of maps and geological data from government agencies, the provision of technical assistance by the government, and to all other legislation affecting the mining industry.

Bibliography and Index

Bibliography

THE BIBLIOGRAPHY comprises works cited in the text and its appendixes, plus selected publications which offer good supplementary reading to these works in the context in which they were cited. The bibliography is designed to facilitate further reading but, by and large, with the same balance among topics reflected in the body of the book. In a survey that covers as much ground as the present one, it is impossible to anticipate the needs for depth and predict the curiosities of every reader. Guiding the reader halfway through the many specific alleys such as resource availability, processing, mineral legislation, corporate finance, taxation, and the maze of commodity and national problems requires a bibliography easily ten times longer. Specialized bibliographies are available on certain subtopics (commodities and marine resource, for instance) or by agency (UNCTAD, the United Nations) and can be found attached to some of the authoritative works cited. In addition to consulting these, readers who wish to delve deeper into the subject may benefit from a few observations.

The best information of an impartial character on the problems of mineral resource development in the developing countries is in the archives of the international agencies with long operational experience in this field, such as the United Nations, the UN Development Programme, and the World Bank. Declassifying and systematizing the information will open to the student a vast storehouse of knowledge.

The best sources of information on developed country policies include the annual reports of the large mining companies and, in the United States, the records of Congressional committee hearings.

If the voluminous output of the U.S. Geological Survey and Bureau of Mines is the standard source for factual information on reserves and resources as well as on technological trends, even for the developing countries and the centrally planned economies, it is because in most cases there is nothing better. UN efforts in this area, though expanding, are grossly inadequate.

Meetings, seminars, and symposia organized by the United Nations or professional societies, especially those of an international character, such as the World Mining Congress, provide a rich source of analytical information on specific problems and juxtaposition of views, as well as for state-of-the-art surveys. Regrettably, some of these are published with a long delay and slide immediately into obscurity.

An indispensable source—but one frustrating to follow and difficult to use on an ad hoc basis—is the daily, weekly, and monthly professional (mining, engineering, and commercial) press. Its news character reduces bias and provides a running account of developments without prejudgments. It is interesting to note that although much of it is directly or indirectly subsidized by the industry, editorially some of the press has been ahead of the industry in recognizing the need for, and advocating a change in, the rules of the game in favor of the developing countries.

No true understanding of the problems and operations of the mining industry can be gained without access to the best source of all—people. An unfortunate gulf separates the policymaker in government from the man in the industry—and by that we do not mean the private mining company, but the man working in this sector or studying it in government, business, universities, or the United Nations. One reason for this is that the latter, perhaps with the exception of the university professor, has seldom the motivation, even less often the time, and rarely the forum to communicate his experience and views. Some of them retire—some are forced to retire—without having occasion to do so, though this should be an obligation, not just an optional service.

Analytical information on the problems of mineral resource development in the developing countries and work by analysts from the developing countries is limited and will remain so for some time. Much of the information is one-sided; yet, with careful study, a discerning analyst can find in it the basis for independent judgment on a number of issues.

Recognition of the inadequacy of the information base, coupled with an unprecedented explosion in the need for information, has led to an avalanche of proposals for institutional arrangements designed to improve the collection, dissemination, and analysis of information at both the national and international levels. Two bills on a new natural resources information system are pending before the U.S. Congress. Similar proposals for an expanded flow of information on the multinational corporations, technology, and natural resources are under implementation or consideration at the United Nations. These efforts merit international support. Their success requires mutual trust, collective action, and emphasis, from the very beginning, on quality rather than quantity.

Books, Journals, and Conference Papers

Adam, Robin G. "Currency Exchange Fluctuation—Their Impact on the Mining Industry," *Engineering and Mining Journal* (October 1974).

American Bureau of Metal Statistics, *Yearbook,* fiftieth annual issue for the year 1970, New York, June 1971.

Annales des Mines, January 1975 [an issue devoted to mineral raw materials and economic relations] and June 1975 [an issue devoted to the economics of raw materials and recycling].

Banks, F. E. "An Econometric Model of the World Tin Economy: A Comment," *Econometrica,* vol. 40, no. 4 (July 1972).

Beckerman, Wilfred. *In Defence of Economic Growth.* London: Jonathan Cape, 1974.

Bergsten, C. Fred. "The Threat From the Third World," *Foreign Policy,* no. 11 (Summer 1973).

———. "The New Era in World Commodity Cartels," *Challenge* (September–October 1974).

———. "The Threat Is Real," *Foreign Policy,* no. 14 (Spring 1974).

Brooks, David B., and P. W. Andres. "Mineral Resources, Economic Growth and World Population," *Science,* vol. 185, no. 4145 (July 5, 1974).

Canada, Government of, Department of Energy, Mines, and Resources. *Departmental Terminology and Definitions of Reserves and Resources: Interim Document.* Ottawa, June 30, 1975.

———, Department of Energy, Mines, and Resources. *Mineral Area Planning Study: Mineral Development Sector.* Mineral Policy Series. Ottawa, April 1975.

———, Geological Survey, A. R. Berger (ed.). *Geoscientists and the Third World: A Collective Critique of Existing Aid Programs,* Paper 34–57. Ottawa, 1975.

———, Information Canada. *Towards a Mineral Policy for Canada— Opportunities for Choice.* Ottawa, 1974.

"Canadian Data–Yield Graphs to Speed Mine Feasibility Studies," *Engineering and Mining Journal* (December 1969).

Carlson, Jack W. "Reliable Minerals Supply for the Future," *Mining Congress Journal* (November 1975).

Carman, John S. "Forecast of United Nations Mineral Activities." Paper delivered at World Mining Congress, Lima, Peru, November 3–8, 1974.

———. "Notes and Observations on Foreign Mineral Ventures," *Mining Engineering* (September 1967).

————. "Notes on Impediments to Mining Investments in the Developing World." Paper prepared for Association of Geoscientists for International Development, Bagauda, Nigeria, September 1975.

Charles River Associates, Inc. "The Contribution of the Nonfuel Minerals Industry to International Monetary Flows." Cambridge, Mass., 1968.

————. "Economic Analysis of the Copper Industry." U.S. Department of Commerce Publication, PB 189 927. Washington, D.C., March 1970.

————. "An Economic Analysis of the Aluminum Industry." Cambridge, Mass., March 1971.

Clarfield, Kenneth W., Stuart Jackson, Jeff Keeffe, Michaele Ann Noble, and A. Patrick Ryan. "Eight Mineral Cartels: The New Challenge to Industrialized Nations." New York: McGraw-Hill, 1975.

Connelly, Philip. "Resources: The Choice for Importers," *International Affairs* (October 1974).

Cranstone, D. A., and H. S. Martin. "Are Ore Discovery Costs Increasing?" *Canadian Mining Journal* (April 1973).

Drake, P. J. "Natural Resources *versus* Foreign Borrowing in Economic Development," *The Economic Journal* (September 1972).

Drolet, Jean-Paul. "The Demand for Canada's Mineral Resources." Paper presented at the International Symposium on Canada's Nonrenewable Resources, Toronto, March 25, 1974.

Dunn, James R., and Harry L. Moffel. "Mineral Explorations in the U.S.: Problem (!) and an Answer (!)," *Mining Congress Journal* (November 1975).

Evans, J. B. "How Bill 31 Will Affect an Actual Copper Mine," *The Northern Miner* (June 6, 1974).

Fischman, Leonard L., and Hans H. Landsberg. "Adequacy of Nonfuel Minerals and Forest Resources," in Roland G. Ridker (ed.), *Population, Resources and the Environment*. Washington, D.C.: U.S. Government Printing Office, for The U.S. Commission on Population Growth and the American Future, 1972.

Fortune Magazine, various issues.

Going, P. "An Industrial Analysis of Exploration Activity," *Canadian Mining Journal* (April 1973).

Guccione, Eugene. "Mine Financing: From Bad to Worse." Paper presented at the Rocky Mountain Energy–Minerals Conference, sponsored by the U.S. Bureau of Land Management, Billings, Montana, October 15–16, 1975; (mimeographed).

Herfindahl, Orris C. "The Long-Run Cost of Minerals," in *Three Studies in Mineral Economics*. Washington, D.C.: Resources for the Future, 1961.

————. David B. Brooks (ed.). *Resource Economics; Selected Works of Orris C. Herfindahl*. Baltimore and London: Johns Hopkins University Press, for Resources for the Future, 1974.

Hotelling, Harold. "The Economics of Exhaustible Resources," *Journal of Political Economy* (April 1931).

International Economic Policy Association. "Interim Report of the Study on U.S. Natural Resources, Requirements and Foreign Economic Policy." Washington, D.C., July 18, 1974.

Krasner, Stephen D. "Oil is the Exception," *Foreign Policy* (Spring 1974).

Kruger, F. G. "Mining: A Business for Professionals Only," *Mining Engineering* (September 1969).

Landsberg, Hans H., Leonard L. Fischman, and Joseph L. Fisher. *Resources in America's Future*. Baltimore: Johns Hopkins Press, for Resources for the Future, 1963.

Lanz, Edward L. "Impact of Environmental Regulation on Mining," *Mining Congress Journal* (November 1975).

LaQue, F. L. "Deep Ocean Mining: Prospects and Anticipated Short-Term Benefits," in *Pacem in Maribus*, The Center for the Study of Democratic Institutions, Occasional Paper, vol. 2, no. 4. Santa Barbara, Calif., June 1970.

Lewis, John P. "Oil, Other Scarcities, and the Poor Countries," *World Politics* (October 1974).

Lovering, T. S. *Minerals in World Affairs*. New York: Prentice-Hall, 1943.

Lowell, T. B. "Copper Resources in 1970," *Transactions*, American Society of Mining Engineers (June 1970).

MacGregor, Wallace, and Edward L. Vickers. "Capital and the U.S. Resources Crunch," *Engineering and Mining Journal* (September 1974).

McInnes, David F. "Estimates of World Metals Depletion: Background for Metals Policy Planning." Firbank Fell, A Centre for the Study of Alternative Societies, December 1973.

McKelney, V. E. "Mineral Resource Estimates and Public Policy." *United States Mineral Resources*, Geological Survey Professional Paper 820, U.S. Department of the Interior. Washington, D.C., 1973.

Malmgren, Harold B. "The Raw Material and Commodity Controversy," *International Economic Studies Institute Contemporary Issues*, no. 1. Washington, D.C., October 1975.

Meadows, Donella H., Dennis L. Meadows, Jorgen Randers, and William W. Behrens III. *The Limits to Growth*. A report for the Club of Rome's project on the predicament of mankind. New York: Universe Books, Potomac Associates, 1972.

Metal Statistics 1973. New York: Fairchild Publications, 1973.

Metallgesellshaft, A. G. *Metal Statistics*.

Mikdashi, Zuhayr. "Collusion Could Work," *Foreign Policy*, no. 14 (Spring 1974).

————. "A Comparative Analysis of Selected Metal Exporting Industries." Vienna, March 1971 (mimeographed).

Mikesell, Raymond F. "Financial Considerations in Negotiating Mine Development Agreements," *Mining Magazine* (April 1974).

————. *Foreign Investment in Copper Mining: Case Studies of Mines in Peru and Papua-New Guinea*. Baltimore and London: Johns Hopkins University Press, for Resources for the Future, 1975.

————— and associates. *Foreign Investment in the Petroleum and Mineral Industries*. Baltimore: Johns Hopkins University Press, for Resources for the Future, 1971.

—————. "More Third World Cartels?" *Challenge* (November–December 1974).

—————. *Nonfuel Minerals: U.S. Investment Policies Abroad*. The Washington Papers, vol. 3, no. 23. Beverly Hills and London: Sage, 1975.

—————. "Rate of Exploitation of Exhaustible Resources: The Case of an Export Economy." Paper presented at the Second Trans-Pacific Seminar on "Minerals Across the Pacific: Bridge or Barrier?," sponsored by the Australian Society for Latin American Studies, Melbourne, Australia, June 20–22, 1975 (mimeographed).

Moran, Theodore H. "New Deal or Raw Deal in Raw Materials," *Foreign Policy*, no. 5 (Winter 1970–71).

National Academy of Sciences. "Mineral Resources and the Environment." A report prepared by the Committee on Mineral Resources and the Environment (COMRATE), Commission on Natural Resources, National Research Council, Washington, D.C., 1975.

National Institute Economic Review. London.

"The No-Growth Society," *Daedalus*, Journal of the American Academy of Arts and Science, vol. 102, no. 4 (Fall 1974).

"No Looking Back." *Mining Journal* (November 22, 1974).

Okita, Saburo. "Natural Resource Dependency and Japanese Foreign Policy," *Foreign Affairs* (July 1974).

Peach, W. N., and James A. Constantin. *Zimmermann's World Resources and Industries*. 3d ed. New York: Harper & Row, 1972.

Prain, Sir Ronald. *Copper: The Anatomy of an Industry*. London: Mining Journal Books, 1975.

"The Problem of Reference Prices," *Metal Bulletin Monthly* (August 1974).

Resources for the Future. "Resource Terminology: An Examination of Concepts and Terms and Recommendations for Improvement," John J. Schanz, principal investigator. Palo Alto, Calif.: Electric Power Research Institute, August 1975.

Roth, Alton, ed. "The Crisis in World Materials, A U.S.–Japanese Symposium." Newark, N.J.: Rutgers University, Graduate School of Business Administration, September 1974.

Smith, Frank Austin. "Waste Material Recovery and Reuse," in Ronald G. Ridker (ed.), *Population, Resources and the Environment*. Washington, D.C.: U.S. Government Printing Office, for The U.S. Commission on Population Growth and the American Future, 1972.

Société Quebecoise d'Exploration Minière. *Annual Reports*.

Solow, Robert M. "The Economics of Resources or the Resources of Economics," *American Economic Review* (May 1974).

"Soviet Eye on Mining." *Mining Journal*, vol. 285, no. 7304 (August 15, 1975).

Spangler, Miller B. *New Technology and Marine Resources Development*. New York: Praeger, 1970.

Sumitomo Shoji Kaisha, Ltd. "Survey of Non-Ferrous Metals Industries in China." Tokyo, 1972.

"Survey of Mine and Plant Expansion [1974]," *Engineering and Mining Journal* (January 1975).

Sutulov, Alexander. *Minerals in World Affairs.* Salt Lake City, Utah: The University of Utah Printing Services, 1972.

Takeuchi, K. "CIPEC and the Copper Export Earnings of Member Countries," *The Developing Economies,* vol. 10, no. 1 (March 1972).

————, and Bension Varon. "Commodity Shortage and Changes in World Trade," *Annals of the American Academy of Political and Social Science* (July 1975).

United Kingdom Overseas Geological Survey. *Statistical Summary of the Mineral Industry.*

U.S., Congress. Joint Committee on Defense Production. *Potential Shortages of Ores, Metals, and Minerals, Fuels and Energy Resources, Etc.* 92nd Cong., 1st sess., August 2, 1971.

U.S., Congress, Subcommittee on Fiscal Policy of the Joint Economic Committee. *The Economics of Recycling Waste Materials.* Hearing. 92nd Cong., 1st sess., November 8 and 9, 1971.

U.S., Congress, House Committee on Banking and Currency. Report of Ad Hoc Committee on the Domestic and International Monetary Effects of Energy and Other Natural Resource Pricing. *Meeting America's Resource Needs: Problems and Policies.* 93rd Cong., 2nd sess., November 1974.

U.S. Council on International Economic Policy. *Critical Imported Materials.* Washington, D.C.: U.S. Government Printing Office, December 1974.

U.S. Department of Commerce, Office of Business Economics. *Balance of Payments: Statistics Supplement.* Various issues.

————. *Survey of Current Business.* October 1968.

————. *Commodity Data Summaries.* Various issues.

U.S. Department of the Interior, Bureau of Mines. *Mineral Facts and Problems.* Washington, D.C., 1970.

————. *Minerals and Materials.* Monthly survey, various issues.

————. *Minerals in the U.S. Economy: Ten-year Supply-Demand Profiles for Mineral and Fuel Commodities.* Washington, D.C., 1975.

————. *Minerals Yearbook.* Washington, D.C., 1973.

————. *Mining and Mineral Policy 1975.* Annual Report of the Secretary under the Mining and Minerals Policy Act of 1970. Washington, D.C., 1970.

————. Office of Minerals Policy Development. *Critical Materials: Commodity Action Analyses—Aluminum, Chromium, Platinum and Palladium.* Washington, D.C.: March 1975.

————. *United States Mineral Resources.* Geological Survey professional paper 820. Washington, D.C., 1973.

U.S. Department of State, Bureau of Public Office, Office of Media Services. *Special Report: International Collusive Action in World Markets for Nonfuel Minerals.* Washington, D.C., 1974.

U.S. National Commission on Materials Policy. *Material Needs and the Environment Today and Tomorrow.* (Final Report of the Commission). Washington, D.C.: U.S. Government Printing Office, June 1973.

――――. *Materials Requirements in the United States and Abroad in the Year 2000.* A research project prepared by the Wharton School, University of Pennsylvania. Washington, D.C.: U.S. Government Printing Office, March 1973.

"U.S. Exploration Is Very High Risk, Development More Costly," *World Mining* (November 1971).

Varon, Bension. "Coke and Coking Coal Availabilities. A Potential Problem or Not?" World Bank Staff Working Paper, no. 135. Washington, D.C., August 3, 1972.

――――. "Enough of Everything for Everyone, Forever?" *Finance & Development* (September 1975).

――――. "Ocean Issues on the International Agenda," in *Beyond Dependency: the Developing World Speaks Out,* Guy F. Erb and Valeriana Kallab, eds. Washington, D.C.: Overseas Development Council, 1975.

――――. "Review of the World Nickel Situation." World Bank Staff Working Paper, no. 108. Washington, D.C., July 1, 1971.

――――. "Slow Sailing at Law of the Sea: The Implications for the Future," *Finance & Development* (March 1975).

Varon, Bension, Jacques Nusbaumer, and others. "The International Market for Iron Ore: Review and Outlooks," World Bank Staff Working Paper, no. 160. Washington, D.C., August 1973.

Varon, Bension, and Kenji Takeuchi. "Developing Countries and Non-Fuel Minerals," *Foreign Affairs* (April 1974).

Vernon, Raymond. "Foreign Enterprises and Developing Nations in the Raw Material Industries," *The American Economic Review* (May 1970).

Walter, Ingo. "A Discussion of the International Economic Dimensions of Secondary Materials Recovery." *International Economic Studies Institute Contemporary Issues,* no. 2. Washington, D.C., December 1975.

Walthier, Thomas N. "Problems of Foreign Investment in Natural Resources." Paper presented at the International Minerals Acquisition and Operations Institute, October 1974, Denver, Colorado; processed.

World Bank. "Commodity Trade and Price Trends." Washington, D.C., August 1974; processed.

――――. "Report on the Limits to Growth." A study by a Special Task Force of the World Bank. Washington, D.C., September 1972.

World Bureau of Metal Statistics. *World Metal Statistics.* Various issues.

Yates, P. Lamartine. *Forty Years of Foreign Trade.* London: George Allen and Unwin, 1959.

Zwartendyk, Jan. "Defining Mineral Wealth: Just What Are We Talking About?" *The Northern Miner* (November 30, 1972).

――――. "The Life Index of Mineral Reserves—A Statistical Mirage," *The Canadian Mining and Metallurgical Bulletin* (October 1974).

————. "Problems in Interpretation of Data on Mineral Resources, Production, and Consumption." *Natural Resources Forum*, vol. 1, no. 1 (October 1976).

United Nations Publications

Advisory Committee on the Application of Science and Technology to Development. *Natural Resources of Developing Countries: Investigation, Development and Rational Utilization.* Report. (E.70.II.B.2). New York, 1970.

Commission on Transnational Corporations, Report, 1st. sess., March 17–28, 1975. (supp. no. 12 E/5655,E/C.10/6). New York, 1975.

Comprehensive Plan of Action for Coordination of Programmes within the United Nation Systems in the Field of Natural Resources Development. Report of the Secretary-General. Addendum on Mineral Resources. (E/C.7/47/add.2.). New York, February 10, 1975.

Committee on Natural Resources. *Problems of Availability and Supply of Natural Resources. Survey of Current Problems in the Fields of Energy and Minerals. The World Mineral Situation.* Report of the Secretary-General. Tokyo, March 24–April 4, 1975. (E/C.7/51). New York, 1975.

————. *Report, 4th sess.,* March 24–*April 4, 1975.* (supp. no. 3, E/5663, E/C.7/56). New York, 1975.

————. *Permanent Sovereignty Over Natural Resources.* (E/C.7/53). New York, January 31, 1975.

Conference on Trade and Development. *An Integrated Programme for Commodities: Specific Proposals for Decision and Action by Governments.* Report by the Secretary-General. Committee on Commodities. (TD/B/C.1/193). Geneva, December 8, 1975.

————. (TD/B/C.1/Iron Ore/CONS/R.2). February 23, 1972.

————. *Measures to Expand Processing of Primary Commodities in Developing Countries.* Report by the Secretariat. Committee on Commodities. (TD/B/C.7/197). Geneva, December 8, 1975.

————. *Problems of the Iron Ore Market.* (TD/B/C.1/Iron Ore, R.L). New York, December 8, 1969.

————. *Problems of Raw Materials and Development.* Report by the Secretary-General. 6th special sess. of the General Assembly. (TD/B/488). New York, 1974.

Development Programme, United Nations Revolving Fund for Natural Resources Exploration. *Operational Procedures and Administrative Arrangements.* (DP/142). New York, October 24, 1975.

Economic and Social Affairs Department, *The Acquisition of Technology from Multinational Corporations by Developing Countries.* (ST/ESA/12). New York, 1974.

Economic and Social Council. *Official Records,* 59th. sess., Resolutions and Decisions, supp. no. 1, July 2–31 1975. (E/5740). New York, 1975.

*Economic Implications of Seabed Mineral Development in the Interna-
tional Area,* May 1974, (A/Conf.62/65) and follow-up report, same
title, February 18, 1975, (A/Conf.62/37). New York, 1975.
Evolution of Basic Commodity Prices Since 1950. Study of the Problems
of Raw Materials and Development. (A/9544). April 2, 1974.
General Assembly. *Official Records,* 6th. special sess., annexes. New
York, April 9–May 2, 1974.
———. *Problems of Raw Materials and Development* (Centre for Economic and Social Information). Declaration and programme of action
adopted by the 6th. special sess. (ES1.E21). May 12, 1974.
———. *Multilateral Trade Negotiations,* Note by the Secretary-General.
Preparatory Committee for the special sess. on development and inter-
national cooperation, 3d. sess. (E/AC.62/14/rev.1). August 18–22,
1975.
———. *Resolutions.* 7th special sess., September 1–16, 1975, press re-
lease GA/5315. September 16, 1975.
The Growth of World Industry. 1973 edition. New York, 1975.
*The Impact of Multinational Corporations on Development and on
International Relations.* (E/55///rev.1.ST/ESA/6). New York, 1974.
*The Impact of Multinational Corporations on Development and on
International Relations.* Technical Papers: Taxation. (ST/ESA/11).
New York, 1974.
*Implications of the Exploitation of the Mineral Resources of Interna-
tional Area of the Seabed:* Issues of International Commodity Policy.
(TD/B/C.1/170). New York, January 8, 1975.
Interregional Seminar on the Application of Advanced Mining Tech-
nology. *Proceedings.* May 21–June 3, 1973, Ottawa, Canada. (DP/
UN/INT-72-064). New York, 1975.
Interregional Workshop on Negotiation and Drafting of Mining Develop-
ment Agreements, Buenos Aires, November 2–18, 1973. *Conduct of
Operations and Development Goals.* (ESA/RT/AC.7/14, 11.10.73).
Paper prepared by David N. Smith.
———. *Financial Considerations in Negotiating Mining Development
Agreements.* (ESA/RT/AC.7/4, 17.9.73). Paper prepared by Raymond
F. Mikesell.
———. *Nationalization.* (ESA/RT/AC.7/18, 18.9.73). Paper prepared by
Pierce N. McCreary.
———. *Processing.* (ESA/RT/AC.7/12, 3.10.73). Paper prepared by the
Secretariat.
———. *Social Considerations and Environmental Protection.* (ESA/RT/
AC.7/7, 17.9.73). Paper prepared by Donald McLoughlin.
———. *Taxation and Incentives.* (ESA/RT/AC.7/9, 27.9.73). Paper pre-
pared by Alun G. Davies.
Marine Questions: Use of the Sea. (E/5650). New York, April 30, 1975.
Mineral Resources of the Sea. (E/4973). New York, April 26, 1974.
Monthly Bulletin of Statistics. Various issues.
Multinational Corporations in World Development. (ST/ECA/190).
New York, 1973.

Non-Ferrous Metals: A survey of their Production Potential in the Developing Countries. (E.72.II.B.18). New York, 1972.

Projections of Natural Resources, Reserves, Supply and Future Demand. (E/C.7/40/add.2). New York, December 5, 1972.

Seminar on Mining Legislation and Administration, Manila, 1969, *Proceedings.* (E/CN 11/I and NR/L 90). New York, November 17, 1969.

The Significance of Basic Commodities in World Trade in 1970. Study of the Problems of Raw Materials and Development. (A/9544/Add. 1). New York, April 4, 1974.

Small Scale Mining in the Developing Countries. (ST/ECA/155). New York, 1972.

Statistical Yearbook. Various issues.

Survey of World Iron Ore Resources. (ST/ECA/113). New York, 1970.

Yearbook of International Trade Statistics. Various issues.

Index